WINDSHIELD WILDERNESS

Cars, Roads, and Nature in Washington's National Parks

DAVID LOUTER

Foreword by William Cronon

UNIVERSITY OF WASHINGTON PRESS

Seattle and London

Windshield Wilderness: Cars, Roads, and Nature in Washington's National Parks is published with the assistance of a grant from the Weyerhaeuser Environmental Books Endowment, established by the Weyerhaeuser Company Foundation, members of the Weyerhaeuser family, and Janet and Jack Creighton.

University of Washington Press
PO Box 50096, Seattle, WA 98145
www.washington.edu/uwpress

Library of Congress Cataloging-in-Publication Data
Louter, David.
Windshield wilderness : cars, roads, and nature
in Washington's national parks / David Louter ;
foreword by William Cronon.
p. cm. — (Weyerhaeuser environmental books)
Includes bibliographical references and index.
ISBN 0-295-98606-9 (hardcover : alk. paper)
1. National parks and reserves—Public use—
Washington (State)   2. National parks and reserves—
Washington (State)—Management.   3. Automobiles—
Environmental aspects—Washington (State)
4. Roads—Environmental aspects—Washington (State)
I. Title.   II. Weyerhaeuser environmental book.
SB486.P83L68 2006   333.78'3—dc22   2006004335

For Rebekah, Arendje, and Mara

CONTENTS

MAPS

FOREWORD

Look to the Wilderness

WILLIAM CRONON

Lucky indeed is the book with a title so perfect that it manages to convey with just two strikingly unexpected and arresting words the core of the argument that its author wishes to make to readers. David Louter's *Windshield Wilderness: Cars, Roads, and Nature in Washington's National Parks* is such a book. What it has to say about the changing role of automobiles in the twentieth-century American experience of wild nature will be of interest to anyone who cares not just about the three parks whose histories it explores—Mount Rainier, Olympic, and North Cascades—but parks and wild places all across the nation. Let me explain why.

Many who encounter the phrase "windshield wilderness" for the first time may experience it as a contradiction in terms, an oxymoronic play on words that, however clever, succeeds in calling attention to itself only by being perversely nonsensical. As we typically understand it in the early twenty-first century, wilderness is a large tract of land distinguished above all else by the dominance of nonhuman nature and the relative absence of human influence. Furthermore, as the environmental historian Paul Sutter has brilliantly argued in his book *Driven Wild: How the Fight against Automobiles Launched the Modern Wilderness Movement* (published in the Weyerhaeuser series in 2002), the struggle to protect wilderness in the United States has historically had as one of its most vital objects the protection of wild places from the incursions of roads and automobiles.

Ever since the passage of the much-celebrated Wilderness Act of 1964, wilderness in this country has had at the core of its legal definition the concept of *roadlessness*. In a key section declaring the "Prohibition of Certain

Uses" that were understood to be inherently hostile to wilderness protection, the act's authors thought it necessary to mention only two critical threats: "there shall be no commercial enterprise and no permanent road within any wilderness area." And just to make sure that readers of the new law would understand how essential it was to prevent any form of motorized transport from ever intruding into legally designated wilderness, the paragraph on prohibitions ends with the admonition that "there shall be no temporary road, no use of motor vehicles, motorized equipment or motorboats, no landing of aircraft, no other form of mechanical transport, and no structure or installation within any such area."[†]

If all these cars, boats, trucks, and planes were to be prevented from transgressing the legal boundaries of wilderness, then surely, by definition, no wilderness should have anything whatsoever to do with *windshields*. Yet here we have an author who proposes to write a book about wilderness as seen through the windows of an automobile. What on earth could this wrong-headed person possibly be up to?

The answer is that David Louter, who works as a historian for the National Park Service in the Pacific Northwest, has used the three great national parks of the state of Washington to produce an invaluable case study of the radical shifts in attitudes toward automobiles that affected most national parks in the United States over the course of the twentieth century. At the very beginning, national parks like Yellowstone and Yosemite were promoted by the railroads in an effort to increase western passenger traffic and ticket sales. As a result, most tourists reached them via train. Only in the second decade of the twentieth century did visitors start to arrive in automobiles, but from that point onward, car-based tourism grew steadily and became ever more important. When the National Park Service was created in 1916 as the agency with primary responsibility for managing the parks, its first and second directors, Stephen Mather and Horace Albright, put enormous energy into promoting the parks and encouraging as many people as possible to visit them. When this impulse toward maximum accessibility was coupled with the cheap labor for road construction made available by the Civilian Conservation Corps during the New Deal, the result was a large-scale proliferation of highways leading to and through the national parks. These included some that to this day remain among the most spectacular anywhere in the United

---

[†]Wilderness Act of September 3, 1964 (P.L 88-577, 78 Stat. 890; 16 U.S.C. 1121, 1131-36), Section 4(c).

States: Going to the Sun Highway in Glacier National Park, the Zion–Mount Carmel Highway in Zion, the Blue Ridge Parkway in Shenandoah, Trail Ridge Road in Rocky Mountain National Park, and so on.

It was precisely these new roads in the 1930s that led a group of activists who most valued the backcountry experience of primitive nature to conclude that the National Park Service was itself becoming one of the greatest threats to wilderness in the United States. This is Paul Sutter's argument: that the founders of the Wilderness Society, and those who worked to pass what would eventually become the 1964 Wilderness Act, were appalled by the nationwide decline in roadless places and so began working to protect those places from reenacting the pernicious example of national parks that were entirely too accessible to cars. For these activists, it was patently obvious that windshields were not only the wrong way to experience wilderness, but in fact represented a deep threat to the wilderness experience itself.

In *Windshield Wilderness*, David Louter's first case study is Mount Rainier National Park, founded in 1899. Not least because Rainier was unusually accessible to the adjacent metropolitan populations of Seattle and Tacoma, its managers were among the first in the nation to push roads deep into the heart of their park, so that tourists could ride high up the mountainside without ever leaving the comfort of their automobiles. By 1910, the first segment of construction was completed on a road that was intended to completely encircle the mountain, enabling visitors to drive to the very edge of the glaciers.

In those early years, few doubted the wisdom of such facilities. Quite the opposite. Early park managers actively embraced the automobile as an ideal way to expose a growing number of Americans to wild nature. Roads were carefully designed to provide a beautifully unfolding series of views of glaciers, rain forests, and wildlife habitats, the windshield in effect serving as the screen on which images of wild nature were projected for maximum visual impact. Mount Rainier National Park thus nicely demonstrates the road-building tendencies of the Park Service that wilderness advocates began to criticize in the 1930s. Louter is well aware of the ways this highway-centered park experience can be criticized, but he asks us also to appreciate how and why it came into being. More importantly, he shows how it enabled national parks to express shared cultural values about the beauty of the natural world at a time when Americans increasingly saw automobile ownership as a symbol not just of high American living standards, but of American democracy and nationalism as well. By so doing, he demonstrates that despite its apparent contradictions, "windshield wilderness" became a very real vehicle for educating the nation's citizens about the beauty and power of their national landscape.

Part of what David Louter offers readers is a series of intriguing and surprising insights into the ways that auto-based experiences of the natural world shaped American encounters with the national parks over the course of the twentieth century. But an equally important facet of Louter's overarching argument is that the national parks themselves began to respond in unexpected and intriguing ways to mid-century critics who argued against road construction in wilderness landscapes. Louter's second case study, Olympic National Park, became a national park in 1938, and its early development was delayed by the Second World War. By the time managers got around to extending automobile access in the 1950s, they had become sensitized to potential threats to park resources that might be caused by the very cars they themselves were inviting to enter. The famous Hurricane Ridge Road was their response to this dilemma: a magnificent road traveling high above timberline, but consciously intended *not* to take visitors into the heart of the park. Instead, Hurricane Ridge Road skirted the edge of the park's wildest areas by carrying tourists to overlooks from which they could gaze into wilderness (through their windshields if they so chose) without either themselves or, worse, their automobiles actually intruding into or damaging that wilderness. The road instantly became one of the park's main attractions and represents a transitional period during which the debates that would ultimately culminate in the 1964 Wilderness Act were getting under way.

Louter's third case study, North Cascades National Park, clinches his argument about changing Park Service attitudes toward visitor experiences of wild nature. Although Hurricane Ridge Road avoided intruding into the wild heart of Olympic National Park, it was nonetheless very much in the tradition of the great high-altitude roads built by the Park Service within the boundaries of the national parks, which became a trademark feature of the tourist experience starting in the 1920s and 1930s. North Cascades, however, was established in 1968, four years after the 1964 Wilderness Act, and it was created as a new kind of national park that would make wilderness protection central to its mission. Here, the key road from which motorists could experience the new park was not itself located within the boundaries of the park. Like Hurricane Ridge Road, it skirted the boundary of the wilderness, but unlike Hurricane Ridge, it was located outside the park proper. Park planners and managers still worked hard to design and choreograph tourists' experiences so that whether inside or outside of an automobile, on or off a road, they gained a sense of the natural areas through which they were traveling. But now, because of the new legal jurisdictions established by both the 1964 Wilderness Act and the 1968 act creating North Cascades National Park, the symbolic importance of preventing cars from entering the protected park landscape became greater than ever before.

The true value of *Windshield Wilderness* becomes apparent just here, as we contemplate the distance that the Park Service and the American people traveled—both physically and conceptually—on the long road that leads from Mount Rainier through Olympic to North Cascades. Many other parks and wilderness areas lie along that road, which is why the insights of this book reach so far beyond the boundaries of Washington State. In David Louter's skilled hands, we arrive at journey's end with two important insights. One is an affirmation of Paul Sutter's argument that in the middle decades of the twentieth century, the defense of roadless wilderness became an essential expression of American environmental values. But another equally important lesson is that the experience of nature in the national parks was profoundly shaped by the changing view through the windshields of our most beloved and despised national vehicle, the automobile. One might even argue that the lessons learned through all those windshields reinforced the values that ultimately encouraged so many Americans to seek deeper, more intimate experiences of the natural world by leaving their cars behind. Whether they drove to the heart of wilderness at places like Rainier, or gazed at it from afar at places like the Olympic Peninsula or North Cascades, they learned to love the lands that lay before their eyes. Whatever the apparent contradictions, that love remains an abiding part of American culture and is the bulwark on which national parks and wilderness areas now depend for their defense.

ACKNOWLEDGMENTS

This book began as a title with a lot of promise, and if it comes close to its potential, it is only because so many people have helped me along the way. My father, Herman Louter, was a big influence, not because of any particular interest in national parks or history, but because he owned a 1965 blue Buick Wildcat. It was in this car that my family took vacations when I was young, leaving behind the smog alerts of Los Angeles summers and heading north along that great river of concrete, Interstate 5, for the milder and seemingly pristine Pacific Northwest. On one trip, we visited my first national park, Crater Lake, and that trip has been a source of inspiration for this study. I would also like to thank my mother, Marlene Louter, who always said I could do this, and she was right. Thanks as well go to my brother, Greg, who helped me find my first car—a 1967 VW Beetle—that took me to western landscapes such as Glacier and Yellowstone.

Throughout this project, friends and colleagues helped me understand what it means to be a historian and how not to take myself too seriously. At the risk of forgetting some, I would like to thank Maggie Miller, Kathy Morse, Jay Taylor, Linda Nash, Matt Klingle, Gordon White, Cicely Muldoon, Mike Reynolds, and Amy Schneckenburger for their insights and humor. Although this study is entirely my own, my work as a Park Service historian and my interactions with other professionals shaped my understanding of national parks. I am extremely grateful for the advice and knowledge my coworkers in Seattle have shared over the years about historic architecture and landscape design, among other observations about the agency and its culture. So thank you Kent Bush, Fred York, Jim Thomson,

Gretchen Luxenberg, Cathy Gilbert, Laurin Huffman, Hank Florence, Wendy Chin, Susan Dolan, Erica Owens, and Kirstie Haertel. Michael Hankinson and John Hammond deserve recognition as my mapmakers and graphic consultants. I extend a special and heartfelt thanks to Stephanie Toothman, my supervisor. She offered encouragement and advice, based on her own experience as a historian and program manager, and took a chance on a graduate student with a book project.

Over the years, other colleagues in the Park Service have offered encouragement and support as well. Among them are Steve Mark, Art Gomez, Paul Gleeson, Dwight Pitcaithley, Jon Jarvis, and John Reynolds. I am especially indebted to Ethan Carr and Richard Sellars, both of whom willingly shared early versions of their own work on national parks and offered advice. They helped build a road I could follow, so to speak. The Park Service's Historic American Engineering Record program documented the historic roads and bridges of the national park system. No study involving park roads would be complete without this work and the efforts of those who guided it, namely historians Tim Davis and Todd Croteau and photographer Jet Lowe.

Archivists and librarians played an invaluable role in the completion of this project. Without the help of archivists at the National Archives in Washington, D.C., at the Pacific Sierra branch in San Bruno, California, and at the Pacific Alaska branch in Seattle, Washington, I would not have unearthed materials for this study. Nancy Hori, the Park Service librarian in Seattle, allowed me to have free run of her collection and for that I am grateful. I also benefited from the tireless assistance of park archivists, curators, and cultural resource managers such as Deborah Osterberg, Gay Hunter, Kelly Cahill, and Jesse Kennedy at Mount Rainier, Olympic, and North Cascades national parks. I owe a special thanks to Tom Durant, photo curator at the Harpers Ferry Center, for finding two historic images of Mount Rainier. And finally, the University of Washington Special Collections contained a wealth of sources that became the foundation for my research.

I am also thankful for my encounters with other scholars. Early in this project, Ted Catton offered sound advice, and his administrative history of Mount Rainier, written for the Park Service, has proven to be an invaluable resource. Moreover, his own work on the parks of Alaska provided me with new insights into the meaning of national parks. Similarly, I have benefited from the work of, and thoughtful criticism by, Mark Spence, Hal Rothman, David Wrobel, Virginia Scharff, Paul Sutter, and Peter Blodgett. Most of all, I am extremely grateful to John Findlay, Richard White, and Bruce Hevly,

Acknowledgments

who advised me on this project when it first began at the University of Washington; they helped me shape what it is today. John Findlay was particularly helpful. He thoughtfully read and commented on every draft and helped me craft a work of which I can be proud.

Portions of this book have appeared as essays in other publications, and I appreciate receiving permission to reprint them here. An earlier and shorter version of chapter 1 was published as "Glaciers and Gasoline: The Making of a Windshield Wilderness, 1900–1915" in *Seeing and Being Seen: Tourism in the American West* (University Press of Kansas, 2001). An excerpted version of chapter 3 was published as "Wilderness on Display: Shifting Ideals of Cars and National Parks" in *Journal of the West* (Fall 2005). The opportunity to publish these earlier works sharpened my ideas, and Nancy Jackson and Steve Danver were gracious and kind, and made the experience rewarding.

At the University of Washington Press, Julidta Tarver is renowned for her patience, wit, and editorial skills. While I am grateful for all these qualities, I am most indebted to her ability, like a good sailor, to help new authors navigate uncharted waters. Bill Cronon's attention to storytelling and scholarship are also renowned, and his close reading of this manuscript, along with his guidance and tireless enthusiasm, made this a much better book. Working with Bill was such a great experience that I would like to do this all again.

Because the writing of history can be a solitary endeavor, I am grateful for the music of the Counting Crows, whose songs helped inspire me to write through the rain, and for the poetry of Richard Hugo, who found his inspiration driving the Montana landscape in a big Buick.

This book is for my family, to whom I owe the greatest debt. My wife, Rebekah Brooks, has encouraged and supported me emotionally and financially throughout the duration of this work. She has sacrificed her own time, her weekends, and her vacations so I could write and research. A geologist, she has helped me see parks and nature differently, to appreciate the small clues that yield large meanings. She has also willingly gone car camping (not in a Buick) as part of my research. I cannot thank her enough. Along the way our two daughters, Arendje and Mara, joined us. Able travelers and campers, they are a constant source of wonder, distraction, and joy. I can only hope that this study in some small way repays them for the time I have been away.

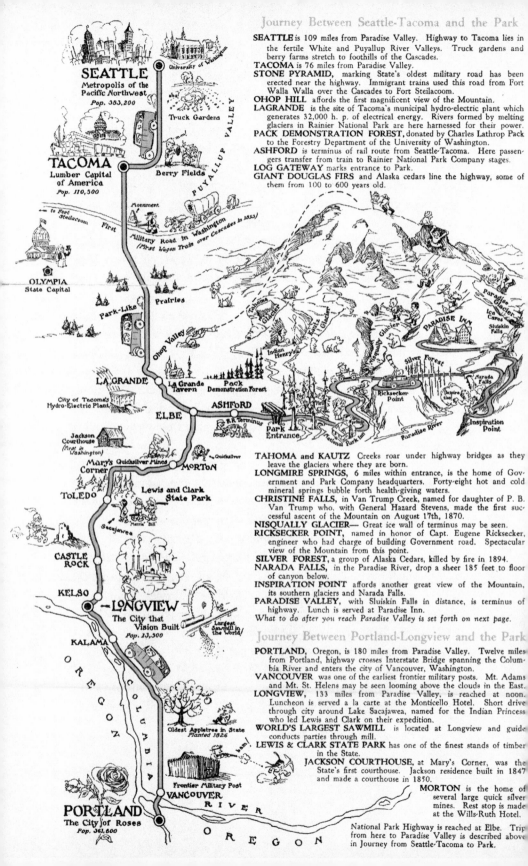

SEATTLE
Metropolis of the
Pacific Northwest
Pop. 365,200

TACOMA
Lumber Capital
of America
Pop. 110,500

OLYMPIA
State Capital

LA GRANDE

City of Tacoma's
Hydro-Electric Plant

ELBE

ASHFORD

Park
Entrance

Jackson
Courthouse
(Most in Washington)

Mary's
Corner

TOLEDO

MORTON

Lewis and Clark
State Park

**CASTLE
ROCK**

KELSO

LONGVIEW
The City that
Vision Built
Pop. 13,300

KALAMA

Oldest Appletree in State
Planted 1826

Frontier Military Post

VANCOUVER

PORTLAND
The City of Roses
Pop. 361,600

OREGON

COLUMBIA

RIVER

OREGON

SEATTLE is 109 miles from Paradise Valley. Highway to Tacoma lies in the fertile White and Puyallup River Valleys. Truck gardens and berry farms stretch to foothills of the Cascades.

TACOMA is 76 miles from Paradise Valley.

STONE PYRAMID, marking State's oldest military road has been erected near the highway. Immigrant trains used this road from Fort Walla Walla over the Cascades to Fort Steilacoom.

OHOP HILL affords the first magnificent view of the Mountain.

LAGRANDE is the site of Tacoma's municipal hydro-electric plant which generates 32,000 h. p. of electrical energy. Rivers formed by melting glaciers in Rainier National Park are here harnessed for their power.

PACK DEMONSTRATION FOREST, donated by Charles Lathrop Pack to the Forestry Department of the University of Washington.

ASHFORD is terminus of rail route from Seattle-Tacoma. Here passengers transfer from train to Rainier National Park Company stages.

LOG GATEWAY marks entrance to Park.

GIANT DOUGLAS FIRS and Alaska cedars line the highway, some of them from 100 to 600 years old.

TAHOMA and KAUTZ Creeks roar under highway bridges as they leave the glaciers where they are born.

LONGMIRE SPRINGS, 6 miles within entrance, is the home of Government and Park Company headquarters. Forty-eight hot and cold mineral springs bubble forth health-giving waters.

CHRISTINE FALLS, in Van Trump Creek, named for daughter of P. B. Van Trump who, with General Hazard Stevens, made the first successful ascent of the Mountain on August 17th, 1870.

NISQUALLY GLACIER— Great ice wall of terminus may be seen.

RICKSECKER POINT, named in honor of Capt. Eugene Ricksecker, engineer who had charge of building Government road. Spectacular view of the Mountain from this point.

SILVER FOREST, a group of Alaska Cedars, killed by fire in 1894.

NARADA FALLS, in the Paradise River, drop a sheer 185 feet to floor of canyon below.

INSPIRATION POINT affords another great view of the Mountain, its southern glaciers and Narada Falls.

PARADISE VALLEY, with Sluiskin Falls in distance, is terminus of highway. Lunch is served at Paradise Inn.

What to do after you reach Paradise Valley is set forth on next page.

PORTLAND, Oregon, is 180 miles from Paradise Valley. Twelve miles from Portland, highway crosses Interstate Bridge spanning the Columbia River and enters the city of Vancouver, Washington.

VANCOUVER was one of the earliest frontier military posts. Mt. Adams and Mt. St. Helens may be seen looming above the clouds in the East.

LONGVIEW, 133 miles from Paradise Valley, is reached at noon. Luncheon is served a la carte at the Monticello Hotel. Short drive through city around Lake Sacajawea, named for the Indian Princess who led Lewis and Clark on their expedition.

WORLD'S LARGEST SAWMILL is located at Longview and guide conducts parties through mill.

LEWIS & CLARK STATE PARK has one of the finest stands of timber in the State.

JACKSON COURTHOUSE, at Mary's Corner, was the State's first courthouse. Jackson residence built in 1847 and made a courthouse in 1850.

MORTON is the home of several large quick silver mines. Rest stop is made at the Wills-Ruth Hotel.

National Park Highway is reached at Elbe. Trip from here to Paradise Valley is described above in Journey from Seattle-Tacoma to Park.

WINDSHIELD WILDERNESS

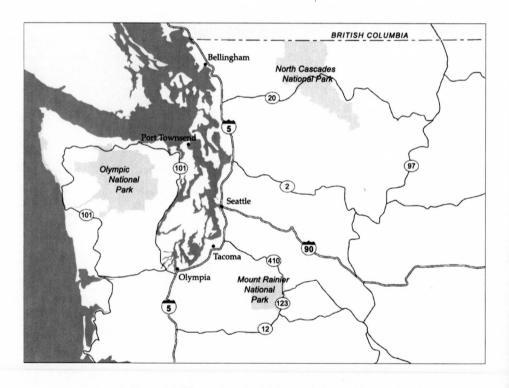

MAP 1. Western Washington's major highways, cities, and national parks

INTRODUCTION

Nature as We See It

When we visit national parks, we drive. And with few exceptions, national parks welcome us with open gates and splendid scenery. At a park like Washington's Mount Rainier, we leave behind urban sprawl, the roadside blight of strip malls, and the patchwork of fields, clear-cuts, and other signatures of people at work in nature. We pass beneath a massive log portal and enter a landscape for the car in nature. It is a landscape that seems pristine. The road travels through a dark forest, passes through meadows, and gradually ascends the mountain in a long series of turns that, like stanzas in a poem, reveal an unfolding panorama of glaciers, rock, and sky. Conforming to the topography and edged with guard walls of stone, the road seems to belong to the landscape. It frames our view. It is how we see the park. It is how we know nature in this place.

"seems pristine," but there is a road

the road plays a role ←

This vision of national parks and automobiles reflects how many millions of Americans encounter their national parks. Although a park road may look "natural," a great deal of thought and effort has gone into making it appear this way, particularly through landscape architecture. Still, we are willing to suspend disbelief that a park road intrudes on, or is harmful to, the environment because it appears to fit the scene so well and presents the scenery to us. I find national parks attractive for these reasons. They intrigue me with their natural beauty. Yet I am left wondering why autos seem so familiar in an otherwise primitive landscape. And what does this say about the meaning of national parks?

We can make sense of automobiles in national parks by thinking of their presence as a story about space and time. Automobiles and the highways they travel have shortened the distance and time it takes to reach national parks. They have brought the cities in which we live and the parks we visit closer together. In our minds as well as on our journeys out of town, the places we live and the natural places we visit merge. They have become part of the same mental as well as physical geography. Autos and highways have made it possible to think of national parks—to understand their meaning— not as wild places reserved from progress but known because of it. Although this notion began early in the twentieth century and has changed over time, it is still with us. It is a legacy of knowing nature through machines.

When the automobile first appeared in national parks one hundred years ago, it changed the way most Americans would encounter these protected areas. Throughout the twentieth century, people would interpret parks from a road and through a windshield. A twentieth-century phenomenon, the automobile helped reinvent the nineteenth-century idea of national parks as products of America's cultural achievements and vestiges of the nation's disappearing wilderness for a modern, mobile audience. For Americans of the Progressive Era, this new way of knowing national parks did not necessarily signal the destruction of nature, but the beginning of something promising. The presence, and acceptance, of autos in a national park embodied the hope that nature and technology could be blended into a new kind of aesthetic, one that would solve the social dilemma brought forth by our ambiguous relationship with the natural world. Thus, coming to terms with the automobile, like coming to terms with technological progress itself, redefined the meaning of national parks as places of *windshield wilderness*, where it was possible for machines and nature to coexist without the same industrial transformation that was affecting other parts of the nation. One made it possible to appreciate the other.

We can think of parks in this way because each generation responds to parks within the context of its time. The national park idea is a flexible notion; we "dispossess" parks of native peoples to protect them as wilderness and we allow native peoples to "inhabit" parks to protect them as wilderness. Notions about the ways we know nature through work and leisure are also flexible.[1] Perhaps the greatest example of this conceptual flexibility is the way automobiles have shaped our perceptions of parks as wilderness reserves (open to cars). Early in the twentieth century (and perhaps still today), automobiles provided Americans with the authentic experience they desired from the natural world. Automobiles supplied not only the vehicle by which middle-class Americans got back to nature but also the vehicle by which they knew nature itself. Granted, the relationship between nature and autos (and the roads developed for them) was delicate, but through regulated use and thoughtful development parks offered a way to control the advance of modern life, which so often came at the expense of wild places.

What evolved was a model of national parks in which automobiles and the highways they traveled seemed to be a part of nature. Ideally, autos and highways helped create national parks for a modern audience. It was an optimistic notion that served as a guiding ideal for the management of the national parks beginning in the second decade of the twentieth century. The development of parks for auto tourists was, and remains, visible in the rustic architecture and landscape design of the nation's oldest parks, among them Yellowstone, Yosemite, and Mount Rainier. But more than achieving the appearance of "harmony" with nature, the development of parks for motorists is instructive for understanding what parks meant to a modern society and within the context of the motor age. Parks were not only reservoirs of wilderness, characterized by an uninhabited, pristine nature, to which Americans retreated to escape their urban-industrial lives. They were also landscapes in which people could engage wilderness in a new way, in which automobiles and highways seemed to be mutually beneficial. As Stephen T. Mather, the National Park Service's first director, envisioned, roads would not necessarily divide parks into different zones of primitive and modified nature. Instead, roads would transform parks into singular landscapes of wild beauty. Although our opinions have changed about his vision of national parks and nature, the model continues to have a powerful hold on how we imagine national parks.

In this study, I trace how this concept of national parks has developed over time and has informed our understanding of national parks. I approach the problem through three case studies: Mount Rainier, Olympic, and North Cascades national parks. The parks, which are located in western Washington, lie roughly within a two-hour drive of Seattle and Tacoma, the region's two largest cities. The parks represent not only the state's array of natural wonders, but also present a chronological record of the changes that have taken place in the way Americans think about national parks as wilderness in the twentieth century. These parks reflect shifting ideas of wilderness as scenic, roadless, and ecological reserves.

In the period from 1900 to the early 1930s, the introduction of automobiles to Mount Rainier, the first park to admit cars, fostered a new preservation ideal in which it seemed possible to commune with nature by car.

Throughout the 1920s, the Park Service shaped the park for motor tourists. Agency leaders and landscape architects expanded upon the ideal of knowing nature through machines with the ideal of the highway in nature, suggesting that Mount Rainier was not really complete, it was not really a national park, until it could be experienced by motoring Americans. It was entirely possible, Mather argued, to design park roads to enhance, not diminish, the wilderness values of parks. Roads, in a sense, could be natural; machines and nature could coexist. In this way, Mount Rainier could meet the needs of the nation's modern, mobile audience, whose expectations about nature were tied to their machines.

The establishment and early development of Olympic National Park from the late 1930s to the late 1950s changed all of this, it seemed. The park model developed at Mount Rainier no longer satisfied a growing number of preservationists who regarded wilderness as "roadless." Largely in response to what they saw as the Park Service's overdevelopment of parks during the work relief programs of the 1930s, especially concerning roads, these constituents wanted wilderness parks established. Preserving wilderness as unmodified nature was really the true purpose of national parks, they asserted. Although Olympic was set aside as one of the nation's first "wilderness parks" and no roads would cut through its center, highways still informed how people thought of the park as wilderness and of the need for its protection. Moreover, the Park Service approached the management of Olympic in a way similar to that of Mount Rainier. It was possible, even if visitors could not literally drive into the park interior, to have a wilderness experience from an automobile. They could look into the park from the vantage point of Hurricane Ridge, reached by a modern road. In this sense, the Park Service carried forward the ideal of encountering nature from a car at Olympic, retaining the notion of wilderness as something people could view from the road, yet modifying it for a new set of expectations about wilderness as roadless.

The postwar wilderness movement and one of the accomplishments of that movement, the establishment of North Cascades National Park, reshaped the notion of windshield wilderness still further. While North Cascades was established as "true wilderness," off-limits to roads, the park campaign produced another version of the ideal of national parks as seamless landscapes for highways in nature. North Cascades was part of a national park complex, in which two recreation areas acted as the park's wilderness buffers. The recreation areas contained a small village and Seattle City Light's

Introduction

hydroelectric dams, reservoirs, and two company towns. They also contained a modern highway and primitive roads, which allowed tourists to experience the wild landscape of North Cascades in a familiar fashion: they could drive through it. Because windshield tourists could not drive "into" North Cascades National Park, and because the signature features of the national park were beyond the sight of the highway, however, tourists' impressions of the park as a wilderness would have to come from the recreation areas. Many would gain a sense of the park's wildness by driving the state highway through one of the recreation areas.

Beginning in the late 1960s, the Park Service approached a rather daunting task for an agency wedded to the idea that wilderness was a scenic experience viewed from a road. The agency had to convey to a public, few of whom would ever step out of their cars into the backcountry, the significance of the wilderness park they could not see. Ultimately, park managers would come to consider the entire park complex as part of the same "wilderness" landscape, to interpret the meaning of the park from the state highway, and to convey the wilderness ideal through films shown at the park's visitor center. By the late 1990s, it was still possible to integrate roads and wilderness in the form of a virtual park.

Although this study focuses on the parks in Washington, it brings a different perspective to all national parks by exploring what it means to view them from the road and through a windshield. This study builds and expands upon traditional interpretations of national parks—as symbols of the nation's remarkable endowment of natural wonders and scenic beauty. It also builds upon more recent interpretations of wilderness as a cultural construct, rather than as a pure state of nature. At some level, all of these interpretations suggest that national parks are products of human design; national parks reflect an ideal of nature as a wild landscape untouched by humans. But, as many studies remind us, this perception of parks has been highly selective. Though cherished as sublime areas of uninhabited wilderness, national parks were once home to native peoples who used the natural environment we now consider untouched. Likewise, rural residents from communities bordering national parks like Yellowstone cut wood, grazed livestock, and hunted game in them before, and for a time after, Congress set these areas aside and eliminated such practices. And in the case of the Alaska parks, native peoples continue to use resources for subsistence without diminishing the wilderness values of those parks.[2]

While these studies challenge treasured notions of wilderness as the last frontier or as original nature, they also underscore the importance of investigating why Americans are so selective in how they imagine parks as wilderness. The definition of "wilderness" itself has been contested in the twentieth century. One narrative, as advanced by scholars such as Paul Sutter, argues persuasively that wild nature is intrinsically roadless and that in many ways it is the antithesis of national parks. For national parks, which were set aside largely to preserve unmodified nature, underwent considerable road development and other so-called improvements to accommodate tourism, recreation, and the new leisure class in the early twentieth century. As Sutter notes, it was this development of national parks for auto tourists—America's new outdoor enthusiasts—and the failure of park managers to control growth that stimulated the modern wilderness movement, namely with the formation of the Wilderness Society in the 1930s. National parks came to symbolize, then, the importance of roadlessness in America—not just as a method of protecting the natural world from industrial forces but as an option to modern notions of leisure and mobility.[3]

On the other hand, the narrative proposed here suggests that many Americans do not have as strict a definition of wilderness. They like "wild" nature but are less restrictive about its meaning. To many traveling Americans, national parks represent—in the past as well as the present—their expectations about and experiences with a wild landscape; "wilderness" in this sense is something they encounter while driving. This narrative more accurately describes the core experience of many park visitors and is reflected in the history of the agency charged both with accommodating those visitors and with the preservation of nature in national parks. Thus for some, parks were the antithesis of wilderness (as roadless), but for many others, parks were (and still are) wild nature. Although seemingly polarized, these perceptions actually lead to a bifurcated definition: one branch for roadless advocates, the other for mass culture.

Imagining parks as wild nature with roads and cars relies, as observed above, on the flexibility of the national park concept. Not only is it possible to remove native groups from parks and call them wilderness, but it is also possible to preserve national parks and modify them for visitors in autos—and still to consider the parks "wild." Considering parks in this way, however, requires that we think of them not as reservoirs of pristine nature removed from human history but as historical creations. Nature, to be sure, exists outside of human control as the living world around us. But nature is also cultural. It is an idea that refers to a set of actual things that "humans *"nature" — "things humans have not made"*

have not made," yet at the same time we also believe that we can know the nature we have not made. We can "see, feel, and touch it." We describe landscapes like national parks as "natural," because in these settings we believe that when we look at mountains, rivers, and wildlife, we are "seeing nature."[4]

Parks might be natural places, but we have altered them significantly. We have built hotels, campgrounds, trails, and roads. Besides screening out native peoples, we have eradicated unpopular wildlife species, stocked lakes and streams with our favorite fish, and watched bears feast on garbage. Still, we marvel at the parks' timeless canyons, the glacier-carved mountains, and the incomparable valleys as remnants of primordial North America. The ability to perceive national parks as wild despite changes wrought within them displays a romantic vision of nature. It is a vision, as one scholar suggests, that has "contributed to a sort of widespread cultural myopia" that enabled late-twentieth-century Americans to "ignore the fact that national parks enshrine recently dispossessed landscapes."[5] It is a myopia, I would add, that allowed those same Americans to overlook the ways automobiles shaped their impressions of parks as wilderness. In this respect, parks are not vestiges of American wilderness frozen in the past but are instead wild landscapes we have transformed. Parks represent a kind of unity of humans and nature; they are wilderness remade.[6]

National parks can be defined largely by how we have interacted with and thought about them over time. And for most of the twentieth century, cars have mediated our interactions with parks. While many historians have appreciated the role of autos in national parks, they have tended to see cars as one of the main tools for the abuse of nature in parks. The story of national parks is one about the natural world in decline. It is a classic struggle driven by the management paradox of preservation and use. Perhaps the most forceful in asserting this view has been Alfred Runte. Runte, who wrote the now classic study on the national park idea, suggests that our attempts to protect and enjoy national parks, especially the earliest parks like Yosemite, have created a long record of modification for tourists at the expense of the parks' primitive qualities.[7] It is a compelling and influential interpretation. In his recent history of the National Park Service's approach to preserving nature, for example, Richard Sellars asserts that the agency has been unable to use science to adequately protect the parks. How parks looked was often far more important than the health of their natural systems, which was less apparent to the eye.[8]

Although these scholars recognize that parks are also emblems of American culture, and that ideas about them have shifted, they tend to limit us to conceptualizing parks as shadows of the past. Yet a history of automobiles in national parks, at least in Washington, suggests that this conclusion might be too simple. Instead, we could benefit from looking at parks through the lens of another preservation principle, one that considers preservation as a dynamic process, one that accepts the human and natural elements of the parks as part of the same mental and physical landscape.[9] In this way, we can see attempts to accommodate autos by designing roads (and other park structures) so that they appeared natural as part of a much larger process of making—not destroying—national parks. Road building created more than avenues of travel; it created a relationship with nature in parks. In this relationship, roads produced a national park model that was attractive to most modern Americans because people toured natural wonders in their cars. This ability gave people a sense that their presence in nature was not an artificial intrusion. True, it was an illusion—but no more than the American wilderness ideal itself. The ideal of being a part of, but not disturbing, the natural world speaks to how Americans imagine their place in nature and reconcile their relationship with it. Leo Marx described this ideal as the "middle landscape," and more recently Jennifer Price has called it a mixture of "nature and artifice."[10] It is an ideal that allows us to appreciate how twentieth-century realities have shaped national parks and that allows us to recognize our connections with nature in them.

1 / GLACIERS AND GASOLINE

Mount Rainier as a Windshield Wilderness

5th N.P.
1899

In the early 1920s, a national park brochure observed that driving around Crater Lake was not "a joy ride, but a pilgrimage for the devotees of Nature." Touring the lake by car was "a spiritual experience—nothing less."[1] In time Americans would come to question the presence of cars in national parks and their compatibility with wilderness. But at the turn of the century, autos offered a fresh perspective on national parks. Indeed, they helped foster a principle of preservation in which it seemed possible to commune with nature in a car. As auto use rose in national parks, park patrons and managers began to consider the meaning of national parks within the context of the motor age. They began to consider how to reconcile machines in park settings. They were not interested in excluding machines from parks to promote a wilderness experience. Instead, they started to fashion a new set of mental perceptions about national parks in which automobiles made the experience seem possible.

Of all the early parks, Mount Rainier stands out in understanding this process. The nation's fifth national park, established in 1899, it set the pace for interpreting national parks in the motor age. By the time the National Park Service was created (1916), Mount Rainier had not only allowed the first cars into a national park, but also had provided access by road and car in such a way as to emphasize the view from the road and the road as part of a scenic narrative. In this way, Mount Rainier illustrates the transition from an older way of knowing parks, by horse power, to a new way of knowing parks, by motor power. The park is also important in understanding the transition to the motor age because it did so with such apparent ease

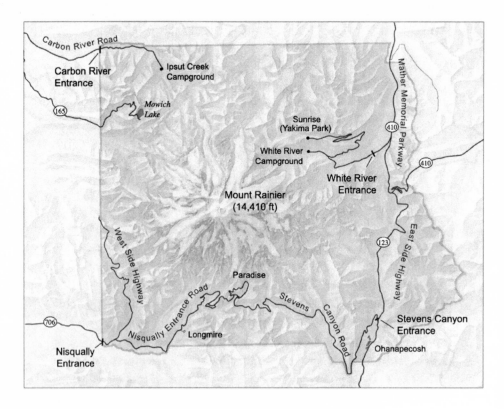

MAP 2. Road system of Mount Rainier National Park

and speed. This was partly because it lacked the long history of railroad patronage common to other western parks, where transportation companies attempted to retain control of park services and accommodations. But the main reason was that Mount Rainier served a motoring audience sooner than other parks. Mount Rainier was in closer proximity to urbanites than any other park of its time. The park's main patrons were residents of Seattle and Tacoma, who could visit the park in a day by car and typified a new generation of park visitors; they were middle-class, urban Americans whose perceptions of the park were tied to their machines.

At Mount Rainier and other parks, reconciling machines with nature relied on a number of factors. The process required thinking of roads not as the antithesis of primeval nature but as constructions that enabled people to know primeval nature better. Park roads were built with the idea that they both organized and protected park scenery. The process also required thinking of parks, and the landscapes they preserved, as best seen

Glaciers and Gasoline

from and experienced through a car. Because automobiles increased the pace and range of park tours, and enabled more people to visit national parks, Americans came to associate autos with appreciating national parks and the natural world. Finally, reconciling automobiles in national parks required thinking of motoring Americans not only as the main audience for parks, but also as essential to their preservation. For better or worse, many agreed that autos popularized national parks, making them truly democratic by opening them to more Americans. Moreover, autos promoted the use of parks for the appreciation of their scenic wonders and in turn protected them from resource development. In the nation's emerging consumer culture, parks had economic value as tourist attractions and wilderness reserves. In these ways, coming to terms with autos contributed to the notion that in the relationship between national parks and automobiles there was potential accord between the machine and wilderness.

THE VIEW FROM THE ROAD:
SCENERY, PARKS, AND PRESERVATION

Before autos ever appeared in national parks, there were roads. Roads, physically and conceptually, paved the way for the transformation of parks into special places for automobiles and nature. At the turn of the twentieth century, roads were shaped to be appropriate for parks, but parks also shaped roads—their routes and views—and were even identified as ideal settings for laying roads out. Roads symbolized a form of modernity, in that their construction altered the primitive to make way for human use of nature, and employed the technology of an industrializing society. The justification for and design of roads were key elements of an ideal of preservation *through* development, which considered roads not as intrusions but as enhancements.

Within the context of nineteenth-century ideas of nature, advanced by park designers such as Frederick Law Olmsted, roads were expressions of the natural world as "scenery," artistic compositions of the picturesque and sublime, and not nature as wild and unpredictable. In this sense, roads provided a scenic narrative: they organized and selected views for park visitors. As Olmsted noted in his recommendations for Yosemite in 1865 (when it was a state park), public parks should be open to everyone but their scenery preserved from "injury." Roads allowed this to happen. They protected these reserves by regulating use—concentrating people in specific areas—and presenting nature. In this way generations of tourists would not overrun the park; traveling Olmsted's proposed valley loop road, they would discover the same Yosemite, its "finer points of view" arranged in a predetermined and visually appealing sequence. Without roads, visitors would not have been able to encounter a national park. In the late nineteenth and early twentieth centuries, army engineers constructed roads in Yellowstone and Mount Rainier, for example, that conformed to these standards. Routed like paths in a garden, roads were considered less as a disturbance and more as a dramatic contrast to each park's primeval setting. Roads, in effect, "produced" the space we know as a national park.[2]

The early development of Mount Rainier National Park's road system reflected the notion that a road was a form of protection for, and an essential element in appreciating, the national park. Construction began on the park's first road, to the subalpine meadows known as Paradise, shortly after the park's creation in response to rising visitation and increasing calls for better access. Paradise was popular because it offered access to the south side of the mountain, considered the easiest route to the summit. But it was even more attractive for its close views of the mountain's glaciers and famous subalpine floral display. Mount Rainier and its unique attributes fit the model for a park envisioned in terms of the nineteenth century: as a cultural icon.[3] Mount Rainier's roughly square boundaries enclosed a relatively small area (some 320 square miles) and focused attention on the principal feature: the 14,410-foot, glacier-clad volcano that dominates the skyline of western Washington. In the late 1890s, the naturalist John Muir observed that Mount Rainier possessed all the qualities of an ideal national park, with its sublime and picturesque scenery. The "noblest" of all the Pacific Coast volcanoes, Mount Rainier evoked feelings of awe, he wrote, for its "massive white dome rises out of its forests, like a world by itself." In contrast to this immense physical presence, a "mountain wreath," "a zone of the loveliest flowers, fifty miles in a circuit and nearly two miles wide," encircled Mount Rainier and beckoned outdoor lovers with its beauty. "Nature," Muir concluded, had created between the dense woods and deep ice "the richest subalpine garden I ever found, a perfect floral elysium."[4]

In May 1903, Assistant Engineer Eugene V. Ricksecker, who was in charge of Mount Rainier's road project locally, selected a route up the Nisqually River valley that would lead visitors to Paradise. This way up the mountain was already popular with tourists and climbers. The road entered the park near its southwestern corner and led to Longmire, which had been attracting visitors since the turn of the century with its medicinal springs and views of the mountain. And from there, the road wound up the mountain's shoulders to Paradise. In addition to taking advantage of its popularity, Ricksecker justified his selection of the route because it would open the park to the greatest number of people. The roadway offered the main connection with Tacoma, the largest city near the park.[5]

Besides these practical considerations, Ricksecker was particularly responsive to the quality of the road's design because it would contribute greatly to how tourists perceived the mountain as a national park. Reflecting the basic philosophy noted above, the engineer chose a route intended to display the park's sublime and picturesque scenery. He also expressed concern for protecting the natural environment through which the road would pass. In this, he was indebted to the work of Major Hiram M. Chittenden. Chittenden, his supervisor, oversaw the construction of Yellowstone's system of roads and bridges from the late 1880s to the early 1900s. Chittenden, himself indebted to park designers like Olmsted, established an ideal of construction in which roads did not mar the park landscape; roads should instead lie gently on the land. Chittenden believed that all road work should enhance the visitor's appreciation of scenery. Roads organized the park tour, the natural scenes and wonders, that visitors would see. And as part of this goal, he thought it essential that road builders consider the aesthetic impacts of construction.[6]

In his survey, Ricksecker portrayed the road to Paradise as different from other roads because it was in a national park. Its location and design would emphasize its scenic rather than commercial purpose. He envisioned it "solely as a pleasure road" for "the enjoyment of the people." It would make "more accessible the summit of Mt. Rainier, and its surrounding grandness." Rather than taking "the shortest practicable route" between two terminals, the road instead would rise from Longmire and reach Paradise through a meandering series of switchbacks that conformed closely to the mountain's topography and connected several points of outstanding scenery. It would take visitors through lowland forests and up the south flank of the mountain, past the snout of a glacier, rushing waterfalls, and striking vistas, until reaching the alpine meadows of Paradise.[7]

Like those employed in developing Yellowstone's roads, Ricksecker's plans showed an interest in both preserving and presenting the mountain's scenic grandeur in such a way as to make the road appear part of the mountain. He explained that it would follow "the graceful curves of the natural surface of the ground," for these were "most pleasing and far less distractive than the regular curves laid with mathematical precision." Other construction details would contribute to the road's rustic appearance as well. To diminish the sense of barrenness and artificiality that a swath of some sixty feet would create through dense forest, Ricksecker directed that a few of the finest trees should be left standing. He also noted that no borrow pits (holes created for fill dirt) should be made and that no material from excavations for the road cut would be used to build the road surface, reducing unnecessary scarring. His choice of the mountain's ubiquitous volcanic rock for surfacing the road added to the natural appearance, as did his selection of native stone for the construction of retaining walls and guard rails, and wood for the road's many bridges.[8]

Ricksecker's construction specifications combined the practical with the pleasurable to ensure that park visitors traveled safely and comfortably, and that their attention was drawn to the scenery instead of to the road. By allowing the road to follow "its own course" as much as possible, Ricksecker believed that the road would not only appear natural, but the traveler would also be "kept in a keen state of expectancy as to the new pleasures held in store at the next turn." In order to ensure the road's "natural" quality and to make travel along it enjoyable, the engineer settled on a gentle gradient. Following a standard set by Chittenden and the army engineers in Yellowstone, the grade of 4 percent would accommodate wagons and other horse-drawn vehicles. The grade and mode of travel in turn influenced what scenic features were seen from the road. The route should link "all points of interest that lend themselves readily to the scheme," the engineer noted, without adding too much distance. Ricksecker recognized that in order to maintain the attention of wagon-bound travelers, changes in scenery "should be kaleidoscopic. Steep stretches where teams must walk soon become monotonous and pall upon the senses. Light grades offer no excuses for the teamster to walk his horses."[9]

For this reason, Ricksecker conceived of travel along the road, up one of the nation's highest mountains, as an unfolding panorama, one he and his crews pieced together on the ground and then rendered on a map. The engineer described this process as one in which the road transported the traveler from forest floor to alpine meadows in a gradual climb in which each foot of elevation gain created a more expansive view of the mountain and surrounding terrain. Speaking of the section of road above Nisqually Glacier, for example, Ricksecker observed that an "extended view of the lower Nisqually country opens up; the first close view of the mountain and its

Southeasterly slopes is obtained, and a superb view of Nisqually Glacier [meets the eye]. . . . The trees are sparse, just thick enough to keep one alert to . . . the best views."[10]

Despite the imagined naturalness of the road, nature itself appears only as tapestry in Ricksecker's writings and, for that matter, in those of Chittenden and other park designers of the period. Nature is the scenic canvas of forests, glaciers, and waterfalls that the road crosses. In the setting of such a natural icon as Mount Rainier, the road appears minuscule but symbolizes by its mere presence the triumph of technology in the wilderness. It is this element that illustrates best how Ricksecker and others of his time viewed the road and the mountain as complementary forms of the sublime. The road was, in a sense, a stage that dramatized the unfolding scenic narrative. By its sheer scale, Mount Rainier did not appear threatened by the road, while at the same time the road transformed the mountain into a spectacular backdrop.[11]

The contrast between road and mountain, among other things, underlay Ricksecker's concept of the road to Paradise specifically, and of a road system for the entire park generally. He envisioned Mount Rainier as having an extensive network of roads. In time, he thought that many of the local routes leading into the park should be improved. In addition to the Nisqually River valley, the engineer learned of a number of access routes into the park during the initial stages of his survey, among them a trail up the Carbon River from Fairfax, a wagon road and trail up the White River from Enumclaw, and a wagon road up the Naches River (near what is today Chinook Pass) from Yakima. He also expressed the possibility of a road into the park from the southeast by way of a wagon route and trail along the Cowlitz River and Ohanapecosh Creek. Along with the Nisqually entrance, the routes would eventually form the principal entrance points into Mount Rainier—at the square park's four corners.[12]

More importantly, Ricksecker imagined a scenic road encircling the mountain that would eventually link up with these entrance roads. The engineer, who made his proposal in December 1904, explained his vision in idealistic rather than practical terms. A high-elevation road around the mountain, constructed as close as possible to the permanent snowline, would offer diverse and alternating scenery. In contrast, a lower route passing primarily through forest, as recommended by another army survey, would be "more or less monotonous." Since a section of the road he surveyed already passed through forest, the engineer believed that it would be "with a certain sense of relief that the tourist will welcome the coming into the open with the opportunity to see out and over such an expanse of rugged country as is here to be seen, and I can imagine no more thrilling exhilaration than a ride along the summit of the Cascades and the glacier dividing ridges."[13]

By mapping the route in his mind and on paper, the engineer made the road encircling the mountain seem more real and further suggested the intimate connection between the road and natural landscape. His vision in many ways was farsighted—a road around the mountain would intrigue park administrators and park supporters for some time to come, in part because it would bring the mountain to the people. Although it reflected Chittenden's plan for the Grand Loop Road in Yellowstone, Ricksecker's proposal also expanded upon the concept. Ricksecker's road would encircle the park's primary feature, the volcanic cone, and provide as many views of it as possible. It would present the mountain from a well-graded road, incorporate it into a familiar type of experience and setting, and thus enable visitors to know the mountain better ostensibly without harming it.[14]

But the reality of road construction demonstrated the limits of this vision. Work on the twenty-five-mile road to Paradise began in 1904. Ricksecker had seriously underestimated the cost of construction, and from the outset road work encountered the difficulties presented by short seasons, rough terrain, and contract labor. Chittenden was called on to oversee the project in 1906 and, as Ricksecker's superior, would be often credited with its construction and that of the proposed road around the mountain.[15] Chittenden concluded that Ricksecker's design details—the road's width of twenty-five feet and its complex "system of berms and drains" for example— were entirely too elaborate, refined, and expensive for a park road in "this wild and rough country" and were better suited to a city highway. The senior engineer also thought that the wagon road between Ashford and Longmire, essentially the park's entrance road, was the worst he had ever traveled. Chittenden ordered Ricksecker to revise construction standards and adjust priorities to make reconstruction of the lower portion of the road his highest priority. Ricksecker complied, and by the following year the road from the park entrance to Longmire had been improved. By 1908, road construction had been completed to the snout of Nisqually Glacier, making the route the first American road to reach a glacier. By 1910, the Nisqually Road (as it was later called) was complete as far as the Paradise Valley, but the section above Nisqually Glacier was too narrow for safe travel and would not open to automobiles until 1915.[16]

The road to Paradise was by no means a first-class road, and it would undergo considerable renovations for more than a decade after its completion. Its location, however, was its most enduring and significant quality. In 1910, Superintendent Edward S. Hall praised Ricksecker for building a road with a gentle grade that "passes all points of interest" and proclaimed it a "very creditable piece of engineering" that was "one of the finest scenic roads in America."[17] Park visitation rose dramatically, from approximately 8,000 in 1910 to 35,000 in 1915, a telling sign of the new road's popularity despite its narrow width, sharp turns, and poor drainage. More importantly, automobiles were largely responsible for the surge in visitation and the park's popularity. Even though they could not travel all the way to Paradise, autos soon outnumbered horse-drawn vehicles, signaling the opening of the motor age in the park.[18]

KNOWING NATURE THROUGH MACHINES

The appearance of automobiles expanded rather than diminished the purpose of park roads as envisioned by Ricksecker and Chittenden. These engineers may have designed roads for visitors touring national parks in horse-drawn carriages or wagons, but the completion of roads, especially Mount Rainier's road, coincided with the dawn of the motor age. While tourists in motorized buggies did not experience park scenery at the slower pace of horse-powered conveyances, they did experience parks in a similar fashion, viewing nature from the road. Roads continued to function as scenic corridors and scenic narratives, making it possible to think of automobiles not just as an acceptable way of seeing national parks but perhaps as the best way.

The coming of the automobile to national parks reflected the way Americans generally embraced the auto as a way to return to nature. After 1910, thanks to Henry Ford, the auto became more affordable and more reliable for middle-class Americans. In 1910, for example, less than half a million people owned cars in the country. By 1913 that number had more than doubled, and by 1920 it had reached 8 million. Although greeted with some apprehension as a token of modern life and industrialization, the automobile enabled Americans to encounter nature on their own. As the rise of auto touring and auto camping starting in 1910 demonstrated, finding "primitive" nature by the road with a modern machine was not only possible, it became a national pastime. In the new social order, middle- and upper-class

Americans perceived that they were becoming more removed from the natural world in their daily lives. At the same time, they enjoyed steadily more leisure time for visiting nature. In the emerging consumer culture of the time, automobiles were for more than utilitarian purposes. Like other goods for purchase, they were "imbued with symbolic value that promised adventure, escape, leisure, drama, the 'good life.'" However contradictory it may seem today, they offered the means for these Americans to leave behind their problems and reclaim a firsthand experience with nature.[19]

The automobile, the very symbol of technology destroying an older way of life, offered mobility and freedom. It promoted individualism and a closer and more "intimate" experience with the natural world in a time when industrial capitalism—symbolized by the railroad in the nineteenth century—was changing that world forever. Freer to move or stay where they pleased, and to go where they could pilot their machines, motor campers were engaging in a more democratic version of the back-to-nature movement of the late nineteenth century.[20] They found an authentic experience with the natural environment in an age when technological advances seemed to alienate people from rather than bring them closer to nature. And national parks, more than any other public lands, represented the ideal of the auto as an enabling technology. As national park advocate Enos Mills wrote in 1913, autos in parks were essential to the nation's "general welfare," for they provided tourists "contact with nature and with people out of doors."[21] Parks may have been vestiges of an ideal American wilderness free of human influence, but they were also vestiges of an ideal wilderness as we most commonly encountered and understood it—as nature by the road.

True, as we look back on the complex reality of twentieth-century life, the automobile was a "necessary evil" because it increased public interest in national parks, protecting them from one kind of exploitation while opening them to another. It is also ironic that the automobile industry would form the backbone of the modern capitalist system that motor campers sought to escape in the out-of-doors, and that the automobile would drag modernity along with it into the nation's hinterlands.[22] But automobiles, at least in the first two decades of the twentieth century, did not seem to conflict with wilderness preservation; they provided a way to experience nature through leisure.[23] More importantly, this perception of autos suggests a developing preservationist norm of knowing nature through automobiles that was, at least initially, not considered problematic.

Popular interpretations of automobiles' introduction to national parks,

Glaciers and Gasoline

though, tend to cast their arrival in a negative light. The appearance of autos in parks, according to some, was similar to the serpent in the garden or was an unfortunate political compromise that has impaired parks' wilderness values. In time, parks like Yosemite illustrated the automobile's destructive powers. As one critic observed in the late 1960s, the automobile "had brought more downgrading changes to Yosemite Valley than the previous five thousand years of erosion. Each day it was cramming a medium-sized city into a valley meant for a hamlet."[24] Although other treatments of automobiles in parks are more sympathetic, they underscore the acceptance of cars as symbolic of the nation's new political and social order. Their owners represented a powerful constituency—with the attention of Congress—without which national parks would not have survived. "As the automobile prospered," wrote the biographer of Stephen T. Mather, the first director of the National Park Service, "so did the national parks."[25]

While these interpretations are informative, our appreciation of national parks increases if we consider the park road as the container for the automobile.[26] Roads not only framed park landscapes for auto tourists, but they also controlled where autos could travel. The introduction of autos into national parks, then, began an attempt to reconcile these machines with nature, so that automobiles became part of an experience that made the landscapes they crossed seem more authentic. Rather than distance motorists from nature, roads and autos made nature seem real; they afforded many the closest contact with the natural world they had known, and perhaps would ever know.

But roads alone could not reconcile cars to wilderness. As machines of the modern age, autos were greeted initially with displeasure at worst and uncertainty at best in park settings. Park officials worried that autos would disturb visitors and threaten their safety when autos and horses met on the same roads—roads designed with horses rather than four-wheeled machines in mind. In 1900, for instance, when the first car chugged into Yosemite, park officials banned automobiles primarily for these reasons.

Park administrators may have overreacted. Although considered "noisy and disruptive menaces," notes historian Anne Hyde, automobiles were unlikely at the time to overrun the park. Yosemite's roads were poor, and prior to 1910 motoring was an uncertain enterprise. It was a novel sport limited to a "few wealthy enthusiasts" who could afford expensive and unpredictable cars and who had the time, patience, and courage to travel the nation's rough roads. In 1911 at Mount Rainier, the first car reached Paradise Valley over the recently completed Nisqually Road in an unimpressive fashion. The touring car, carrying President William Howard Taft, became hopelessly bogged down in mud above Nisqually Glacier and was dragged to Paradise by mules.[27]

Despite these concerns about automobiles and the reality of motor travel, the secretary of the interior allowed autos into Mount Rainier in 1908, making it the first park officially to admit automobiles. The decision also made Mount Rainier instructive for understanding how federal officials and park patrons would adjust to the presence of cars through regulation. Bowing to public pressure from automobile clubs, the secretary allowed autos into Mount Rainier, but only after drafting a long list of rules restricting hours of operation, speeds, and general conduct. Above Longmire, for example, automobiles were limited to use between 9:00 and 11:00 AM and between 3:30 and 5:30 PM. The speed limit was set at six miles per hour, except on straightaways when no horses were in sight, where speed was allowed to reach fifteen miles per hour. Horse teams also had the right-of-way, and drivers, when approached by teams, were to pull over to the outer edge of the road until teams safely passed.[28]

Other parks adopted varying forms of Mount Rainier's regulations. The prescriptive measures characterized the Progressive Era approach to problems initiated by technological innovations; they offered a sense of control about a changing relationship with nature, and even improved opinions, such as those of park managers, about the value of autos in parks. Mount Rainier's acting superintendent, Grenville Allen, initially recommended against allowing autos into the park because they would be a "great annoyance" and would pose "some danger to the public." Drivers not only would negotiate roads used by horses, but also would pilot their machines around numerous blind curves, past steep embankments, and over narrow bridges. After one season, however, Allen announced that the regulations "protected motorists from considerable danger," that visitors derived "a great deal of pleasure" from driving into the park, and that the machines were generally accepted by the public.[29]

Roads and regulations aided but did not complete the rapprochement between technology and wild nature. These rules, for example, emanated from deeper concerns about the meaning of national parks in the motor age. The appearance of autos signaled for many the end of an older, perhaps more genuine way of knowing national parks that included travel by railroad, extended stays in fine hotels, and leisurely tours of the parks by wagon

Glaciers and Gasoline

or stage. For countless others, however, the motor age initiated the only way they would know parks: as playgrounds for mobile modern Americans. With its ability to shatter older barriers of distance and travel time, the automobile not only changed people's lives outside of parks and how people got to parks, but also reconfigured how they toured the parks. Cars reordered the spatial relationships within parks and fostered new kinds of expectations about encounters with nature.[30]

This shift in how Americans toured parks was not altogether positive, some argued, for it fragmented their park experience and thus their image of national parks. Rather than make time to see the entire park, tourists might visit only the most popular sites. Like reading a chapter instead of an entire book, their understanding of the park would lack depth. This was a common complaint at the first national park conference, held at Yellowstone in 1911 and convened by the secretary of the interior to address issues common to the administration of all parks. Louis W. Hill, Great Northern Railway president and chief promoter of Glacier National Park, for example, complained that autos turned national parks into mere day trips. Tourists could reach points of interest faster than by horse and spend more time at them rather than on a stage. Hill said that he would be "embarrassed" to drive his car into Yellowstone. The trip would occur too quickly, the pace too fast. "I could take the car, make the trip, and be back for lunch," Hill noted. "Now, what kind of trip would that be?" Hill, who carried his machine around on his train, could justify driving a private auto into Yellowstone only if it were part of a longer driving tour of the West, a somewhat misleading comment considering the poor quality of the region's roads.[31] What really bothered Hill and those who catered to tourists was the threat autos posed to the hegemony of the railroad-supported concessions in Yellowstone as well as other western parks.[32]

Others warned that autos cheapened the park experience. By speeding along a park road, visitors would lose touch with nature. In 1912, hearing of the recent debates over admitting autos into parks, especially Yosemite, British ambassador to the United States Lord James Bryce warned against it. "If Adam had known what harm the serpent was going to work," Bryce wrote, "he would have tried to prevent him from finding lodgement in Eden; and if you stop to realize what the result of the automobile will be in that wonderful, that incomparable valley, you will keep it out." Bryce's argument for national parks was within the tradition of the English garden and its American counterpart, the nineteenth-century public park. At higher rates of speed, he observed, the "focus is always changing, and it is impossible to give that kind of enjoyment which a painter, or any devotee of nature, seeks if you are hurrying past at a swift automobile pace." The automobile wasted scenery.[33]

Bryce's comments, often cited for their great foresight, spoke to the romantic and nostalgic responses many Americans felt with the coming of the automobile to national parks, particularly with the displacement of horse and wagon travel. Curiously, those who waxed poetic about horse coaches selectively overlooked complaints by passengers about the choking dust and jarring discomfort of a drive over rutted park roads. More importantly, Bryce's views misread another component of reconciling machines with parks: the democratizing influence automobiles would have. Cars transformed parks into places not open only to the select elite who could afford to travel by train to parks and spend days in them, but rather as places open to the majority of Americans (who owned or traveled in automobiles). Autos helped make national parks public spaces, as envisioned by individuals such as Frederick Law Olmsted. According to Robert M. Marshall, chief geographer of the U.S. Geological Survey, people should have the right to choose when and how they toured the parks. This right alone, he suggested, merited granting the privilege of autos in parks.[34]

By their actions, Americans in general agreed. By the early 1900s, railroads brought tourists to within less than fifteen miles (and a short stage ride) of Mount Rainier and Yosemite, but within a few years, automobiles surpassed this and other forms of transportation to and into the parks. It was a pattern that would be repeated in other parks. As auto ownership soared, motorists became a formidable force in national park affairs; they developed a well-formed coalition of special-interest groups, including auto clubs as well as business and political leaders, supporting the use of autos in all parks. In 1912, for instance, Seattle and Tacoma formed a park advisory committee that would be highly influential in Mount Rainier's administration and development, especially in encouraging its accommodations for the motoring masses.

Perhaps the most widely known example of these groups' influence was the pressure auto enthusiasts exerted to open Yosemite to cars. At the national parks conference held in Yosemite in 1912, Secretary of the Interior Walter L. Fisher recognized that automobiles had come to stay in national parks. His comments were influenced by the presence of well-organized automobile clubs, automobile manufacturers and agents, good-roads boosters, and commercial organizations at the conference. Their representatives had been inundating the secretary's office with telegrams and letters requesting that their machines be admitted to Yosemite. They spoke a language politicians understood. Economically, the appearance of automobiles in Yosemite was free advertising and would boost car sales; auto travel to the park would promote the construction of better roads and increase tourism to the immediate area and California as a whole. Moreover, auto enthusiasts and their organizations represented a powerful voting bloc. Senator Frank Flint, for example, testified that the Automobile Club of Southern California, with 4,500 members, was the largest in the nation. His state had the second highest ownership of automobiles, next to New York; there were approximately 84,000 cars on the road, and in California there were more cars per capita than in any other state. (The population of California was more than 2.3 million in 1910.) All of this added clout to his club's keen interest in opening Yosemite to automobiles.[35]

In 1913, Secretary of the Interior Franklin K. Lane, when he lifted the ban on autos in Yosemite, acknowledged the importance of cars in the administration of national parks and in making them "as accessible as possible to the great mass of people."[36] Lane was a Californian who replaced Fisher, and his decision is often cited as the turning point for the presence of autos in parks, while the early acceptance of autos in Mount Rainier goes unmentioned. Nevertheless, Lane's decision refined the meaning of national parks in the auto age and underscored how cars would lend justification for protecting parks as economic engines for tourism. The debates over autos in Yosemite occurred around the same time that scenic preservationists, led by J. Horace McFarland, president of the American Civic Association, and John Muir, president of the Sierra Club, were fighting to protect national parks from consumptive uses, the ravages of logging, water power projects, and grazing. The most flagrant infringement, of course, occurred when Secretary Lane approved San Francisco's proposal to dam the park's Hetch Hetchy Valley. Coincidentally, his decision came in the same year he lifted the ban on autos in Yosemite.[37]

While the introduction of cars into Yosemite may have highlighted the importance of roads, regulations, democracy, and tourism in the way Americans came to terms with machines in wild landscapes, Hetch Hetchy raised the technology-nature issue to another level. The battle over Hetch Hetchy was the clarion call for scenic preservation nationally, while at the same time the juxtaposition of automobiles and a dam in a national park setting usually goes unnoticed. However, while the dam was symbolic of the destructive power of technology, autos seemed to offer a way to actually commune with nature in a national park.

John Muir and his Sierra Club embraced the automobile as a way to expand the political support for parks and to counter arguments for purely utilitarian uses of parks with their own that auto tourism to national parks would promote economic growth.[38] Muir was a complex thinker who valued nature as well as technology. He may have preached the value of nature over civilization, but like Ralph Waldo Emerson a half century before, Muir entertained the possibility of harmony between nature and machines. As Emerson reasoned, the machine in the landscape (which in Emerson's time was symbolized by the train) was not an unresolvable conflict, at least philosophically. How could it be, if technology was a product of man and man was a product of nature? Moreover, Emerson suggested, it was not a question of whether nature was pristine or defiled. Technological innovations created new landscapes, which required consideration within a larger perspective. Everything was part of the same great "Order" of being and possessed its own beauty and value. Evidently, Muir saw automobiles the way Emerson saw trains. Cars seemed to present a lesser menace than grazing sheep in Yosemite or flooding one of its valleys. In fact, the presence of autos seems to have assured the ascendancy of a then new preservationist norm that accommodated nature and automobiles. This vision excluded the industrial extraction of natural resources, but incorporated the modern machine into the enjoyment of the natural world through outdoor recreation and nature tourism. In this light, parks were a kind of national commons for nature and machines.[39]

This strain of thought casts the introduction of automobiles into national parks in a different light. Like Emerson's train, the automobile brought people to nature in national parks, where the possibility of an accord between the machine and wilderness outweighed the potential for destruction. Viewed in this way, national parks were ideally suited for automobiles; the main question was not if but when parks would make the change from horses to autos. For parks like Yellowstone, which admitted cars in 1915, the transition was difficult because they had to break free of railroad hegemony over travel to the park and its tourist facilities. In addition, remote parks like Yellowstone would not see more auto tourists until road and automobile improvements after World War I made long-distance motor travel inviting to a larger audience. Yosemite, on the other hand, made the transition more easily because, despite its age, it did not have a major railroad patron and was poorly developed for tourism. Moreover, Yosemite was attractive to auto users because, as one historian notes, "it was the only major western park located within easy driving distance of two major urban centers—Los Angeles and San Francisco."[40]

A PARK FOR THE MOTOR AGE

If Yosemite was within "easy driving distance" of Los Angeles and San Francisco, then Mount Rainier was but a brief errand into the wilderness for residents of Puget Sound. The park made the transition to automobiles with great celerity and with little conflict primarily because of its proximity to Tacoma and Seattle, a distance of about sixty miles; the majority of park visitors resided in these cities. Like Yosemite, Mount Rainier lacked a railroad patron. The Northern Pacific Railroad, which advertised Mount Rainier in the late nineteenth century, had its image tarnished during the park campaign because many contemporary observers suspected that bribery underlay the government's generous settlement for the railroad's land in the park. Afterwards the Northern Pacific would play only a limited role in developing visitor services for the park. The Tacoma Eastern Railway had better luck. It offered service to the park by 1904, but the automobile quickly overtook it as the dominant mode of travel to and within the park by 1910. That year, of the nearly 8,000 visitors to the park, almost twice as many came by auto as by train or stage.[41] As the Seattle photographer and conservationist Asahel Curtis remarked, the main reason for the automobile's acceptance was that the national park's "short distance" from Seattle and Tacoma made it "possible for many to make the trip to the mountain parks in their own machines."[42]

While Mount Rainier's situation was perhaps unique, in that from the beginning it was influenced by its close relationship with urban centers, it was not simply an "urban park." Mount Rainier provides perhaps the best example of how motor travel shaped what people thought of, and how they responded to, national parks. Seattle and Tacoma residents saw Mount Rainier within the new physical and mental geographies created by automobiles. In this respect, they imagined Mount Rainier as a national park in much the same way other Americans would imagine parks in more remote settings. It was a reservoir of the primitive that was not separate from but an integral part of an increasingly urban and industrial nation.

Both cities energetically supported the park's establishment and later promoted its development and participated in its administration—especially the improvements for automobile tourists—through the Seattle-Tacoma Rainier National Park Advisory Committee (later known as the Rainier National Park Advisory Board), which was formed in 1912. In a sense, the joint committee arose out of each city's claims on the mountain as a symbol of its community's scenic beauty, quality of living, and regional superiority in the late nineteenth and early twentieth centuries. The Puget Sound cities displayed an interest not only in promoting Mount Rainier for tourism but also in incorporating the region's spectacular mountain scenery into the amenities each city offered. As the automobile and improved roads made Mount Rainier a short motor drive from each city, these conditions opened new opportunities for tourism in the nearby Cascades. Seattle also incorporated the mountain and other surrounding mountain ranges into its plans for a series of parks and boulevards (designed by John C. Olmsted) as early as 1903, and the city featured Mount Rainier prominently in the Alaska-Yukon-Pacific Exposition in 1909. For its part, Tacoma laid claim to the mountain and tried to change its name to Mount Tacoma, setting off a feud with Seattle. In addition, Tacoma's local "good roads movement" brought together an array of interested parties—automobile owners, bicycle clubs, boosters, and businessmen—who concentrated on improving the county road, the Mountain Highway, from Tacoma to Mount Rainier. By 1913, the state legislature had passed a bill to turn the county road into a state highway, to be designated as the "National Park Highway."[43]

Residents of Seattle and Tacoma integrated Mount Rainier into their lives by visiting the park in record numbers, quickly making it one of the most heavily toured by automobiles. In 1915, for example, almost half of Mount Rainier's visitors (approximately 15,700) came from Seattle and Tacoma, the numbers split nearly evenly between the two towns. Mount Rainier managers estimated that most tourists from Seattle and Tacoma either piloted their own cars or were passengers in private cars. Moreover, in 1915 Mount Rainier passed Yosemite in visitation, with 35,166 visitors to 33,452, making Washington's park second only to Yellowstone. Mount Rainier overtook Yosemite in part because the war in Europe kept tourists at home, but increased visitation to Mount Rainier during this time is also notable because it came during California's expositions in San Diego and San Francisco, when Yosemite was a major attraction. Although the fairs were a stimulus for opening Yosemite to automobiles, the number of private autos entering Mount Rainier was also greater than in Yosemite. Nearly 23,500 machines entered Mount Rainier, while close to 21,000 entered Yosemite.[44]

At the turn of the twentieth century, Seattle and Tacoma's role in shaping Mount Rainier as a destination typified the way western cities exerted influence well beyond their boundaries, whether exploiting surrounding hinterlands for natural resources or for their appeal to tourists. Denver residents, for example, laid claim to the Estes Park country several hours north of the city. Denverites boosted their town as the starting point for auto tours of the West, and their promotion of Estes Park for motoring popularized the area and played a major part in the establishment of nearby Rocky Mountain National Park in 1915.[45] More importantly, the patronage of Seattle and Tacoma illustrates a trend for national parks in the motor age. Mount Rainier may have been a park in the nineteenth-century sense of the word, with its emphasis on scenic grandeur. But at the same time it was a new version of the national park ideal, primarily because its audience represented a new generation of park visitors: twentieth-century urban, middle-class tourists. It was an audience that "got back to nature" in its own machines, on its own terms, and on its own schedule. Unlike their nineteenth-century counterparts, these visitors were concerned less with Mount Rainier as a symbol of national heritage and the social status that resulted from visiting such a place. Instead, the new type of visitors sought experience in nature as individuals who emphasized recreation and self-fulfillment over the collective contemplation of the mountain's deeper cultural significance.[46] And their perception of the park was mediated by their machines. The auto not only shaped their understanding of Mount Rainier as a national park; it strengthened their sense of what national parks should be.

These conditions suggest why Mount Rainier was treated as an anomaly at the national park conferences. As Assistant Secretary of the Interior Carmi A. Thompson observed at the first conference in 1911, Mount Rainier possessed conditions that were "entirely different" from other, more remote and often older national parks, and automobiles were "entirely advisable." The park contained but "one point of interest," Thompson argued, "that great mountain standing there as it does a lofty citadel, snow capped and bordered with glaciers." Tourists were interested primarily in seeing and climbing "that lofty mountain, so there can be no possible objection to taking them to the base of the mountain as quickly as possible and as comfortably as may be."[47] After a visit to the park that year, Thompson appeared to be carried away with the potential of the new machines. He promised to support a road all the way to Mount Rainier's summit. Impressed with the park's new road and the accessibility of such natural wonders as its glaciers, he exclaimed to a Tacoma audience, "I, like the average man, like to climb mountains in an auto." "Yours," he added, "is the only one obliging enough to let me."[48]

Although the assistant secretary's plans never materialized, they demonstrated how automobiles transformed people's perceptions of national parks, especially in terms of the spatial relationships between the park and its visitors. As the time and effort it took to reach the park decreased, people began to think of Mount Rainier within the context of their new automobility. As early as 1909, Milnor Roberts, from the University of Washington, noted that one could look at pictures of snow-mantled mountains and polar regions in magazines, but "the remoteness of these scenes lessens our chances of ever seeing them." Mount Rainier, on the other hand, was close at hand, "a wonderland of glaciers and snow in our own country." It was so easily reached by automobile that its reputation was spreading. A party "leaving Seattle or Tacoma in the morning," he wrote, by evening could pitch camp at timberline in "the shadow of the great peak" and with a view of "the vast forest wilderness."[49]

Moreover, the automobile seemed to enhance rather than diminish tourists' perceptions of the national park. The experience of driving into a park contradicted expectations that cars would ruin the experience. Passing through the park's portal, visitors were forced to slow down, to leave behind the "exhilaration of speed" in exchange for the "calmer glories of nature." Throttled down, their high-powered machines transported them over a "perfect road" winding through a dense forest and then up the mountain past waterfalls and glaciers.[50] If anything, the automobile compelled tourists to recognize that when they entered a national park, they were in a special landscape. The contrast of machines in the natural setting of a park, it seems, triggered this response, and a new set of metaphors appeared to describe the experience. A *Sunset* pictorial published in 1912, for example, enthusiastically depicted motoring in Mount Rainier as an encounter between "Glaciers and Gasoline."[51]

When thrown together in national parks, primeval nature and modern technology could even elicit reactions of wonder that bordered on the spiritual. In a more detailed account the following year, Carpenter Kendall observed that the "new-fangled dynamics" of the automobile enabled him to go "motoring on the mountain" and delight in its ageless mysteries.

Glaciers and Gasoline

Ascending Mount Rainier by automobile, Kendall noted, transported him through "a deep cathedral wood" with air "heavy with silence, as of prayer," past the "anthem of the river," and within reach of the "glistening peak which lifts its shining crest into the heavens." Far from being a disruptive influence, his machine's engine was "muffled against the dense wall of trees," allowing him to hear the "sound of falling waters" and see "graceful" cataracts appearing from some "unknown height and shooting under a rustic bridge." His automobile and the wild surroundings made the experience seem entirely "natural." As Kendall concluded, "If a landscape architect with his very best degree under his arm had planned these choice bits, they could not have been more perfectly set."[52]

By making national parks easier to reach and encounter, automobiles made it possible to consider in positive terms the experience of visiting a park in a car. Increasingly, automobiles helped to satisfy middle-class desires to seek restorative encounters with the natural world found in national parks and other scenic landscapes. Because most middle-class Americans could afford to be away only for short periods of time, the automobile expanded the range and opportunities for their vacations, which added to its popularity. Meanwhile, western communities and boosters, like those of Seattle and Tacoma, touted their region's scenic grandeur as a drawing card for tourists and supported auto tourism and national parks as essential parts of their economic development. Enos Mills, who was the chief advocate for Rocky Mountain National Park, for example, stressed that autos were essential to the future of national parks and western tourism. Cars enabled "most people" to reach the parks swiftly, covering the long distances in the West that separated population centers from these natural wonders. Mills went so far as to say that autos were better than horses for seeing national parks. Horses were more destructive of scenery than automobiles; horses required too much attention, trampled and overgrazed meadows, and needed too many facilities for their care. Cars, on the other hand, made camping inexpensive and comfortable. For these reasons, the automobile was a preferred means of transportation in national parks; it not only brought people into closer contact with nature but tended to tighten the bonds between urban centers and these wild landscapes.[53]

This new orientation expanded upon the original concept of seeing a national park from a road, as espoused by nineteenth-century park designers and engineers, to include automobile travel. Motoring was a means of knowing nature that embraced the park within a new geography created by the highway and automobile. The greatest expression of this new vision was the interest in building a road encircling Mount Rainier, as proposed by army engineer Eugene Ricksecker during the construction of the government road to Paradise. In 1911, for example, writer John Williams suggested that with the completion of the first park road, the next phase in opening the park to public use would be to fulfill "Mr. Ricksecker's fine plan for a road around the mountain." Williams's illustrated tourist guide, *The Mountain That Was "God,"* included Ricksecker's revised map of the park, which showed the engineer's proposed eighty- to one-hundred-mile route around the mountain. The planned road branched off from Christine Falls on the Paradise road and worked its way around the mountain, providing access to as many of the "great 'parks'" as possible and reaching the "snout of each glacier" before returning to the Paradise Valley.[54] Although Williams argued that a road around the mountain was essential, in part, for Mount Rainier's "proper policing" and "its protection from forest fires," he underscored the importance of the road to understanding the mountain as a whole and for providing better access to the mountain from other parts of the region.

In 1912, the Seattle-Tacoma Rainier National Park Advisory Committee presented the road-around-the-mountain as a key component of its nine-point policy for the "development and exploitation" of the national park. Concerned chiefly with improving the park's road system, the joint committee described the road proposal in terms similar to those of Williams. However, the group also stressed the planned road's relationship to other road projects that would increase the number of park entrance roads, namely in the park's three undeveloped corners. These areas were more than "natural entrances" for "an encircling road system." They were avenues that would eventually bring the park closer to Puget Sound's "two principal cities."[55]

The committee's involvement shows how central the automobile was in the park's development and meaning. Without a railroad patron for Mount Rainier, the group considered its role in park policy as a practical matter of regional and commercial interests. Ultimately, it expected the federal government to protect and improve the national park for public enjoyment, and it expected the government to carry out those actions in a way that would match its own commitments to the construction of roads leading to the park.[56] The committee's interest also highlights how the natural world and the modern age were seen to go hand in hand. Mount Rainier was not wilderness isolated from the influence of modern life and inventions like the automobile, but a wilderness that was there because of such inventions—growing more connected all the time to urban areas through roads and automobiles.

In their responses to public pressures and the increased mobility of park patrons, park administrators aided in strengthening this bond. They began to portray the park differently in annual reports. In 1913, they no longer described the park—its geography, natural features and amenities for visitors—as in isolation from, but rather in relation to, the Puget Sound cities. Administrators began to include the park's orientation to Seattle and Tacoma in their descriptions of the park's physical setting. They emphasized the distance from the Puget Sound cities to the park's main entrance and the "thoroughfare" leading to the park and its connection with the road to Paradise. They continued to document who traveled to the park by horse and wagon or on foot, and how many people came to "camp." But they paid closer attention to the type of automobile tourists entering the park, whether in a private car or auto stage, and for a time stopped reporting the number of mountain ascents.[57]

Park administrators also initiated surveys for a road system to encircle the park, reflecting the interests of groups like the Seattle-Tacoma park committee. As envisioned by both park administrators and park supporters, the park, county, and state road systems, both existing and proposed, would advance together. Roads would thus further incorporate the park into the surrounding region; they would form networks not only for economic growth but also for inspiration. As suggested by Superintendent Ethan Allen, the main goal of the road surveys was "the complete encirclement of the mountain park" by automotive roads, to "make it accessible from all directions."[58] William G. Steel, founder of Crater Lake National Park (1902) and president of Crater Lake Company, observed that a similar road survey for his park was essential to expanding visitation; such a road would enable tourists from around the West to see this rather remote park. "Our park is a new one," he concluded, and the automobile "is our only means of salvation."[59]

By 1913, the first surveys for a motor route encircling Mount Rainier were under way. Park officials expressed interest in carrying a road from the park's southwest corner to the east side of the park (along the park's southern border) to take advantage of a proposed state highway over Chinook Pass. The highway, which began in Seattle, would cross the park's northern boundary and bring a flood of east-west travel from across the state. Plans for the highway also stimulated interest in building a road across the northern slopes of Mount Rainier. A road across this section of the park would form another segment of the around-the-mountain route and shorten the distance to this area for Seattle and Tacoma residents. In 1915, park officials, anticipating pressure from tourists to use a mining road at Glacier Basin to access the park's northeastern corner, considered building a road across the northern slopes to connect the road at Glacier Basin with Carbon River to the west.

Administratively and conceptually, the Carbon River proposal brought the road project full circle. It had long been assumed that the Carbon River area, located in the northwestern corner of the park, would be the next area developed after the southwestern corner. The area lay closer to Seattle and it was thought that the Northern Pacific Railroad, with a rail line in the vicinity, might be induced to develop the area. Moreover, some considered the northwest side of Mount Rainier to contain the park's "grandest" scenery.[60] After inspecting the proposed route, Supervisor DeWitt L. Reaburn doubted that a north-side road would be "very promising on account of the high and rugged character of the region" and the "enormous expense" of building a "long and tortuous road." A survey of a road up the Carbon River to Cataract Creek near the snout of Carbon Glacier seemed more promising. Reaburn noted plans for locating a hotel and other services in the area with "a magnificent view of the Mountain and Carbon Glacier." The area, he anticipated, could also serve as a connecting point for a west-side road. Perhaps the greatest selling point was that a road to the area would decrease the distance to the park from Seattle by forty-one miles and from Tacoma by twenty-one miles.[61]

Although roads would make the park accessible from every direction, the goal of the road system was to bring the park closer to those living in Seattle and Tacoma. In 1915, there was only one road, the road to Paradise Valley, in Mount Rainier National Park. Still, the introduction of autos—controlled through regulations, conveyed over a road designed for scenery—popularized the park and enabled modern Americans to experience it and to know the nature it preserved in a novel way that became central to the understanding of national parks in the early twentieth century. Perhaps more than any other park of its time, Mount Rainier represented this ideal. Its urban patrons considered the mountain a symbol of their region's and cities' scenic beauty and a source of tourist revenue. They also thought of the park in terms of their new mobility. The automobile not only brought the park closer to them physically; it also altered how they thought of it conceptually. Their road proposals suggest that they interpreted the park within the

Glaciers and Gasoline

context of the nation's urban industrial order, an order in which business and nature preservation coexisted. They also suggest how the park was being mapped in a new kind of mental geography. Mount Rainier was not an isolated reservoir of wilderness preserved from progress, but was known because of progress.

Most of all, the acceptance of autos in national parks in the first fifteen years of the twentieth century embodied the optimistic belief that nature and technology were mutually beneficial. It fostered a new preservation ideal of communing with nature by car that would fully blossom with a federal agency dedicated to the care of parks in 1916. National parks, illustrated by Mount Rainier, were cultural constructions of nature, abstract notions made real through use. In the nineteenth century, those notions centered on parks as symbols of America's cultural achievements, selections of the western landscape's most sublime natural icons, which were to be viewed and contemplated. In the early twentieth century, those notions centered on parks increasingly as places for outdoor recreation, enclaves of nature to be reached by and known through machines.

2 / THE HIGHWAY IN NATURE

Mount Rainier and the National Park Service

Knowing nature through machines presented an ideal way of thinking about and experiencing national parks. Although largely unproven, the idea of the automobile as an enabling technology, displayed so well at Mount Rainier, was powerful. It centered on the belief that park roads not only conveyed auto tourists through a physical landscape, but also framed their perception of the park as a wild landscape that could be encountered by automobile. Knowing nature through machines also inspired the management of national parks under the National Park Service. This ideal strongly influenced the agency throughout the 1920s, under the leadership of its first two directors, Stephen T. Mather and Horace M. Albright. From 1916, when the agency was founded, to 1933, when the federal government was reorganized, they promoted the development of national parks for automobile tourism in part to realize the parks' full potential as places where machines and wild nature came together.

The Park Service leaders, however, did more than advertise parks as ideal places to commune with nature by car; they transformed parks into landscapes for the highway in nature. Maintaining and expanding upon traditions of nineteenth-century park management, Mather and Albright employed landscape architects and engineers to design parks, especially their road systems, in the "rustic" style. Through the use of native materials and appropriate location and scale, park facilities gave visitors the impression that autos, roads, and other amenities did not intrude on the natural scene. Instead, they seemed to be a part of nature. In this way, agency leaders advanced the notion that national parks were not only reservoirs of wilderness, characterized by uninhabited, pristine nature, but also were landscapes in which Americans could engage wilderness in a new way, as part of the motor age.

MATHER'S VISION: PARKS AS NATURE BY THE ROAD

The Park Service nurtured the ideal that autos and highways were a part of nature primarily because the agency was a product of the twentieth century. Its establishment coincided with the rise of the motor age, the popularity of auto travel by the middle class, and the growth of a national highway system. Although it was formed in response to threats to parks, like the damming of Yosemite's Hetch Hetchy Valley, the Park Service promoted the improvement of parks for auto tourists to defend against similar threats. Preservation *through* development made sense to Park Service leaders.[1] They did not see themselves turning away from the wilderness philosophy of the naturalist John Muir. They instead saw themselves embracing a new, mobile audience and shaping parks to meet its expectations about nature. It was an audience whose values were also influenced by the world of consumption and the mass market. In the late teens and twenties, Park Service leaders enthusiastically marketed parks to a mobile nation, tailoring the agency's message to appeal to a passion for the outdoors as a source of American values as well as individual experience. Mather, who spearheaded the advertising campaign, suggested that the true purpose of national parks lay in their use by, not their reservation from, motoring Americans. By driving into nature's wonders, Americans would find sustenance for the soul and physical well-being.[2]

In the time-honored tradition of government agencies using their successes to ward off outside control, the Park Service used the advent of auto tourism and the vast increase in auto owners to its own political advantage. Mather and Albright were also attempting to blend national parks with American life.[3] In tune with Progressive Era beliefs and the period's obsession with business, these men's concept of national parks was not simply about the intrinsic values of protected areas. The agency leaders not only could qualify the meaning of parks as symbols of the nation's cultural heritage, but also could quantify their meaning as sources of a new tourist industry. These conditions allowed Mather and other agency officials to jubilantly report increases in park travel as evidence of the public's acceptance of national parks and to characterize the related flood of autos and construction of hundreds of miles of new roads and other facilities for tourists in national parks as signs of success, not failure.[4]

In the minds of Park Service leaders, modifying parks for windshield tourists met the needs of most park visitors and satisfied what they believed auto tourists desired from their experience with national parks. Moreover, Mather and Albright believed that these modifications could in fact preserve wild nature, not necessarily in its original, primeval form, but as Americans had come to know it through recreation, through modern machines. The agency's founding legislation, the Organic Act of 1916, supported this idea. It declared that the purpose of national parks was to protect the "scenery, and the natural and historic objects and the wildlife therein and to provide for the enjoyment of the same in such a manner that will leave them unimpaired for the enjoyment of future generations."[5] Although the language of the act has often been interpreted to mean that the Park Service's mission was about total preservation, the agency's founders and main authors of the legislation, among them Mather and Albright, thought differently. They were urban professionals of wealth and social status, with backgrounds in industry, law, urban planning, and landscape architecture, who interpreted the legislation to mean that parks were "preserved" so long as they appeared pleasing to the eye. This meant that all forms of resource extraction and other actions that would permanently disfigure park landscapes were excluded. But modern machines, road systems, and other amenities for tourists were entirely appropriate in national parks because they could be integrated with, and were essential to informing perceptions of, the parks' wilderness settings.[6]

What usually goes unnoticed about the legislation is that it recognized that national parks were part of a new spatial relationship with nature created by the automobile. Few Americans would experience or understand national parks any other way. In 1910, while scenic preservationists launched a campaign for a park bureau to fend off the Hetch Hetchy assault, Henry Ford's Model T went into mass production. Soon after, automobile ownership began its meteoric rise throughout the country, soaring from less than half a million automobiles registered in 1910 to twenty-three million in 1930.[7] Meanwhile, motor travel became the single greatest reason for the rising popularity of national parks. Visitation rose from 700,000 people and 60,000 autos in 1917 (the first full year of the Park Service's existence) to 2.6 million people and 690,000 autos in 1929. As Mather observed during this period, "we are indebted more than anything else" to the automobile for

ORGANIC ACT OF 1916
ALSO...
year NPS was created

making "the matchless splendors of the national parks . . . the supreme scenic travel magnets of our country."[8]

Cars alone were not responsible for influencing the agency's perception of national parks. Highways were also essential components in shaping the visitation patterns and impressions of parks. They were part of the new transportation and tourist geography reconfiguring the landscape of the nation, especially the American West, home to most national parks. Across the country, the vast increase in drivers sparked continuous calls for road improvements, which began as early as 1905 with the "See America First" movement, and led to the promotion of the first national highway, the Lincoln Highway. Calls for "good roads" also contributed to the first federal aid for road improvements in 1916 (the same year the Park Service act was passed) and to the passage of the 1921 Highway Act, the impetus for which was the creation of a national highway system.[9]

In this emerging highway landscape, national parks would become as we know them today: accessible for a broad sector of the American public and a distinct part of highway travel that provides closer contact with the natural world. In the 1920s, finding primitive nature by the road was a distinct aspect of auto tourism. As one person noted, the "whole countryside" had become a "motorist's park."[10] But as auto tourism increased, along with urban sprawl and commercial development, those who expected pleasing scenes of native trees, flowers, mountains, and lakes discovered instead litter, billboards, ramshackle food stands, and an array of automobile-related services cropping up along the road.[11] The chances of finding roadside beauty diminished, except in national parks, where primeval nature and the open road were part of the same preserve.

National parks became special places for highways and nature because they were federally owned and could be managed to perpetuate the experience of finding nature by the road. Mather, retired millionaire industrialist that he was, seemed to understand this relationship between public roads and public parks and sought to exploit it. Among the first professionals Mather hired were landscape architects and engineers, who virtually guaranteed that park highways would appear "natural." It was their job, Mather instructed, to lay out the roads "so that they will disturb as little as possible the vegetation, forests, and rocky hillsides through which they are built," while providing motorists with opportunities to view the scenic wonders of national parks. Because his agency would take "the greatest care in the protection of the landscape" in road construction, Mather insisted that roads would not degrade the wilderness values of parks. Rather, they would present parks in a way that would appeal to a majority of visitors.[12] This concept of the highway in nature also informed Mather's interest in protecting scenery along the approach roads to national parks and his vision for a national park highway system (the National Park-to-Park Highway). It proved especially powerful in Mather's desire to develop park highways that would reveal the grandeur of national parks and evoke in motorists the sense that they were having an intimate encounter with pristine nature.

Mather's concept of roads, while it won support from members of Congress and the public, was not universally accepted. By the mid-1920s some scenic preservationists worried that accommodations for automobiles were deteriorating, not enhancing, the wilderness values of national parks. In fact it was in response to the growing presence of autos in parks and on other public lands that outdoor organizations began to define wilderness as roadless. Even though Mather (and later Albright) would revise plans for roads in parks and declare his intentions more clearly with statements that roads would not overwhelm the parks to appease critics, his views of wilderness never strayed far from the road.

To address the concerns of wilderness supporters, the agency's first leaders relied increasingly on landscape architects not only to harmonize developments with their natural surroundings but also to resolve the issues wilderness advocates voiced. The idea, however, was never to eliminate roads altogether. Instead, by employing principles of naturalistic design, landscape architects ensured that road routes conformed to the topography of parks as much as possible, allowing tourists to view park scenery without a road scar detracting from that experience. Landscape architects also devised standards for naturalizing park roads through careful construction techniques and the use of native materials. By the late 1920s and early 1930s, the Park Service thought it had found a solution to increasing concerns about its management of parks as wilderness reserves open to automobiles. Landscape architects were in charge of overseeing park developments to ensure a balance between nature and human artifice in the parks. To organize and present their work, they used master plans—comprehensive outlines with conceptual drawings—to identify and schedule development projects and to illustrate how they would affect a park as a whole.[13] In this way, it seemed possible for roads to be part of, rather than intrusions upon, the natural world. It seemed possible, at least in the minds of agency leaders, that Mather's dream could become reality.

The Highway in Nature

CREATING THE IDEAL PARK:
THE ROAD AROUND THE MOUNTAIN

In the 1920s, Mount Rainier figured prominently in both the Park Service's road program and in Mather's vision of national parks. In its development strategies for Mount Rainier, the Park Service proceeded from the notion that a road system around the mountain would create a closer bond between machines and nature. It would produce what Mather thought was a model national park, one that could be toured by car and that would be accessible from the local and state road systems. There was perhaps no greater symbol of the highway in nature as Mather envisioned it than the parkway named for him. Mount Rainier's Mather Memorial Parkway protects a forested corridor of some sixty miles (mostly outside the park). When built, it offered auto tourists a long scenic drive to the park as well as through it. The parkway had been the last field project Mather worked on before suffering a stroke in 1928. According to his biographer, the road was still on his mind as he lay in a hospital bed. Paralyzed on one side of his body and speechless, Mather mouthed the word "Cascade" to Albright. Mather's career, however, was over; he died the following year.[14] But the parkway, dedicated in 1932, memorialized the director and his belief that the scenic approaches to parks, along with the roadside scenery within parks, should be preserved.

Besides honoring Mather as a fallen leader, the parkway was instructive for appreciating his influence on Mount Rainier as well as on all national parks. In his conception of Mount Rainier, Mather demonstrated that he was interested in more than managing parks as a new kind of business venture. He displayed the qualities shared by others who toured parks in the early twentieth century: a passion for mountaineering and motoring. As a member of the Sierra Club, he climbed Mount Rainier in 1905. His ascent left a lasting impression and drew him back to scale peaks in the West almost every summer to "soothe and refresh himself."[15] Many of those trips, and his later tours of national parks as their director, were conducted in part by automobile. Thus, he saw in the auto something more than a source of political strength for the parks. He saw it as a source for placing people into closer contact with the natural world within national parks.

As early as 1916, Mather pressed for a road system that would encircle Mount Rainier with this goal in mind. After touring the northwest corner of the park the year before with members of the Seattle-Tacoma park committee, he was convinced that a road up the Carbon River valley was essential to the park's future. In his role as director of parks under the secretary of the interior, Mather initially used the trip to dramatize the purpose of parks, the need for their management by a federal bureau, and the importance of a strong alliance between the federal government and local business leaders in their administration. (Mather persuaded members of the committee, for example, to form the Rainier National Park Company and to build an inn at Paradise, which opened in 1917.) Mather suggested that a Carbon River road would open up a lightly visited part of the park to motorists. But he also envisioned it as an entryway for another road, one that would go around the park. Such a road, he observed, would present motorists with ever-changing views of the "great mountain." It would be "a scenic highway unsurpassed in the world."[16]

Although Mather's proposal carried forward the views of early road designers like Eugene Ricksecker and park patrons like the Seattle-Tacoma park committee, he was also fashioning a way to think about not just one park but all parks as part of a great circuit tour. Mather may be better known for opening parks to cars and turning them into urban villages. But he also saw in the nation's expanding highway network a way to link parks together as a system, both conceptually and physically. In doing so, he not only would build on the reputation of parks as scenic assets and sources of national identity—what historian Marguerite Shaffer calls "sacred national landscapes"—but would also expand on their draw for domestic travel and a growing tourist industry.[17] Roads would lead to and through the parks, and automobiles would be the mode of conveyance that drew them together. The national park director's purchase and improvement of Yosemite's Tioga Pass Road in 1915, for example, was intended to take advantage of the growing popularity of cross-country auto travel. Mather's act allowed more cars to enter Yosemite, symbolizing for some critics the beginning of the end of its wilderness values. Yet, in Mather's vision, the Tioga Road would join Yosemite, General Grant, and Sequoia national parks together, especially if they could not be expanded into one large park, as he wished.[18]

The most famous example of this idea was the park-to-park highway. Shortly after dedicating the Tioga Road, Mather enthusiastically endorsed a national park-to-park highway, promoted by boosters, that would link the major western national parks in a loop road. Mather worked with the Yellowstone Highway Association, later reorganized as the National Park-to-Park Highway Association, to promote this great circular highway. Dedicated in 1920, it would allow travelers to visit national parks in nine states over a well-marked and mostly paved series of roads covering some six thousand miles. The road system, as Mather and others described it, would bring the isolated reservoirs of American wilderness and scenic grandeur into a much closer relationship with the nation's growing metropolitan character. It would transform parks into pearls strung along an extended highway awaiting the discovery and pleasure of motorists. It would further reorder notions of travel across space and through time introduced by the automobile, for tourists theoretically could tour the wonders of not just one park but of all parks within a relatively short period of time.[19] Tourists could think of parks and highways as part of the same public landscape.

While Mather's endorsement of what he called the world's "greatest scenic drive" was partly a practical response to the growth of tourism, the highway's conception and mapping also responded to the continued rise of auto camping as a popular way of retreating to and engaging nature.[20] As one writer informed readers of *Sunset* in 1917, automobiles provided "an elemental contact with the reality of nature. . . . There is more than 'scenery' to be complacently inspected; there is the life and atmosphere of the West to be lived."[21] This back to nature movement turned the roadside into the public space auto tourists used for camping and, more importantly, into a natural landscape they valued for its aesthetic and inspirational qualities. Mount Rainier was part of this landscape. As an auto tourist observed upon seeing the mountain for the first time, "All at once there burst into view a marvelous sight. High up in the air there loomed a tremendous mass of snow and ice that seemed only a few miles away."[22] Mather seems to have recognized that, as opportunities for finding nature by the road decreased elsewhere, national parks would become refuges of the open road in nature's paradise.

The relationship between the circle highway at Mount Rainier and the one around the West was important, Mather suggested, because he wanted to place tourists in the proper frame of mind to appreciate parks. Under ideal circumstances, the entire park highway tour would have been one continuous corridor of wonder. To this end, Mather expended a great deal of energy promoting scenic highways leading to national parks. He advised park tourists, for example, to travel over routes like Oregon's Columbia River Highway on their way to Mount Rainier and other western parks. A segment of the park-to-park highway, the Columbia River Highway was renowned for its "scenic grandeur" and imaginative design because it was actually built as a scenic highway and showcased the many waterfalls and vistas along its route. At the same time, Mather was actively involved in protecting roadside scenery, especially "stands of virgin timber," along highways approaching national parks. Driving through a logged-over landscape outside a park's boundaries would not inspire visitors. He wanted park tourists to know they had entered a special landscape when they drove into a national park, but he did not want the transition to be jarring. His work with the roadside beauty movement led to regulations for preserving roadside strips of timber (often within national forests), the establishment of state parks along highways, and the promotion of scenic byways—all leading to park boundaries like the parkway that would eventually bear his name at Mount Rainier.[23]

Mather also employed his concept of the relationship between public highways and parks to convince Congress to finance the improvement of park roads. The federal government had a responsibility to construct "good roads" not only outside national parks but also in them because good roads drew more attention to national parks. Road conditions influenced people's impressions of the parks, Mather reasoned. Tourists paid their admission expecting "enjoyment and pleasure," and protested loudly when dusty and bumpy dirt roads marred their visits. In 1924, Mather's argument was compelling enough that Congress approved the Park Service's first road construction program, a three-year, $7.5 million effort to improve existing national park roads (some 1,060 miles) and to build at least 360 new miles.[24]

The director's vision of national parks as places for the highway in nature inspired his desire to revive the proposal for a motor road around the mountain in 1919. In part, he wanted to ensure better automobile access to the entire park. Mount Rainier continued to be inviting to motoring Americans, especially residents of Seattle and Tacoma. During World War I, for example, the park was briefly the most visited park in the system, and throughout the 1920s it consistently ranked as the third or fourth most popular park for motorists. Along with Mount Rainier superintendent Roger Toll and George Goodwin, the Park Service's chief engineer, Mather agreed with park boosters that Mount Rainier's popularity with auto tourists gave it considerable potential for tourist developments at all four corners. The southwestern entrance was already popular, agency officials noted, and there were already plans for the Carbon River at the northwestern corner. The state highway was proceeding toward the White River at the park's northeastern corner, renowned for views of the impressive Emmons Glacier. Meanwhile, more mineral springs had been discovered in the Ohanapecosh region, near the mountain's south-eastern corner. There, the Forest Service was already allowing concession development just outside the park's boundary.[25]

In their proposals, Park Service officials described the circle road as a way to connect these areas. They used language similar to descriptions used by Mather and others of the park-to-park highway. The road around the mountain would be formed by a series of routes linking the park's most significant points of interest—subalpine meadows, glaciers, and forests—to form a single road system. In this respect, agency plans deviated little from the earlier proposal made by Ricksecker. Goodwin, for instance, shared the young engineer's confidence in drawing a line around the mountain and calculating the distance from one corner of the park to the next. Only now, the circle road was becoming part of the Park Service's official management policy, and the agency conceivably had the political and financial power and expertise to complete the project.[26]

But it was the project's abstract qualities that are most revealing. As proposed, the road is valuable for understanding how the Park Service interpreted the meaning of Mount Rainier—and parks in general—to a modern audience in automobiles, and thus how the project would only enhance the visitor experience and in a sense create the park itself. As Superintendent Toll observed, the scheme was the central element in the "ultimate development of the park." With it the majority of visitors could enjoy the mountain's many wonders in the convenience of their cars without taking an "arduous camping trip." In similar terms, Mather referred to it as an "ideal road system" that, despite its rather grandiose proportions, was not impractical. In an age of great road projects, it was a highway for the future.[27]

In 1924, Superintendent Owen A. Tomlinson submitted a road plan that justified the road system for a variety of administrative reasons, but he also supported the highway as the best way to fulfill the purpose of this and all national parks. Echoing park designers of the nineteenth century, he maintained that without the road around the mountain, Mount Rainier would neither be "accessible to the people" nor maintained in "its natural condition as nearly as possible." Only the southwestern corner of the park, he observed, was open to the public, and for this reason too many visitors were being concentrated in one area, overtaxing existing services. In time, the enjoyment tourists expected here would diminish, as would the natural scenery they came to see.[28] Cars did not destroy wilderness; they protected it.

Tomlinson, whose rationale for the road program echoed Mather's,

interesting thought
process – Agree
or disagree?

asserted that completion of a highway encircling the mountain would bring, quite possibly, an end to the park's road development. It would relieve the existing strain on park services and resources and would assure the greatest enjoyment by the greatest number of visitors. On the one hand, his conclusion was a matter of simple arithmetic. Close to 161,500 people visited the park in 1924, more than tenfold the number a decade earlier, and the number of people crowding into a relatively small area would only increase, he reasoned. On the other hand, he thought the road would provide visitors with the "ideal" way to see Mount Rainier and would be how they derived the most pleasure from it. Granted, spending three weeks hiking around the mountain, leisurely exploring and examining features of interest, had great appeal. But it was only a select minority who could devote that much time to a vacation. It would be more advantageous to see as much of the park as possible by car in a shorter period of time, since the park was "crowded with scenic beauties and natural exhibits."[29]

The superintendent's description of Mount Rainier's road system, and his reasons for it, further reinforced Mather's vision of national parks as elements of a much larger landscape of highways in nature. Mount Rainier was part of a new and evolving automotive landscape; it was directly influenced by the state highways leading to it and the nearby Puget Sound cities, all of which invited more visitors and pressures to build more roads. In turn, the situation focused attention on the poor road conditions in Mount Rainier and cast the park in an unflattering light. As Tomlinson observed, visitors would remember it not as a place away from it all, a vessel of primitive America, but as a place of "dead end roads" and repetitive scenery.[30]

Mather's concept of parks, however, was as problematic as it was imaginative. At Mount Rainier, it was one thing to imagine the circle road and the park it would create; it was another to construct the road. The circle highway, based on the nineteenth-century carriage drive, would have to be built on the mountain's steep and unstable slopes and would require more extensive excavation and construction to carry automobiles than wagons. In this rugged terrain, with the mountain's long winters and heavy snows, the road corridor would be wider and more visible. At best then, as one historian suggests, the circuit scheme was wishful thinking, at worst a visual and environmental disaster in waiting.[31]

Nevertheless, Mather and others who embraced the circular road system could not conceive of experiencing the park any other way. The automobile

The Highway in Nature

had framed their perspective on Mount Rainier and other parks. Driving the park seemed normal. And any aesthetic and environmental concerns—how the road looked and the potential damage its construction would cause to the park landscape—were not as important as the idea of the road itself as an avenue through wonder. Beginning in the early 1920s, the earliest road projects carried out by the Park Service at Mount Rainier, the Carbon River Road and the West Side Road, were disappointments. They met with financial setbacks and environmental obstacles. And though considered the first legs in the road around the mountain, they were incomplete.[32]

Mather, however, pressed on, convinced that these roads, despite their problems, would become part of a larger "ideal road system" for the park. In 1921, for example, when the Park Service began construction of the Carbon River Road, it promoted the route as the "first link of the West Side Road." It would eventually join the northwest and southwest corners of the park and with other road sections would encircle Mount Rainier. Mather was confident that in an age of "enormous road-building projects," this and other elements of the circle road had "no unreasonable or impracticable features." One of the first routes funded under the Park Service, the road traveled six miles within the park by 1924. Yet despite the director's optimism, the Carbon River Road never reached its intended objective, the terminus of the Carbon Glacier, instead ending a mile before it. That year flooding damaged the new road, and the Park Service was forced to build expensive revetments along sections of the road. The following year, the connecting Pierce County road to Fairfax was completed, and a campground for auto tourists opened at Ipsut Creek. But that would be the extent of the road, and proposals for another hotel and services operated by the park's concessionaire came to naught.[33]

Although the Carbon River Road never became the popular motor route that Mather anticipated, it illustrates his approach to building roads in national parks. It possessed qualities he wanted for public highways, in particular the kind of seamless transition a road should make leading to a national park. But achieving this impression, like the construction of the road, was a complex matter. In the first place, Congress would commit funds to new road construction only after the access road from Fairfax was under construction. Further complicating matters, nearly half of the road to the park boundary lay across privately owned timberland, and the rest crossed national forest. The situation, though, inspired the kind of cooperation Mather thought necessary to protect scenic approach roads. In 1921, the

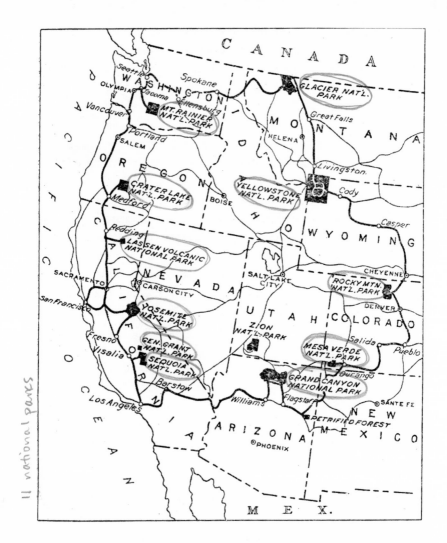

II national parks

MAP 3. National Park-to-Park Highway. In the early 1920s, national parks were part of the nation's new highway geography.

project brought together Mount Rainier's two main support groups, the Mountaineers and the Rainier National Park Advisory Board (formerly the Seattle-Tacoma park committee). Although the two groups would later be divided over the extent of road developments in the park, they convinced the Forest Service and Pierce County officials to begin work on the Carbon River approach road. Meanwhile, the Natural Parks Association of Washington actively sought the protection of roadside forests from Fairfax to the park boundary, and through a land exchange with a timber company, the group helped preserve a section of forest along the road corridor.[34]

Moreover, Mather viewed the problems associated with the construction of this and other park road projects as something that could be solved with the expertise of landscape architects and engineers. In particular, he wanted the Carbon River Road project to succeed because it was one of the first on which landscape architects and engineers had collaborated.[35] These specialists, if anyone, should have been able to overcome the natural forces that damaged the road and, as much as possible, would find a way to make the road a part of the mountain itself. If the agency's road program were to have a future, it depended on them.

The problem with the road, the director decided, lay not in the joint venture of landscape architects and engineers, but in the skills of his chief engineer. Evidently, Goodwin had refused to acknowledge that the road, as designed, was nearly impossible to build because it could not survive the seasonal flooding of the Carbon River. This, and a number of similar incidents, caused Mather to fire him. Mather's long-term solution was not simply to hire another chief engineer but to seek the assistance of an agency of road-building engineers. In 1926, he decided to leave his agency's landscape architects in charge of the design of park roads, but he enlisted the assistance of the federal Bureau of Public Roads to help build them. By taking advantage of the bureau's road-building skill, specifically its engineers, Mather sought to ensure that park roads, like the system planned for Mount Rainier, would overcome any obstacles of nature.[36]

A SEAMLESS WHOLE: ROADS, WILDERNESS, AND PARKS IN THE MOTOR AGE

In the mid-1920s, Mount Rainier figured prominently in the Park Service's first major road program and in arguments against it as well. The new arrangement with the Bureau of Public Roads buoyed Mather's interest in building a "great road" in Mount Rainier and other national parks. He seemed confident that a road would eventually encircle Mount Rainier, even when faced with environmental and fiscal hurdles. By the late 1920s, for example, it became obvious that only the southern half of the West Side Road, the next phase in Mount Rainier's road system, would ever be completed. The steep terrain around Ipsut Pass, near the Carbon River, convinced Park Service officials to revise their plans. To preserve the loop drive experience on the west side, rather than abandon the project altogether, they proposed building an entrance road to Mowich Lake, about the midpoint between the northeast and southeast entrances, and extending the West Side Road from the lake south to the North Puyallup River. From there, tourists could either continue on through the park at the Nisqually entrance or return to Tacoma.[37]

However compelling, Mather's passion for roads and his optimism that they could be built were not universally accepted. Just as the director's road program gathered momentum, scenic preservationists began mounting their own campaign against the program's apparent destruction of the wilderness values of parks. Outdoor organizations reacted to the growing presence of cars in parks by defining wilderness as roadless; they were "driven wild" and were forming a different vision of roads.[38] For these outdoor enthusiasts, the central issue was not that park roads could reconcile cars and wilderness, as Mather suggested. It was whether too many roads, or any roads for that matter, would destroy the wilderness values of a park. In short order, Mather and other Park Service leaders found themselves in the midst of a debate over the meaning of wilderness and national parks. The debate threatened to disrupt the agency's fragile coalition of park advocates, composed of not only outdoor clubs but also auto enthusiasts and business interests who supported tourist developments. More importantly, it pressed Mather to clarify his vision of parks as landscapes for highways in nature.

The debate over roads and cars in national parks suggested that, at least in the 1920s, defining national parks as wilderness areas free of roads was difficult. So much of their identity at the time was related to the notion that they could actually sustain roads and cars without losing their wilderness values. At Mount Rainier, for example, groups like the Rainier National Park Advisory Board believed that modifying parks for auto tourists was appropriate because wilderness was an added but not central feature of national parks. In the eyes of many board members, the purpose of Mount Rainier and other national parks was something beyond a wild and unmodified landscape; it was something waiting to be attained. Mount Rainier was still an unfinished product. In the future, the road system would benefit park visitors by giving them great opportunities to see Mount Rainier and a recreational experience they would value. It would also benefit the park's concessionaire by attracting more customers. To the advisory board's way of thinking, the government was partially responsible for accommodating the needs of the park concessionaires since they assumed the financial risk and provided services the federal government, by itself, could never have provided. The board's chairman, Asahel Curtis, asserted that without roads, parks like Mount Rainier would not be "accessible for all our people." If the Park Service listened to a "very small minority" and left the park in an unaltered state, it would fail to fulfill the democratic purpose of national parks. "Frequent visits to our shrines of natural beauty" not only would reward the tourist industry, he concluded, but also the nation by making people "better citizens."[39]

But to other organizations, like the Mountaineers, the agency's activities displayed a grave disregard for national parks as wilderness enclaves, landscapes that seemed undisturbed by human activities. To them, the Park Service's commitment to concessionaires and road projects was particularly troubling. By the mid-1920s, groups such as the Sierra Club and the National Parks Association joined with the Mountaineers to question the Park Service's aggressive pursuit of new park acquisitions and the associated development of park road systems and other accommodations for visitors. Wilderness proponents disagreed with Mather's earlier statements that parks were "practically lying fallow" without "proper development." In their minds, scenery was not "a hollow enjoyment" without "the ordinary creature comforts," like hotels and roads, as the director suggested. Granted, the Park Service was trying to assure its autonomy by staking its claim to the new growth in outdoor recreation by offering parks as the nation's playgrounds to an increasingly mobile middle class. But Mount Rainier and other parks like Yosemite seemed overwhelmed by auto tourists. The Sierra Club, for example, claimed that the flood of auto tourists into the beloved valley of Yosemite had spoiled it. In midsummer, wrote one critic, the "air is filled with smoke, dust, and the smell of gasoline."[40]

The distinction between getting back to nature in an automobile and wilderness protection, however, was no clearer by the 1920s than it was when John Muir first endorsed the use of machines in Yosemite. The Mountaineers had earlier supported park road development at Mount Rainier on the condition, it seems, that automobiles would take outdoor enthusiasts as close to climbing routes and backcountry trails as possible. Now, after the first road projects were completed or underway, the group wanted to limit the use of autos once within park boundaries to prevent unnecessary development and the loss of the park's wilderness values. Yet they also complained that regulations prohibiting cars "for hire" from entering national parks unfairly restricted their use of Mount Rainier, especially during outings to climb or hike around the peak. While autos "operated for pleasure" could enter national parks, rented vehicles—such as auto stages and freight trucks carrying members and supplies—could not. Thus, once inside the park, the Mountaineers were forced to abandon their rental trucks and to pay a fee to use machines operated by transportation companies licensed to operate in the park. The Mountaineers argued that the regulations unfairly excluded them and many others from accessing national parks and from using the public highways that led to and through them.[41]

Besides debates over access, groups like the Mountaineers believed that Mount Rainier and other parks were becoming too commercial. In 1920, for example, the Massachusetts Forestry Association reported that its members had a disappointing stay at Paradise Inn. "The atmosphere of commercialism about the park is distasteful to many," the organization noted, "and would indicate a greater desire to pay dividends than serve the traveling public." Moreover, as visitation increased, parks were increasingly the scene of a bewildering array of new activities and services. In the late 1920s and early 1930s, for example, park patrons could play a round of golf at Paradise in the summer and watch ski tournaments in the winter.[42]

Worried that the growing commercial flavor and carnival-like atmosphere of national parks were diminishing their status as wilderness reserves and thus making them less authentic representations of the natural world, the Mountaineers and other preservationists began to criticize the Park Service's priorities. The entire reason for improving access to parks, they argued, was to let as many people as possible relate to nature in its primeval state, not to let local business interests reshape them into ordinary landscapes.[43] The Mountaineers, though critical of what they saw as excessive privileges accorded to the park concessionaire, were also expressing disappointment over losing a park they had had virtually to themselves. The park as the club members had known it was rapidly disappearing, and they wanted to reclaim some of their relationship with the mountain before it was too late. It was a process that sharpened their conception of parks as places left untainted by modern life and that led to their suggestion that sections of Mount Rainier should remain unmodified landscapes.

As early as 1926, the Mountaineers proposed that several areas in Mount Rainier be designated as "wilderness areas" free from roads and commercial developments such as hotels and pay camps. The group generally wanted portions of the southwestern and northern sides of the park spared; these included Indian Henry's Hunting Ground, St. Andrews Park, and Klapatche

Park, along the route of the West Side Road, as well as the area between Ipsut Pass and Yakima Park, along the proposed route of the road across the mountain's northern slopes. By following these suggestions, the group believed, the Park Service would no longer be subjecting the majority of the park to "commercial use and development" while keeping only a fraction of it in "its natural wilderness condition."[44]

The Park Service responded to the proposal positively, but not necessarily for the same reasons motivating the Mountaineers. In the park's 1926 development plan, the agency eliminated the road across the mountain's northern slopes. The decision, reached by Superintendent Tomlinson and Thomas C. Vint, the agency's chief landscape architect, emphasized other reasons besides the region's wilderness values. Both men noted that a road across such rugged terrain was unnecessary and unwise, concurring with earlier park managers. Thus, the wilderness proposal created relatively few problems for the Park Service. For them the mountain's north side was simply a place they could not build a road, and as Superintendent Tomlinson observed, this fact qualified the area, along with portions of its west side, for designation as wilderness. He supported the group's proposal for this reason, noting that it corresponded with the Park Service's mission and national park ideals. It would also appease "those concerned with the preservation of natural wilderness areas" and assure them that the agency was "guarding against over development of the national parks." Mather agreed with Tomlinson and, on August 17, 1928, set the areas aside as wilderness.[45]

Even though Mather agreed to establish wilderness areas off-limits to roads, he did not necessarily share the views of the emerging coalition of wilderness advocates that wilderness—and thus parks in general—should be free of roads. He supported wilderness designation at Mount Rainier where it seemed that building a road might be an impossible thing. His decision was also politically motivated, for he needed to hold together the fragile coalition of park supporters. Mather seemed to realize the danger of proceeding without allaying the concerns of wilderness proponents. Beginning in the early 1920s, for example, he claimed that it was not his intention to "gridiron" the parks with roads. Mather, who repeated the statement like a mantra, meant that parks should be accessible at least by one road leading through their most scenic sections. In this way, large areas within each park would remain in a "natural wilderness state."[46] Mather, however, continued to aspire to the belief that wilderness was really a scenic quality, without the deeper meanings associated with wilderness as original nature that some were beginning to suggest. In the case of Mount Rainier, Mather could maintain his convictions. So much of the mountain remained above and beyond the road that it was possible to think of wilderness and roads as compatible.

In Mather's mind, the issue of roads in parks was not one of dividing parks into separate spheres of wild versus defiled lands. The park road system program, he asserted, was really part of a larger landscape preservation program. Through sensitive design and selection of materials, landscape architects would blend these road developments into the natural setting of the parks. They could also beautify existing roads to create a similar effect, a practice that began with Yellowstone's roads in 1924. Roads, it seemed, would not necessarily turn parks into different zones of primitive and modified nature. Instead, roads would transform parks into unified landscapes of wild beauty.

In the mid-1920s, the full expression of this ideal lay several years in the future, when new park roads were completed and existing ones altered. Meanwhile, wilderness supporters pressed the Park Service to revise its concept of national parks as suitable settings for highways in nature. The idea of wilderness as roadless, which they were fashioning during the 1920s, tended to be reactionary. It was a response to modern life and the motor age. It was a different version of the idea cast by an earlier generation, represented by John Muir, who sought to protect the natural world from resource exploitation. As the historian Paul Sutter suggests, the wilderness idea emerged as "an alternative to landscapes of modernized leisure and play, and it was preeminently a product of the discordant internal politics of outdoor recreation."[47] In this respect, the coming of the automobile and the potential for communing with wild nature by car did not appeal to everyone. Some were moved to consider communing with nature without a car, and worked to prevent motorized recreation and roads from invading all public lands. They not only began to define wilderness by the absence of cars and roads, but also tried to reshape national parks to reflect this idea.

This notion of wilderness was different from how Park Service leaders like Mather conceived it. Rather than integrating the machine with a wild landscape, wilderness advocates sought to keep the two apart in official wilderness reserves. In 1924, at the recommendation of the young forester Aldo Leopold, the Forest Service created the country's first wilderness area, the Gila Wilderness in New Mexico, in which mechanized access was prohibited.[48] According to Leopold, later renowned as a wildlife biologist and

The Highway in Nature

as a person who developed ethical rationales for protecting wild and rural lands, wilderness should preserve the past, an America of pioneers and covered wagons, in a landscape uncontaminated by the current trend in automotive recreation. He thought of wilderness as "'unmotorized' nature." By relying on their own wits and instincts, people could know the natural world on its own terms. Automobiles, while satisfying the social impulse to return to the natural world, transformed the experience into sport. People could become more attuned to nature, to feel closer to its primitive essence, Leopold argued, only by engaging it more directly through such physically demanding activities as hiking or hunting. Only then would they realize the value of preserving nature as an end in itself.[49]

The Mountaineers' proposal reflected Leopold's concept with its roadless requirement and challenged the perception of national parks as envisioned by Mather, as wild landscapes open to, and largely undisturbed by, automobiles. The rather novel idea seemed to perplex agency leaders in Washington, D.C., who first reviewed the resolution. They wondered if wilderness was the appropriate designation for park areas free from roads. It seemed hard for them to imagine parks (and wilderness) without roads. Perhaps, they suggested, it would be more exact to describe the entire park as "wilderness subject to the installation of roads, trails, hotels, and other commercial developments." Unlike Leopold's concept of wilderness, Park Service leaders imagined wilderness as a space in which people could travel by modern cars and other means. For them the essential quality of national park wilderness was not unmechanized transportation but simply that parks differed from national forests; parks were closed to timber harvests, hunting, and other forms of resource exploitation. At the same time, Park Service Acting Director Arthur E. Demaray and Assistant Director Arno B. Cammerer proposed a definition of national park wilderness that was even more inviolable than Leopold's definition. The only precedent for national park wilderness areas was the recent creation of such an area in the Yosemite high country for scientific research. The area, however, excluded people (except for scientists) in order to retain nature in its "balanced" state. Since the Mountaineers wanted access to their proposed wilderness areas by horseback or foot, the two men thought that wilderness was the wrong classification. What the climbing club was proposing were areas of nature essentially without human influence. Rather than call them "wilderness," they settled on the bureaucratically bland title of areas "free from road and commercial development."[50]

Although Mather agreed to the term "wilderness area" to describe Mount Rainier's reserves, the wilderness issue was far from resolved. The wilderness question exposed a growing rift between park advocates nationally on the subject of appropriate park developments. At Mount Rainier, for example, the Mountaineers and the Rainier National Park Advisory Board butted heads over the extent of developments. The board and park concessionaire were pressing for the installation of a tramway to and a scenic loop drive around the Paradise Valley. And in the park's 1926 development program, the Park Service unveiled plans to add buildings to Paradise and Longmire as well as to build four new developed areas (and the roads to reach them) at Spray Park, Sunset Park, Yakima Park, and Ohanapecosh Springs.[51]

Complicating matters further was the lack of consensus about the true purpose of parks. Should they be managed exclusively to preserve pristine nature? Or should they be managed for the way many had come to know them, through their windshields? The answers to these questions centered, as they would for most of the twentieth century, on the issue of access, specifically access by automobile. "Certainly," observed Thomas H. Martin, general manager of the Rainier National Park Company, "the spirit of our nation calls for majority rule, and this would mean that the National Parks, and all other public institutions, are held for the interest and benefit of the majority." And since the majority of visitors drove to national parks, he concluded, it was only logical that the government grant them access to the parks by building roads for them. The Mountaineers, however, responded that they were also members of the advisory board and the only ones who had "wholly non-commercial" interests. Their views, then, were important. The Mountaineers were not opposed entirely to roads within Mount Rainier; they just believed that roads served a purpose other than providing tourist revenue. Thus, they endorsed an "adequate road system for the park," one that not only would allow visitors to enter the park and experience its primitive qualities but that also would preserve certain areas of the park as wilderness by making them off-limits to roads.[52]

Wilderness as a roadless concept may have been growing increasingly popular, but its supporters never seemed to stray far from an idea of national parks informed by automobiles. Even park protector Robert Sterling Yard expressed somewhat contradictory views. Yard, who had grown disenchanted with his role in publicizing national parks for Mather by 1920, became one of the most passionate critics of the ways auto tourism, roads, and the related

The Highway in Nature

commercial emphasis of the park experience had corrupted the meaning of parks. As head of the National Parks Association, a group dedicated to protecting parks, he argued that motoring tourists—and to a large degree his former colleagues Mather and Albright—did not really appreciate national parks outside of their recreational attributes. They did not fully grasp the purpose of parks. Yard asserted that their true purpose lay in their scenic magnificence and their ability to evoke awe and reverence for primordial nature. National parks, in short, were museums of "the original American wilderness" and "our gallery of the sublime in American scenery." With the invasion of autos, recreation in national parks had taken on a different tone. It had less to do with the intellectual and spiritual power of nature's temples and more to do with the immediate physical and psychological experience associated with hiking, fishing, and camping. Only by limiting auto-related developments and educating the public so it could fully comprehend and appreciate what Yard saw as the inherent values of national parks would they retain their importance over time.[53]

Ironically, Yard's emphasis on national parks as museums of scenic, inspirational, and wilderness landscapes embraced automobiles, in part, to convey this message. Though he seemed to focus on parks as realms of original nature, Yard considered the "primitive" or "wilderness" qualities of parks to be scenic, too. They could be seen from a road. In this regard, he seemed to share more of Mather's vision of national parks than he admitted. In order to instill in visitors a proper reverence of nature, untainted by cars, Yard and John C. Merriam, president of the Carnegie Institution, incorporated automobiles into the first educational programs for park visitors. They devised plans for automobile-oriented interpretation at parks such as Crater Lake, where visitors would learn about natural history as they drove the road encircling the lake. Visitors at Crater Lake and in other parks could also participate in a new form of interpreting nature, the auto caravan, led by park naturalists.[54]

Meanwhile, wilderness advocates were gaining a stronger voice in national park affairs. In 1927, the *Saturday Evening Post* published an article condemning the Park Service for excessive road construction and characterizing motor tourists as almost mindless participants in the erosion of the aesthetic values of national parks. According to George Vanderbilt Caesar, a member of the Mountaineers who wrote the article, the Park Service's policies were subjecting parks to the "jazzing hordes." Obviously referring to Mount Rainier, he asked, why should the government go to such lengths "to encircle the wilderness with roads?" After all, the great majority of auto tourists had only a superficial interest in the natural world of parks and would not dream of leaving their cars to engage it more closely.[55]

George Horace Lorimer, editor of the *Post*, had long been one of the agency's champions, and this analysis dealt a blow to the Park Service and some of its supporters. They learned that Caesar planned a more explicit essay denouncing road plans for Mount Rainier specifically as the worst example of the agency's overdevelopment of parks. Although Asahel Curtis characterized Caesar's views as "dope," he could not dismiss him as one of the "few misguided individuals" who believed that parks should remain undeveloped; their numbers and voices were growing. The situation moved agency defenders to counter the argument that wilderness preservation and motor roads were "utterly incompatible."[56]

One way to approach this task was to emphasize how much of the park was left in a wilderness condition after road development. At Mount Rainier, noted Thomas Martin, the proposed road system would occupy less than 5 percent of the total park. At nearly any point along the park's highways, a visitor would have to walk only fifty feet from an automobile to be "standing upon ground that is absolutely unbroken, still in its wilderness state." As manager of the park's concession, Martin believed this information placed greater rather than less importance on completing the park's proposed road program. Since the majority of the people who visited Mount Rainier wanted to travel on a "reasonably developed highway system," they deserved to see even such a small part of the park.[57]

In the Park Service's official rebuttal to Caesar's article, among other sources of criticism against its road program, Horace Albright offered a similar perspective. Albright's article, entitled "The Everlasting Wilderness," appeared in the *Saturday Evening Post* in 1928 and, as suggested by the title, reminded readers that his agency's primary mandate was to preserve parks as wilderness. On average the backcountry, whether formally classified as wilderness or not, made up some 90 percent of all national parks. This fact was not simply dumb luck, he implied. The cost of road construction in the mountainous high country of national parks was prohibitive, requiring anywhere from $100,000 to $1 million a mile in places. In no way, he stated, could the Park Service begin to threaten these primeval landscapes: not for the original allocation of $7.5 million for road building in 1924, not even for $75 million. The current road-building program, he asserted, was focused primarily on modernizing older, existing roads for automobile use, such as those in Yellowstone and Yosemite. Even Mount Rainier's "ambitious" program would make only 14 out of 325 square miles available for intensive development. Therefore, the "most beautiful park lands are destined to be left in isolation far away from the roads."[58]

Albright, though, went so far as to suggest that the relationship between roads and parks was governed by a higher force. In many cases, national parks like Mount Rainier were not just "naturally" inaccessible in a physical sense. Their current and future inaccessibility was also providential. It was no random act that parks were set high in the mountains, "fortified behind impregnable fortresses of snow and ice" for half a year or more. This condition more than any other would assure their preservation. It prevents us, he noted, from "binding our most gigantic mountains with ribbons of pavement," thus giving wilderness time to renew itself.[59]

Albright's comments echoed Mather's opinion that park roads were extraordinary. In a sense, they were above criticism. As the director noted while describing the agency's road-building program, a basic philosophy guided their development. Unlike county or state roads, park roads did not have to conform to rights-of-way in the shape of grids or to commercial factors that would force their construction over the shortest route to save money and time. What made park roads so special was that they were shaped to the lay of the land. They not only revealed the landscape; they became a part of it as well.[60]

NATURE AND ARTIFICE: LANDSCAPE ARCHITECTS AND THE NATURAL ROAD

While Mather seemed intent on dodging the debate about the impact of roads on natural systems, he was also trying to move the issue to another level. Mather was attempting to craft an image of parks in which wilderness and technology appeared unified. He justified roads as a way to improve the park experience by allowing more Americans to commune with nature by car without disturbing it. His views, of course, relied extensively on the expertise of landscape architects who guided park developments. Landscape architecture seemingly offered a way to reconcile roads to wilderness, as the designers' work assumed that nature was inherently "balanced." Nature was a visual rather than an ecological condition. Landscape architects cared more about how nature appeared to the eye than they did about what they knew (and could not so easily see) of a road's effects on natural systems. Landscape architects thus conceived of road building through the principles of "naturalistic" design. They might be destroying nature as scenery by clearing forests, blasting hillsides, and grading slopes to make way for roads, but they were also creating something that looked "natural." They were laying out a road that would develop and preserve scenic features while making travel over the road more enjoyable. Their work offered a seeming synthesis between the two sides of the roads versus wilderness debate.[61]

Making roads appear in harmony with wilderness was nothing new at Mount Rainier and other early national parks. Some of the first park roads were constructed using design standards that emphasized concealment as well as scenery. According to Henry Hubbard in the first text on landscape architecture, roads should not only carry travelers through unraveling scenes of beauty, but they should also be inconspicuous. The road, he instructed, "should seem to lie upon the surface of the ground without interruption of the natural modeling." Naturalizing the road entailed hiding road cuts and fills by simulating "the natural surface where possible," or by creating as natural a surface "as the designer can arrange" by planting native vegetation or using some other means available.[62]

In the 1920s and 1930s, the work of Park Service landscape architects, under the leadership of Thomas Vint, grew more sophisticated with the production of standardized plans that adhered to "the principles of harmonious design." Ideally, their plans, which dealt with the design, construction, and treatment of roads, would render a road "invisible" and give the impression that roads caused little damage to the natural world. Moreover, it was this ideal of blending the built and the natural environments, as scholars of landscape design and architecture have noted recently, that informs our perceptions of what national parks should look like. This style of landscape design, according to Linda McClelland, "subordinated all built features to the natural . . . and achieved in each park a cohesive unity that in many cases became inseparable from the park's natural identity." Perhaps most symbolic of this style was the rustic architecture of park buildings and structures, especially the great park lodges like Yellowstone's Old Faithful Inn, with their "rugged proportions, naturalistic siting, and use of native stone and timbers."[63] Attesting to both the popularity and appropriateness of rustic design in a wilderness park setting, the Park Service produced a three-volume portfolio, *Park and Recreation Structures*, that provided general guidelines for developing structures in the rustic style in the late 1930s. What

The Highway in Nature

made rustic design attractive for forested national and state parks, the volumes' editor wrote, was that it used native materials in proper scale, avoided "rigid, straight lines, and over-sophistication," and gave "the feeling of having been executed by pioneer craftsmen with limited hand tools." In doing so, it achieved "sympathy with natural surroundings and with the past." It not only seemed to belong in the woods but also seemed to have ties to America's frontier heritage.[64]

More than a collection of structures that appeared to belong in a park's natural setting, roads, park villages, campgrounds, and other facilities were part of the overall composition—or designed landscape—of national parks. They were essential to the "public's use and appreciation of the parks," as scholar Ethan Carr asserts. "Park design, or landscape architecture," brought all of these elements together, thereby shaping the visitor-use patterns within parks and framing tourists' "visual encounters with the awesome (and certainly 'undesigned') scenery of the larger park landscape." In this way, Carr notes, the designed landscapes within national parks, with their rustic roads and other structures, mediated "between the individual and the vast terrain of the backcountry" and generated the "aesthetic appreciation of landscapes and the emotional communion with the natural world," or wilderness, that we associate with national parks.[65]

With all of this in mind, it seems, Horace Albright could speak confidently that the crisis over wilderness would be resolved because landscape architecture would unite nature and artifice. It could bridge the gap between what he characterized as the two "extremes" in park planning, especially concerning roads.[66] Although landscape architects had been influential in the selection of park roads, it was their involvement with the road renovations and construction at Mount Rainier, among other parks, that offered convincing proof of landscape architecture as a mediating force. By 1929, the Bureau of Public Roads, working with Park Service landscape architects, completed extensive improvements to the Nisqually Road, including the construction of a new road from Narada Falls to Paradise. The old road would be used for uphill traffic and the new road for downhill traffic, thereby eliminating the congestion associated with the single-lane road and long "trains" of autos waiting to ascend or descend the mountain. The renovations made it the "first modern road" available to motorists, who enjoyed driving the "wide curves, easy grades, and smooth crushed rock surface," reported Superintendent Tomlinson. As Albright commented, it was "magnificent."[67]

The "perfection" of the road also related to its natural appearance and to a series of techniques landscape architects employed to integrate the road into its surroundings. Working with civil engineers, landscape architects introduced radial and superelevated, or banked, turns to eliminate steep grades and switchbacks, which would have appeared imposed on rather than part of the natural terrain. They also concealed the road and repaired construction scars by planting slopes and cuts with native vegetation to beautify as well as stabilize them. They customized the color of the surface in places to blend it further with the surrounding terrain and built guardrails of native stone that edged the road like an outcropping of the mountainside. But it was not enough to edge the road with a rock wall. The wall itself was designed to have an irregular stonework pattern and be topped with crenellations to relieve monotony. In this way, it appeared more as part of the landscape than as a wall built for public safety. Similarly, two new bridges, constructed at Christine Falls and nearby Narada Falls, seemingly merged with the escarpment. Their graceful concrete arches and stone-faced veneers framed the picturesque falls for tourists stopped by the road.[68]

By blurring the line between the natural and built environments, the rustic style of park architecture created the illusion that roads emerged naturally from the earth. Among the more successful Park Service projects conveying this impression was Mount Rainier's Yakima Park Road. In the late 1920s, engineers with the Bureau of Public Roads surveyed the sixteen-mile road connecting Yakima Park with the Naches Pass Highway. The new road would take over much of the White River Road, which the Park Service controlled after 1916, and would provide access to the new development planned for Yakima Park, or Sunrise as it came to be known. Superintendent Tomlinson had long supported the project because it would open the northeast corner of the park, connecting the region with the state highway and advancing the larger round-the-mountain tour of the park. The new park road would also relieve crowding at Paradise and provide motorists with a new "'playground' on the mountain." At 6,400 feet, Yakima Park was one of few high-elevation meadows that was wide and level enough to absorb "crowds of people" in automobiles, and one that could be "reached by highway" without great expense. When it opened in 1930, it was the highest place reached by auto in the park.[69]

Like the Going-to-the-Sun Highway in Glacier National Park, the Yakima Park Road was especially important for demonstrating the benefit of park road standards in the construction of new roads. According to park landscape architect Ernest A. Davidson, who supervised the project, the road

The Highway in Nature

needed to be nearly perfect. And in his mind, it was. By constructing the road "gently," Davidson believed he had helped preserve views and scenery that were "so exceptionally fine" they defied "adequate description." The road was significant from a design standpoint because it incorporated a number of innovations to preserve the steep subalpine terrain through which it ran. The Park Service's landscape division was concerned especially with rock excavation and inserted specifications into this and other road contracts to protect "outstanding natural features" from blasting. To carry out the Park Service's requests and prevent rocks and soil from destroying native grasses and forested hillsides below the fill slopes, road contractors limited their use of explosives, erected temporary barriers of trees, and practiced alternative methods of excavation and grading (such as hauling fill material from other road sections). The most notable example of this "Type B" excavation, and the signature feature of the road, was a section known as the Sunrise Ridge Loop. It replaced a planned series of steep switchbacks ascending the upper section of highway as it entered Yakima Park with a longer switchback that followed the ridgeline at 6,120 feet, providing visitors with a more gradual and graceful drive as well as a panoramic view of the Cascades from Oregon to Canada. To enjoy the view, they could stop at the center of the loop, Sunrise Point; it featured native stone guardrails, a parking lot inside the horseshoe curve, and walkways to overlooks. Sunrise Point, considered state-of-the-art by Park Service landscape architects and engineers, was "destined to become one of the best known [scenic points] in our country," noted Davidson.[70]

A PLACE FOR WILDERNESS AND ROADS:
THE PARK MASTER PLAN

By itself, the sensitive treatment of park roads could not quell "extremists" such as Robert Sterling Yard, who were attempting, according to Albright, to influence the management of national parks. In the late 1920s, sensitive design neither slowed calls for more roads nor satisfied demands for wilderness protection entirely. Wilderness designation for the northern slopes of Mount Rainier may have appeased preservationists, who were increasingly defining wilderness by the absence of roads and cars. But setting aside wilderness did not ensure its total protection. There were still calls to complete the road encircling the mountain, as well as pressure to install a tramway from Glacier Bridge to Paradise and to construct the Paradise scenic loop road.

The situation forced the Park Service to decide what limits, if any, to put on automobiles in national parks. Although interest in these two projects fizzled with the Depression and as the agency's attention shifted to Yakima Park, agency leaders decided that they needed to rely on more than fate to reconcile controversial proposals, particularly those involving park roads. The strategy that emerged in the late 1920s and early 1930s to reconcile controversial projects, indeed to reconcile wilderness and roads, was the park "master plan." After he took over for Mather in 1929, Horace Albright looked to the development outline drawn up earlier for Mount Rainier and proposed that all parks should have comprehensive plans to organize the development of park systems—such as utilities, communications, and circulation—as well as detailed plans for developed areas. Moreover, the master planning process, Albright suggested, would also serve the larger goal of completing a park; it would clarify which areas of the park were to be "developed" and which were to remain as "wilderness."[71]

Like other responses to change triggered by automobiles and technology in general, master plans provided a sense of order. Albright endorsed them because they were tools to resolve complex issues and were produced by those professionals best suited for this task, landscape architects. The director had given the authority for general planning to Thomas Vint's landscape division, since, like Mather, he viewed park development as primarily landscape development. As Vint noted, it was the primary mission of the division—and landscape architects—to create a "well-studied general plan for each park, which includes a control of the location, type of architecture, planting, grading, etc., in connection with any construction project."[72]

The landscape division had also proven its mettle in the contest within the agency over the appropriate location of park roads and other developments. A decisive issue emerged around this time, when Vint and fellow landscape architect Ernest Davidson convinced Albright to select the lower rather than the higher route for the Stevens Canyon Road in Mount Rainier. This road was an important link in advancing the road system from near Paradise, around the eastern side of the mountain, and connecting with a proposed east-side highway. Although the high line offered more spectacular views, and was favored by the Park Service's chief engineer, Frank Kittredge, Vint and Davidson argued for the canyon route. In their opinion, the ridge road would become a spectacle of engineering, a "highway hung on 'sky hooks,'" for which the devastation of the surrounding landscape could not be justified.[73] Albright's decision, which came in 1931, was not just about this particular road, but signaled the importance of master planning and was a defining moment for landscape architects. By centralizing park construction under one division, Albright asserted that landscape architecture was the best way to understand national parks.

Defining national parks, then, was now firmly left to landscape architects in the master-planning process. But master plans were more than ideal expressions of regional plans, as one scholar suggests. They were also ideal representations of a national park within the context of the motor age. The decision about which areas in a park were to be developed versus kept wild hinged upon identifying a suitable model for the park's plan. Interestingly, landscape architects did not choose "wilderness," in the sense of a roadless, unmodified country, as Mount Rainier's essential characteristic. Instead, their model for the park was a version of the earlier model of the round-the-mountain road.[74]

The revised loop tour, as envisioned by Albright and illustrated in Mount Rainier's 1931 master plan, would consist of a park highway from the Nisqually entrance to Paradise and from there to Yakima Park by way of the proposed Stevens Canyon Highway (which would eventually connect with the state's Naches Pass Highway). For Albright, the road encircling the mountain was still intact, only a great section of it now lay outside the park on the highways leading from Seattle and Tacoma. Tourists could begin their trips in those cities, drive as they always had to Paradise, and continue on to the park's northeastern corner, making a side trip to Yakima Park, before leaving through the White River entrance and returning home.[75]

This route solved lingering problems. The new road system would improve the park company's business opportunities by providing two centers for visitors; further, the Yakima Park Highway supplied the excursion that concession owners had argued for in their support of the Paradise scenic loop. Similarly, the new system would make the park's administration more efficient, giving managers more direct access to the mountain's northeastern corner, where Yakima Park was destined to be nearly as popular as Paradise. Most of all, it meant that the northern and western slopes of the mountain would remain in a mostly wilderness condition, in the sense that they would be roadless, because, as Albright observed, the new route rendered completion of the West Side Road (and developments proposed for Sunset Park and Spray Park) improbable. As part of this revision, the Park Service abandoned its earlier proposal to extend the road from the North Puyallup River to the new entrance road leading to Mowich Lake (completed in 1935). The new model also assured that development in the park would be confined to areas along the route: Longmire, Paradise, and Yakima Park.[76]

Although the park's road system was not entirely linked in the 1930s, the master plan recognized that it gave shape to the physical boundaries of the park. In order to better administer park roads, Congress moderately enlarged Mount Rainier in 1926 to the south so the park boundaries could embrace sections of the Nisqually Road as it entered the park. More importantly, Congress significantly enlarged the park to the east, to the Cascade Crest, in 1931. The expansion may have made sense ecologically; it included the headwaters of rivers and creeks, as well as the range of the park's wildlife populations. It also made sense in terms of protecting scenic vistas. But the main motivation for expansion was the road system developing around Mount Rainier. That year the state of Washington completed the Naches Pass Highway through the park's northeastern corner. Designated as Washington Highway 410, it traveled south and then east over Chinook Pass and on to Yakima. Albright believed that Chinook Pass was scenically beautiful and was the natural eastern entrance to the park and therefore should be in the park. The road also provided access to the Yakima Park Road and the new developments that opened there that same year. Moreover, without enlarging the park, there would be no route for the road the agency planned to build with the state up the eastern side of the park.[77]

The master plan also recognized that the road system shaped the mental boundaries of the park, preserving Mather's vision of national parks as revealed through highways. The plan recognized that Mount Rainier had become part of the larger public highway landscape in which motorists related to, and formed their visions of, the natural world. The dedication of the Mather Memorial Parkway in 1932, for example, symbolized how automobiles could be reconciled in the park's wilderness setting. The parkway also incorporated highways outside park boundaries into the park experience. As one admirer observed, the parkway led drivers through its wooded isles of primeval forest where they "could seek the peace and inspiration obtained by close communication with nature."[78]

But it was the plan itself that most revealed the mental image of Mount Rainier held by landscape architects and other agency officials, as a place where wilderness and roads encountered each other in relative harmony. In the plan, on maps that rendered the park on paper, roads were drawn in colored pencils; they appeared as small, curvilinear lines in large, open spaces. The layers of maps, shaded with pastels and accounting for all of the park's

The Highway in Nature

current and future developments, offered a comprehensive and orderly picture of the park. Nothing seemed to be in conflict because the park was not a product of nature so much as it was a product of human design.[79]

As an artistic expression of the park, the master plan offered an ideal image of the relationship between roads and wilderness in national parks. The plan, however, did not prevent development, but rather illustrated the kind of park the Park Service wanted to create. Using the master plan, for example, the agency completed Mount Rainier's road system with the construction of the East Side Highway in 1940 and the Stevens Canyon Highway in the late 1950s.[80] Controversial projects such as the final link in the West Side Road also remained in the park's master plan until the late 1930s. As unlikely as this link's construction was, its presence in the plan made the Park Service appear intent on fulfilling an older vision of Mount Rainier's road system, noted landscape architect Ernest Davidson, "to the definite detriment of National Park scenic and wilderness values."[81]

In this respect, Mount Rainier's first master plan would only partially resolve the debates that emerged in the 1920s about the presence of roads and cars in Mount Rainier and their effect on its wilderness values. Whether parks should be managed as wilderness, excluding cars, or should be fully developed for tourism would be debated for some time to come. The plan, though, was a picture in time. And it is important to understand that in the tradition of park planning, a "wilderness area" as it was used in the 1931 master plan generally meant the rest of the park that was undeveloped, beyond roads and open to trails, backcountry use, and other administrative uses. This definition was largely reminiscent of the one Park Service leaders employed when they created the wilderness areas for Mount Rainier in the late 1920s, and what planners meant even though they designated the mountain's northern slopes as a research area in the park's master plan.[82] In this sense, "wilderness" continued to imply a roadless area within a national park open to automobiles. In the late 1930s, the creation of Olympic National Park as roadless wilderness would challenge this view, but for the moment, the issue seemed irrelevant. In the early 1930s, master plans managed to preserve, at least on paper, the potential for wild nature and machines to coexist.

3 / WILDERNESS WITH A VIEW

Olympic and the New Roadless Park

In July 1938, the writer Thomas Wolfe toured the West's national parks in search of inspiration. As he told a friend, he was embarking "on what promises to be one of the most remarkable trips of my life . . . a complete swing around . . . every big national park in the West."[1] Riding with a reporter who was researching a story about parks, Wolfe was like many park tourists in that he traveled by car. He described his experience in a stream-of-consciousness narrative that was like the drive itself, a series of fleeting images of the western landscape. Each sentence read like a turn in the road. At Mount Rainier, the white Ford carried him "up and up to timber/line and to the Sunrise Lodge and light playing marvelously, and blue cerulean, struggling to/break through, and the glaciers level to the eye." Wolfe's "Western Journey," as he called it, lasted two weeks, during which he covered some five thousand miles over the park-to-park highway and passed through eight states and eleven national parks. The purpose of the tour, the "gigantic unconscious humor of the situation," he noted, was to make "'every national park' without seeing any of them—the main thing is to 'make them'—and so on and on tomorrow."[2]

While Wolfe's trip attested to the powerful role of automobiles and highways in bringing Americans to nature in national parks, it was no ordinary journey. In the 1930s, a new generation of preservationists promoted wilderness parks, like Olympic, and maintained that these parks could be wilderness only absent roads. To these advocates, Wolfe's account may have relayed an awareness of the impressive country contained in the national parks he toured, but his trip also revealed increasing alienation between a modern,

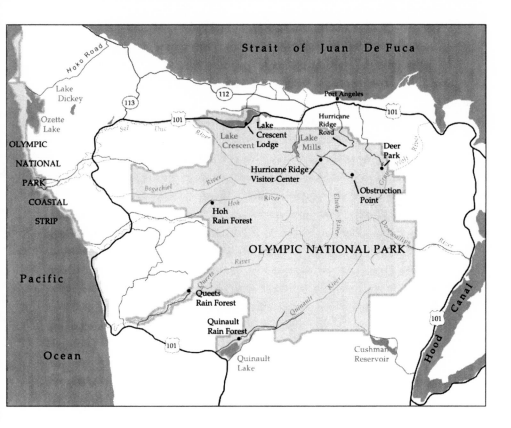

MAP 4. Road system of Olympic National Park

mobile society and wild places. Seduced by speed, Wolfe seemed numb to the intrinsic values of parks, as scenery cascaded through his windshield. He seemed to care more about "bagging parks" than understanding them.

The ideal of the highway in nature, which served as a model for national parks like Mount Rainier in the 1920s, was anathema to this new generation of wilderness advocates. Although the National Park Service seemed to address their concerns with its method of reconciling automobiles and primeval nature using rustic architecture and master planning, the problem was less resolved than it appeared. By the early 1930s, the conflict between automobiles and wild lands in the minds of wilderness activists such as Robert Marshall, cofounder of the Wilderness Society, could not be settled simply by rendering machines and nature compatible in a master plan. To the contrary, Marshall and others argued, the boundaries between autos and wilderness seemed more clearly defined than ever before. In national parks, preservationists asserted that the artifice of rustic roads and designed land-scapes was a destructive force; no matter how appealing to the eye, these developments destroyed the parks' primitive character.[3]

This stronger emphasis on wilderness as roadless was partly a reaction against Stephen Mather's vision for public parks and public highways, but it also reflected the evolution of the highway journey of the teens and twen-ties. An explosion in auto travel during the 1930s, which saw auto owner-ship rise from nearly 26 million in 1931 to 32.5 million in 1940, altered motorists' expectations about the natural world. Simply put, the highways were more crowded. Moreover, paved highways were more common and cars like Wolfe's Ford traveled at higher speeds, further affecting people's impressions of nature by the road. Destinations, more than places along the way, came to occupy drivers and their passengers. And national parks were still favored objectives with the nation's traveling public. Although park visitation lagged in the early 1930s with the Depression, it rebounded by the end of the decade, when 16.75 million people visited the national park sys-tem; roughly half of all autos in the country passed through the gates of the nation's parks. As part of this trend, Wolfe suggested by his actions and motives that rather than being special landscapes for cars and primeval nature, national parks instead had become trophies for American vacations.[4]

Leaders of the new wilderness movement saw roads as damaging intru-sions into parks and championed other, nonmechanical means of experi-encing parks. The establishment of Olympic National Park, on June 29, 1938, just days before Wolfe concluded his western trip, symbolized this new vision. The park was established as a *wilderness* park. It was a national park con-ceived of on a new, roadless model that stood in opposition to the trend represented by Wolfe's journey. Furthermore, in order to justify this new concept, wilderness advocates emphasized that parks were ecological zones rather than landscapes of monumental scenery. All too often—as at Mount Rainier—their boundaries had been drawn to surround a single natural fea-ture and often ignored the ecological relationships needed to preserve the flora and fauna within them. Along with Everglades (1934), Great Smoky Mountains (1934), Shenandoah (1935), and Kings Canyon (1940), Olympic responded to this new perspective.[5]

With the creation of Olympic, the Park Service embarked on a new project, managing a national park as a roadless wilderness. However, it never lost sight of the ideal of parks as primitive landscapes open to cars. While no roads would cut through Olympic's interior, highways still informed how

Wilderness with a View

the Park Service—and by association how the general public—thought of the park as wilderness. For the majority of park visitors still experienced parks from their automobiles. Thus, preserving the "true wilderness" character of Olympic, the Park Service believed, relied more rather than less on roads and cars. The road to Hurricane Ridge exemplifies this approach. Located on the northern edge of the park, it allowed visitors to look into the heart of the Olympics, to see a landscape otherwise invisible from and off-limits to roads and cars. The Hurricane Ridge Road, first proposed with the park's creation, opened in the late 1950s and became one of Olympic's main attractions. With its modern design, the road could accommodate the increasing numbers of postwar auto tourists. Moreover, it allowed park tourists to visit the park in a day, requiring little or no new visitor developments. Its panoramic views, considered by Park Service planners to be far superior to those elsewhere in Olympic, also deflected interest in building new roads in other areas of the park. In this context, the Hurricane Ridge Road remained consistent with the original notion of national park wilderness as something viewed from a road and through a windshield. At the same time, Park Service leaders regarded the road as an innovative way to reconcile autos and wilderness in national parks. They considered it yet another form of wilderness appreciation and preservation.

SHIFTING IDEALS OF WILDERNESS, CARS, AND PARKS: THE NATIONAL PARK SERVICE IN THE 1930S

For the Park Service, Olympic notably differed from parks like Mount Rainier, with its display of one great feature. A large park, Olympic encompassed some 648,000 acres, and with additions authorized in its legislation, it would expand to approximately 900,000 acres over the next fifteen years. Lying on the remote Olympic Peninsula between Puget Sound and the Pacific Ocean, the park preserved a region rich in resources including mountains, forests, coastline, and wildlife. Within the new park's borders were the Olympic Mountains, a radial range of rugged, glaciated peaks dominated by the 7,969-foot Mount Olympus and drained by river valleys arrayed like spokes on a wheel. Extensive old-growth forests of Douglas fir, western hemlock, Sitka spruce, red cedar, and Pacific silver fir blanketed and extended from these mountains. Among the most treasured trees were the moss-covered giants of the rain forests in the valleys of the Hoh, Bogachiel, and Queets rivers running to the sea. Further, the park provided habitat for the rare

Roosevelt or Olympic elk as well as protection from hunters, who once threatened them with extinction.[6]

More importantly, Olympic shifted the Park Service's attention away from managing parks for windshield tourists to protecting wilderness. In the 1930s, wilderness preservationists criticized the agency for neglecting this goal. They argued that the federal government's reorganization in 1933 distracted it from its primary task of preserving the great western scenic parks and diluted the original meaning of national parks as reservoirs of primeval nature. The reorganization more than doubled the national park system, adding national monuments, national recreation areas, battlefields, cemeteries, and historic sites formerly overseen by other bureaus. As part of the New Deal's conservation program, the agency also took a lead role in the nation's recreational planning, which involved surveying and designing new park areas, seashores, parkways, and state and local parks. More than ever, national parks came to be seen as places for ordinary recreation. The parks were also increasingly "under construction." During the New Deal, the Civilian Conservation Corps and Public Works Administration infused the park system with unprecedented labor and capital, enabling the agency to improve facilities such as park roads, trails, and buildings as well as to construct new ones.[7]

The parkway (specifically, a road through and connecting parks) was the most disturbing symbol of the loss of the primitive; viewed by many as destructive, it was the antithesis of wilderness.[8] In fact, it was the Park Service's involvement in building parkways in the eastern United States, such as on Virginia's Blue Ridge, that drove wilderness advocates to action. The agency's proposal for the "Skyway" drive along the crest of the Appalachian divide in Great Smoky, for example, led Marshall, Robert Sterling Yard, and others to form the Wilderness Society in 1935. The first national organization dedicated to wilderness preservation, the society was determined to prevent this and other road-building programs from destroying opportunities for primitive recreation.[9] Landscape architects and others may have embraced the parkway as a thoughtful way to enjoy nature and to control unwanted development; yet no matter how picturesque the landscapes of American parkways appeared, whether scenes of rural America or miles of spectacular scenery, they were "unabashedly contrived compositions," according to one historian. What road proponents overlooked was that parkways and other roads destroyed the primitive in order to create the park-like setting through which they traveled. As Marshall observed, when it came to the primitive, "the landscape architect cannot plan it away."[10]

Wilderness with a View

Objections to parkways, among other issues, sharpened wilderness groups' belief that park roads were incompatible with the primitive. Perhaps the greatest expression of this was the National Parks Association's 1936 proposal to establish a "National Primeval Parks System." These primeval parks would protect the core of the national park system and would be managed the way all parks should be: for the "complete preservation of original conditions." Only within the framework of total protection should the Park Service provide the public opportunities "to see unchanged nature," concluded William Wharton, president of the association.[11]

Although wilderness advocates viewed the Park Service's commitment to automobile-based tourism with alarm, the agency was moving beyond catering to the majority of park visitors. It also began to consider the importance of wilderness parks. The agency's motivation for imagining a park like Olympic, to be sure, resulted from criticism by natural scientists and the emerging coalition of national conservation groups. But dissension came from within the agency's own ranks as well. Through the diligence of George M. Wright, director of the agency's wildlife division, ecology flared briefly but brightly across the horizon of national park administration in the 1930s. Wright, involved in path-breaking wildlife surveys in national parks, stressed the importance of parks as undisturbed natural systems and thus encouraged a new interpretation of park landscapes and the effects on them from roads and construction. Wright and his cadre of wildlife biologists reviewed park projects and assessed their merits in ecological terms. As landscape architects proposed building new roads and modernizing old ones, biologists challenged the assumptions road planners made about the natural world. They pointed out, for example, that a road's location and design must take into consideration more than the visual harmony of a road with its surroundings. They pressed landscape architects to consider a road's disruption to things such as wildlife migration patterns and to protect the integrity of natural systems less visible to the eye.[12]

Although landscape architects such as Ernest Davidson began to call for the protection of wild nature in park development schemes, the Park Service was more likely persuaded to change its ways by Secretary of the Interior Harold L. Ickes.[13] Ickes, appointed by President Franklin Roosevelt in 1933, was deeply interested in protecting national parks as wilderness reserves. The aggressive, one-time Progressive reformer disliked the overcrowded conditions in many parks and cautioned Park Service leaders against catering too eagerly to the comforts of tourists. He especially despised automobiles. In 1933, he exclaimed that if he had his way, he would create a park with no roads: "I would have it impenetrable forever to automobiles," Ickes noted, "a place where man would not try to improve upon God."[14]

Ickes arrived at this view in part because of his genuine love of wild country, rooted in a childhood spent in the wooded areas around his boyhood home in Pennsylvania and strengthened by trips to the West in the years before and after World War I. His association with Marshall also shaped his views. Although he and Marshall were never close friends, Ickes shared with Marshall a "common love of wilderness" and sought his opinion on national park road proposals. The most controversial of the time, as noted above, was the proposed skyline drive through Great Smoky Mountains National Park. When Marshall informed Ickes of his opposition to the project, the secretary vetoed the proposal, and the Park Service abandoned the project in 1935.[15] Ickes made similar decisions regarding road plans for western parks. At his insistence, for example, the Park Service chose a lower route for the final segment of Rim Drive at Crater Lake and eliminated the West Side Road from Mount Rainier's master plan.[16]

Throughout his tenure, Ickes championed wilderness in parks, and his interest fueled the Park Service's rivalry with the Forest Service as the nation's leader in outdoor recreation. He pledged to establish wilderness areas in existing national parks through congressional action and to create large primitive areas—particularly Everglades, Isle Royale, Kings Canyon, and Olympic—as new wilderness national parks that would have a minimum of tourist facilities and that would remain practically roadless. Like Marshall perhaps, Ickes believed that the Park Service was more capable of preserving primeval forests and other primitive landscapes than the Forest Service. These new parks, managed by an agency with a preservation mission and created by an act of Congress, could protect the nation's disappearing wild lands better than an agency dedicated to the rational use of the nation's resources. Most new parks, like their predecessors, were drawn from national forest lands, and their creation triggered administrative quarrels over jurisdiction and management philosophies. Olympic was the most famous battle of its time; the creation of the park removed the center of Olympic National Forest from Forest Service administration. Part of the forest had been set aside as Mount Olympus National Monument in 1909 to protect the region's rare elk. For more than three decades, however, the forest (including the monument) had been managed not as a wilderness reserve but as a working forest. Under this management scheme, For-

Wilderness with a View

est Service officials asserted that they could provide for timber harvests, outdoor recreation, and protection of the forest's primitive values—all in a seemingly harmonious way.[17]

The Forest Service lost the Olympic battle, in a sense, because it still had a great deal to prove about the compatibility of these uses. More importantly, it lost because of the Park Service's new attention to roadlessness. At the same time, while most accounts of Olympic's creation describe it as an impressive victory for a national park as roadless wilderness, they undervalue how the Mount Rainier model influenced the conception of Olympic as wilderness.[18] Even though the Mount Rainier model was out of favor and the Park Service imagined Olympic as a wilderness park, the agency continued to search for ways to convey a familiar message: that the potential for harmonizing automobiles in a park's wilderness setting existed.

A WILDERNESS FEELING:
PLANNING OLYMPIC AS A ROADLESS PARK

In 1938, the Park Service issued the first master plan for Olympic National Park in which it expressed a bold vision: Olympic would be roadless. The master-planning team, led by Secretary of the Interior Ickes, noted that Olympic had been set aside to protect "one of the finest remaining scenic and wilderness areas of the nation . . . for the benefit of future generations." No roads crossed into the interior of the park, and it was "entirely unnecessary," the team concluded, to build any more. Moreover, there were enough roads leading to, or a short distance into, the park. Most were unimproved, extending up river valleys draining the Olympics, and provided reasonable access to the park's four sides from U.S. Highway 101, which encircled the peninsula. The planners saw no reason to improve these low-standard and seasonal routes, even though they had to be traveled slowly. Here the Park Service departed from past practice in which a road created an unfolding scenic narrative of a park's natural wonders. At Olympic, the message was that to enjoy the primitive, visitors needed to leave their cars behind—get out and walk or ride horseback over the park's trails leading from the end of the roads. Olympic was a "WILDERNESS PARK" to be maintained in "WILDERNESS" conditions, the plan declared. If visitors wanted "cushion travel," they should seek out other parks or public lands.[19]

Despite this tough stance, Park Service planners made one important exception. Although there would be no attempts to provide all-season driving at higher elevations, the team endorsed the construction of a seven-mile road connecting the Hurricane Ridge Road, from where it ended at Obstruction Point, with the Deer Park Road. Both roads provided access from Highway 101, near the park's northern boundary, and Port Angeles, the peninsula's principal city. Like most of the roads serving the park, these were built by the Forest Service as truck trails for administrative purposes. Given its multiple-use mission, the Forest Service intended a wide variety of possible uses for these roads, including fire suppression, future timber harvests, and recreational developments. For the Park Service, however, the connection would have a single purpose: a one-way loop to satisfy auto tourists for whom national parks, even wilderness parks, were places they could drive. The new road, planners wrote, would "permit excellent views of the high interior country," namely Mount Olympus and the Olympic Mountains, and "will guarantee to all people, even invalids, an opportunity to see the beauties of the park, and to actually pass through it."[20]

With the above exception, the master plan may have emphatically excluded roads, but highways figured prominently in the Park Service's conception of the new park. On the one hand, the plan minimized the significance of roads, signaling a kind of closure to years of debate over park standards and wilderness values vis à vis roads. As if to remove any lingering doubts about the Park Service and its history of highway construction, Secretary Ickes publicly declared that the agency would "keep [Olympic] a wilderness." He insisted that visitors—the majority of whom were able—should expend some effort to see the park. "Too many of us," he observed, "want a predigested breakfast food for our stomachs and a previewed national park for our eyes."[21]

On the other hand, the master plan, even with Ickes's strong endorsement, was somewhat deceptive. It asserted a simplistic concept of the national park as roadless wilderness; yet for several decades roads and cars had been the most influential factors in shaping people's ideas of parks as wilderness refuges. The plan may have emphasized a new wilderness park model, but it wanted that model adapted from the traditional concept of a national park. Ironically, the Park Service would rely more rather than less on presenting an impressive sample of Olympic National Park to America's motoring masses in order to protect and convey the park's wilderness grandeur. By allowing park tourists to view the untamed interior of the Olympics by car, agency leaders believed they stood a better chance

Wilderness with a View

of gaining support for wilderness preservation policies and against new road construction and other developments in the park.

The agency's approach to its administration of Olympic partly resulted because the Park Service never saw its mission as protecting wilderness as a landscape unmodified by humans. At the very least, it interpreted landscapes as having human values. In this sense, Secretary Ickes's comments suggested that Park Service leaders had fully embraced wilderness as a roadless concept when in fact they were still grappling with the whole idea of a wilderness park. In the 1930s, agency officials acknowledged that parks deserved more complete protection. But as Park Service director Arno B. Cammerer stated, the old rule of park preservation still applied. To protect the cherished areas, there must be an "economically justifiable and humanly satisfying form of land-use" that could compete with arguments for resource development.[22] Even after years of justifying national parks as landscapes preserved through development, the Park Service was not secure politically. It still had to consider utilitarian issues, especially when usurping lands from the Forest Service.

Cammerer, who replaced Horace Albright as director in 1933, agreed with his predecessors about parks as wilderness reserves. As democratic institutions national parks should have something for everyone, he argued, be it spiritual, scientific, recreational, or commercial. These qualities distinguished national parks as wilderness reservoirs, he suggested, because unlike national forests, parks did not allow the economic development of their resources. Instead, they provided for public enjoyment of their "inherent natural characteristics" through appropriate developments. Roads were still essential. They not only enabled visitors to see a representative section of a national park, they also saved "even larger sections of wilderness for the relatively few who enjoy wilderness." Even though the history of roads in parks like Mount Rainier suggested that even "thoughtful" road developments encouraged more visitation and tourist developments, roads, he urged, were still tools for wilderness protection.[23]

Cammerer, however, expanded upon Mather and Albright's conception of wilderness as a seamless landscape of machines and nature. In response to preservationists who argued that there were clear boundaries between wilderness and autos, Cammerer suggested that this idea was too abstract. Wilderness, like parks, combined the human and the natural and was made real through use. Tangible evidence of this was the construction of a road; it could save a forest for the general public to "actually view its beauties," and thereby avert its destruction through timber harvests, mining, or grazing. Thinking, perhaps, of newly created parks such as Olympic, with its forests withdrawn from production, the director noted that in the long run a road may be a "small price" if it countered rational arguments to use public lands for resource development. In other words, the physical presence of a road to identify and display a wild landscape could ensure that landscape's protection. "People do not know what wilderness is," the director concluded, "until they have a chance to go through it." And most would go through it on a road.[24]

The trouble with this argument, however, was that agency officials had difficulty expressing the true meaning of wilderness for parks. According to Cammerer, a road could make and protect a park as wilderness, but a park was not by itself necessarily wilderness. As the landscape architect Thomas Vint observed in 1938, "wilderness values" were becoming important assets to national parks. Vint, who became the agency's chief of planning in 1934, thought that in the "current enthusiasm" for the protection of wilderness, the expression "wilderness area" had been abused and its meaning confused, especially within the context of the park master plan. A "national park" and a "wilderness," he asserted, were not the same. Although national parks were, in part, products of American concerns for the preservation of wilderness and original nature, they were places for, and to be enjoyed by, people. Vint eschewed the definition provided in Forest Service policies governing primitive areas or in the Copeland Report of 1933 that emphasized the absence of permanent structures and mechanized transportation. Instead, he favored *Webster's* "rather clear and extreme" definition of wilderness as an uninhabited, "pathless waste of any kind."[25]

Vint was suggesting that national parks were more than wilderness areas. They were places for humans in nature, and to simply erect a barrier around them to protect their primitive qualities would not "solve the national park problem." Only a qualified definition of wilderness as a scenic landscape inspiring viewers with its primitive qualities would fulfill the purpose of national parks. A wilderness experience in a national park was largely a form of visual recreation, restricted to the rider, hiker, sightseer, or motorist; consumptive forms of recreation, like hunting, were prohibited. Rather than excluding developments like trails and roads from parks to preserve them as undefiled wilderness, it would make more sense to limit the number of people who could enter them. This would restrict developments to serve park tourists and would preserve the natural terrain. The

Wilderness with a View

Park gates, c. 1920, welcomed auto tourists and symbolized the transition to a special landscape for cars and nature. Special Collections, University of Washington Libraries, UW 24498

In this classic 1914 photograph of travel along a forest road near Mount Rainier, Asahel Curtis captured the close contact with nature motorists discovered in national parks in the early 20th century. Special Collections, UW, A. Curtis 29848

The appearance of cars in national parks raised the potential for harmony between technology and the natural world. Auto tourists discovered new opportunities for intimate encounters with nature, such as at the snout of Nisqually Glacier on the "Road to Paradise" in Mount Rainier, c. 1915. Mount Rainier National Park Archives

Destination of auto tourists and the first road into the park, the Paradise Valley afforded visitors close views of the mountain and lodging at Paradise Inn. Mount Rainier National Park Archives

View from the road, 1932. In parks like Mount Rainier, park planners designed roads to present the parks' scenic beauty to motorists in an unfolding scenic narrative. National Park Service Historic Photograph Collection

(Facing page) In the 1920s, car camping in national parks illustrated the popularity of auto travel as well as the close ties between people and nature. Special Collections, U W 15119

A SECTION OF PARADISE VALLEY CAMP GROUND.
Rainier National Park

First Park Service director Stephen Mather, far right, and second director, Horace Albright, far left, pictured in 1925 with Mather's Packard. Mather, a supporter of auto tourism and highway development, traveled by car when visiting parks. Note the license plate. National Park Service Historic Photograph Collection

(Facing page, bottom) "The Vanishing Wilds—Scenic Highway," c. 1925. In the early 20th century, Americans discovered wild nature along highways, and as opportunities for this diminished in the 1920s, parks took on added importance as reserves for the highway in nature. Special Collections, U W, Pickett 3128.

Roads designed for scenic views. This image, taken around 1903 during Mount Rainier's first road survey, depicts the proposed route of the road to Paradise, where it would cross the Nisqually River near the Nisqually Glacier. Mount Rainier National Park Archives

Building roads to appear as if they were part of the natural scene was a signature of Park Service landscape design. At Mount Rainier, the Sunrise Ridge Loop, along the Yakima Park Road, was an important example, offering spectacular views, stonework, and a ridgeline approach to Yakima Park (Sunrise) that avoided unsightly switchbacks. Mount Rainier National Park Archives

Nature and artifice. This contemporary view of Christine Falls Bridge in Mount Rainier demonstrates the principles of landscape design that sought to harmonize the built with natural environments in national park road construction. HABS/HAER Collection, Library of Congress

(Facing page, top) Landscape architects tried to prevent the violent activity of road building from creating the destruction seen here during construction of the Yakima Park Road in the late 1920s and early 1930s. Mount Rainier National Park Archives

Reconciling nature preservation with visitor developments, Park Service land-scape architects created "master plans" for national parks, the first being Mount Rainier in the early 1930s. Mount Rainier National Park Archives

Scenes like this of a road through the Olympic Peninsula illustrate the dense forests and primitive environment that greeted motorists in the 1920s. Special Collections, U W, A. Curtis 47442

North Fork of the Quinault Road, 1941. Logging operations like this had greeted auto tourists traveling through the Olympic Peninsula, motivating some to seek protection of the region's forests as a national park. Olympic National Park Archives

(Facing page, bottom) Postcard from the edge of wilderness. Opportunities for viewing the Olympic Mountains from vantage points like Hurricane Ridge attracted motorists and outdoor enthusiasts in the 1930s and 1940s. Special Collections, UW 17041

In the late 1930s and 1940s, Park Service planners determined that a new road to Hurricane Ridge was necessary to view Olympic National Park. The old single-lane road, leading up from the Elwha River Valley, was too difficult for modern cars with "low slung automatics" to drive. Olympic National Park Archives

The Hurricane Ridge Road, seen here c. 1959, exposed visitors to the mountain environment and panoramic views of Olympic National Park, offering a stage from which to view a wilderness no roads could cross. Olympic National Park Archives

Designed to accommodate modern cars, the Hurricane Ridge Road, seen here in 1958, allowed visitors to see the park in less than a day, eliminating the need for overnight facilities and accomplishing the Park Service's goal of preserving wilderness through development. Olympic National Park Archives

Visitors to Olympic Park approach the lodge and explore the area around Hurricane Ridge in this contemporary photograph. HABS/HAER Collection, Library of Congress

(Facing page, bottom) More than mountains and forests awaited motorists at Olympic National Park along the coastal strip, seen here c. 1940s. Although some of the coast was accessible from Highway 101, the Park Service opposed plans to extend a parkway along its entire length. Olympic National Park Archives

President Franklin D. Roosevelt, seen here on his tour of the Olympic Peninsula in 1937, was a major influence in the establishment of Olympic National Park. Olympic National Park Archives

"Stehekin"   Fields Hotel.

Stehekin Valley, seen here c. 1910, was often likened to Yosemite for its alpine scenery and dramatic relief. Located at the head of Lake Chelan near the mouth of the Stehekin River, Stehekin is accessible only by boat, foot, or air. It retains much of its character from the early 20th century as a place existing beyond the influence of modern life. Special Collections, UW, L. D. Lindsley 24496

Mountain scenery, such as this seen c. 1910 in the upper Bridge Creek Basin north of Stehekin Valley, inspired calls for a national park in the North Cascades early in the 20th century. Special Collections, UW, L.D. Lindsley 24497

Highway 20 and the park few would see from a car, c. 1970. This aerial view, looking generally east, reveals the extreme scale of the North Cascades. Highway 20 cuts across the base of the mountains along the Skagit River in the lower foreground, passes Ross Dam (lower center), and turns to follow Ruby Arm (lower left) toward Washington Pass. Seattle Municipal Archives Photograph Collection

Although a dam created Ross Lake, park supporters considered it to have
wilderness value and urged the Park Service to make it off limits to road
development projects planned for access from Highway 20 in the 1970s. The
only road access to the lake was at its northern end, through the town of Hope,
B.C. Seattle Municipal Archives Photograph Collection

Senator Henry M. Jackson was a key political figure in both the creation of North Cascades National Park and the completion of Highway 20. He is photographed here with the park's first superintendent, Roger Contor. Special Collections, UW, 25664

(Facing page, bottom) Stehekin Valley Road, c. 1963. With no connection to high-ways outside of the valley, the Stehekin Valley Road was, in the minds of some, the perfect park road. North Cascades National Park Archives

Tourists, sightseers, and locals mix in the 1970s on the dock at Stehekin Land-ing. With no outside road access, backpackers and others depended on shuttle vans to drive them up valley for day hikes and longer trips into the backcoun-try. North Cascades National Park Archives

This contemporary view of the Stevens Canyon Highway in Mount Rainier depicts the changes in park highway design and construction between the 1920s and 1930s (lower right) and the 1950s (left foreground). HABS/HAER Collection, Library of Congress

master planning process was intended to accomplish some of this by identifying developments and designated wilderness areas apart from them. The issue was not about classifying the parks as wilderness, Vint concluded, but concerned treating everything outside of a park's developed areas as wilderness. What the Park Service needed to do was confine development.[26]

Vint and other agency officials, though at times engaged in semantics, were arguing that national parks, including a so-called wilderness park, were still visual experiences. Wilderness was a perception as much as a place; it could be observed and contemplated. And even in a park of such proportions as Olympic, it could be appreciated from a car. Opinions such as those of Cammerer and Vint point out that Olympic provided an opportunity not only to fulfill the mandate of a national park as roadless but also the opportunity to enhance the theme of wilderness with a view. Perhaps the most significant aspect of this new phase of park management was that it did not rely on a transmountain road, but instead on a road to the park's edge.

The decision to run a road to the park's border may not have been surprising, given the changing attitudes about roads in parks and specifically Secretary Ickes's opposition to them. But it came at a significant juncture in the Park Service's history. By the early 1930s, the agency had completed what it considered its most "outstanding" road projects. Among its most impressive accomplishments were the Wawona Road in Yosemite, the Trail Ridge Road in Rocky Mountain, the Going-to-the-Sun Highway in Glacier, the Zion–Mt. Carmel Highway in Zion, and Rim Drive in Crater Lake national parks. Significant for their engineering and landscape-design principles, especially within the tradition of landscape parks like New York's Central Park and the profession of landscape architecture, these roads achieved the ultimate goal in scenic preservation. Despite the scale of construction, noted landscape architect Henry Hubbard, park roads "represent the effect that *man has done nothing.*"[27]

Besides being notable for their design standards and heroic engineering, these roads ended the era of scenic highways in national parks for two reasons. First, in 1933 the completion of Trail Ridge Road and the Going-to-the-Sun Road, two transmountain highways, symbolized the fulfillment of the road policy advanced by Mather and Albright in the 1920s. Each park would need no more than one great road that provided a sample of its scenic grandeur, leaving the major portion of the park in its primitive condition. As Albright wrote of the Going-to-the-Sun Road, let it "stand supreme and alone."[28] Second, the Glacier road completed the last section of the

National Park-to-Park Highway, fulfilling Mather's concept of national parks as organized by, and understood from, a highway system. The vast scenic loop highway not only enabled Americans to think of national parks within the context of their motorized mobility, but it also promoted parks, exemplified by the transmountain roads in Rocky Mountain and Glacier, as scenic landscapes through which they could drive. Barring few restrictions, tourists could enter national parks in one fluid transition from public highway to park highway.

ALL ROADS ARE NOT CREATED EQUAL: THE FOREST SERVICE'S BATTLE FOR THE OLYMPICS

The Park Service's decision to oppose a transmountain road in Olympic makes sense given its opposition to parkways and new roads in national parks, the evolution of park road policy, and the completion of the park-to-park highway. At Olympic, however, there were other factors at play. One of the most immediate concerns of park supporters in the 1930s, led by the Emergency Conservation Committee (ECC), an advocacy group based in New York City, was the Forest Service and its apparent disregard for wilderness values. The conservation group asserted that the commercial mission of the Forest Service had failed to protect the peninsula's natural systems, especially its Roosevelt elk and its quickly disappearing old-growth forests. In 1934, one year after administration of Mount Olympus National Monument was transferred from the Department of Agriculture to the Department of the Interior and the National Park Service, the ECC, supported by local groups like the Mountaineers, proposed the creation of Olympic National Park.

The ECC, composed of natural scientists and park advocates, was led by philanthropist Rosalie Edge. Edge's organization used the opportunity of the monument's transfer to call attention to the recent killing of 250 Roosevelt elk on Forest Service lands next to the monument and the need for permanent protection of the rare elk in a national park. Outrage over the "slaughter" fueled support for a park among conservationists in the East as well as the West. Besides saving the peninsula's "wildlife from extinction," the creation of a park would also save a large part of the Olympic country's "magnificent forests from annihilation." Moreover, the conservation group used the opportunity to argue for the preservation of vast tracts of ancient forests not just as habitat for wildlife but also for their own sake. On the peninsula, the nation faced the last chance to save a large remnant of the "wonderful primeval forests" unique to the Pacific Northwest but that were already being "logged off to the very last stick."[29]

National parks were attractive to organizations like the ECC and other preservationists because, despite the problems associated with park management in the 1930s, parks offered a form of permanent protection. Although the Forest Service had pioneered primitive recreation in the 1920s and 1930s, establishing the first wilderness or primitive areas in the country off-limits to mechanized transportation, its designations were impermanent. Forest officials could create, modify, or abandon primitive areas with little public notice, whereas parks were created and protected by an act of Congress. More importantly, the Forest Service's management philosophy—"multiple use"—held that forests were for such things as grazing, water power developments, and timber cutting. Outdoor recreation, from auto camping to backcountry hiking trips in primitive country, was also part of multiple-use management, but such recreation in national forests seemed different to people like Edge because of the agency's philosophy. It did not seem associated with any deeper purpose, such as the need for peace, solitude, and natural beauty in an increasingly "mechanized world." Recreation was a resource just like any other found in forests, and it had to be reconciled with the development of other forest resources over a long period of time.[30]

More unsettling was that the Forest Service often designated primitive areas or other recreational areas within national forests to fend off national park proposals. The agency employed these tactics in the Olympics, where shortly after the creation of Mount Olympus National Monument preservationists proposed a national park. In 1915, for example, Chief Forester Henry S. Graves reduced the 610,000-acre monument by more than half to open it to resource production, but he saved the most rugged and scenically beautiful mountain area to appease national park interests. Graves next ordered a plan for developing the monument's system of trails and roads to provide public access. He wanted to show that his agency was contemplating the same kinds of developments found in national parks, especially a transmountain road up the center of the monument. In this way, he could argue more effectively that the reserve should remain under his agency's control.[31]

Curiously, the Forest Service responded to demands for a national park or a parklike experience with what it seemed to envision as the most significant feature of a national park: a mountain highway. In 1926, the agency commissioned a study of two transmountain roads, one leading north from the Quinault River to the Elwha River, the other leading northeast from the Quinault River to the Dosewallips River. The proposed roads were to have primarily recreational value, enabling motorists to reach the "great interior of the Olympic Mountains," a region now only accessible by trail to hunters, trappers, and mountaineers.[32] Both roads would have cut across the national monument and were later incorporated into a comprehensive recreation plan for the forest in 1929.

Although the recreation plan recommended trails, campgrounds, summer homes, resorts, and especially primitive recreation, it conveyed the idea of a national park by including the two road proposals. With the designation of the Olympic Primitive Area, a 134,000-acre alpine region, off-limits to mechanized transportation, and the establishment of the Snow Peaks Recreation Area, which embraced Mount Olympus National Monument, the Forest Service plan suggested that the roads would not detract from the wilderness character of the region. Fred Cleator, who wrote the plan, observed that the roads "would be inimical to the generally accepted wilderness idea of the high Olympics as a whole, but would leave the proposed primitive area intact, so that immense territories of mountain fastnesses would still be left untrammeled." Even though the plan illustrated the agency's interest in a recreation program, it allowed the Forest Service to manage the forest for work as well as play, and to continue harvesting trees. Ultimately, the plan's intent was to show the agency's detractors that it could manage the region for its wild and scenic qualities as well as its commercial values.[33]

Yet as the park campaign gathered force, the Forest Service was hard pressed to make its case for retaining jurisdiction over the Olympics. In 1936, the agency made its greatest statement of permanence when Secretary of Agriculture Henry A. Wallace officially designated an expanded Olympic Primitive Area (238,930 acres) adjacent to the national monument. Nevertheless, wilderness supporters like the ECC, the Mountaineers, and the Wilderness Society were suspicious. They pointed out that Secretary Wallace or any future secretary could change this decision, particularly if local economic pressures mounted for resource exploitation. They also noted that the new area left out a great body of ancient forests and wondered what this omission portended. They were even more curious about what the agency meant by wilderness. True, the region would be off-limits to timber harvests and other developments as well as to mechanical conveyance. However, plans for the primitive area proposed a spur road on the monument's

Wilderness with a View

north side from Sol Duc Hot Springs to Seven Lakes Basin, providing a "fine view of the high north slopes of Mt. Olympus" and other natural features for motorists. More worrisome was the agency's proposed Quinault-Dosewallips road through the primitive area, cutting across the south side of the monument.[34]

The Forest Service justified the transmountain Quinault-Dosewallips road, which traversed the highly scenic Anderson Pass, in terms similar to those national park planners might have used. Such a road was the best way to bring auto tourists into "closer touch with glacier country." It would also satisfy pressure from local communities, namely those in the vicinity of Grays Harbor to the west and the Puget Sound cities and Hood Canal to the east, to shorten the distance between them and gain a scenic drive as a tourist attraction at the same time. Finally, the road would provide direct access to the high country, reducing the time backcountry travelers spent hiking or riding through the region's "least interesting country." It would thus expand the range and quality of wilderness encounters.[35]

The Forest Service's road proposals, despite their apparent intent to present nature from the road, were viewed by wilderness supporters as disingenuous at worst and simply improbable at best. Given the agency's history and mission, any road could become a logging road. The transmountain road, for example, "would make some of the best timber in the area available" to timber companies, noted Robert Yard. In addition, the road could not be justified on economic grounds or as a public necessity. It would traverse steep and high terrain, making its construction expensive and its scarring of the landscape extensive; and, since snowfall would close it for much of the year, its use would be limited. This latter reality defused arguments that the road was a military necessity for defending Puget Sound; travel on the peninsula could take place over the all-year loop highway (the Olympic Loop Highway, later designated as Highway 101), which took motorists around the peninsula's mountains, through its forests, and along its coastline.[36]

The Forest Service's attempts to prevent the creation of a park by providing a parklike experience were shrewd. Granted, the Forest Service unsuccessfully fought the park proposal by arguing that it could harmonize forest preservation and local economic interests under multiple-use, or sustained yield, management. Yet the agency's willingness to comply with road plans suggested that it was trying to force the Park Service to decide whether the roads should be completed. Both the Seven Lakes Basin and the Quinault-Dosewallips road projects would traverse the monument, which was under

Park Service jurisdiction. If the Park Service approved the roads, especially the transmountain Quinault-Dosewallips road, the Forest Service could argue that there was little difference between the forest and the park, and thus little reason to create a park. If the Park Service disapproved of the roads, then the Forest Service could make the same argument, this time stressing how both provided for primitive recreation.

What confounded the Forest Service, however, was that ultimately the agency was preparing to fight a park like Mount Rainier, renowned for its roads and scenery, rather than a roadless wilderness park. Since Chief Forester Graves's original rationale for reducing Mount Olympus National Monument, forest officials had maintained that the high Olympics were scenically beautiful, and the national monument possessed most of the range's spectacular peaks. In their minds, this fact should have satisfied any desires to create a national park. Meanwhile, the Forest Service downplayed the Olympic range's national park caliber. It asserted that compared to peaks like Mount Rainier in the Pacific Northwest, the Olympics were almost ordinary, no more impressive than other areas. Hardly "superlative," the area was not worthy of national park status. The region's rainy climate, furthermore, often shrouded the range in clouds. Residents of Seattle, forest managers argued, had better views of the snowy peaks from across Puget Sound than they did when they traveled the Olympic Highway. Thousands of motorists, seeking a closer view, traveled the highway only to find that "the mountains have entirely disappeared," observed forest planner Fred Cleator. Without a "few intimate and worthwhile views of the Olympics," the highway offered a largely "tiresome trip through cut-over or timberland." More than the Olympics' average scenery, that the mountains could not be seen easily from cars disqualified the range as a park. Since most national park visitors never left their cars, and doing so was the only way to see the remote Olympic country, forest officials reasoned, why make it a park? Other areas preserved primeval forest along public highways, notably Mather Memorial Parkway at Mount Rainier, and these could satisfy the public's desire to see ancient forests from a road.[37]

Forest Service officials, though, misjudged the changing conception of national parks in the 1930s as wilderness landscapes. Park supporters were interested in the kind of permanent protection a congressionally authorized national park offered for primeval nature, which differed from the Forest Service's administrative safeguards for wilderness. The Forest Service also overlooked changes within the Park Service itself toward wilderness preser-

Wilderness with a View

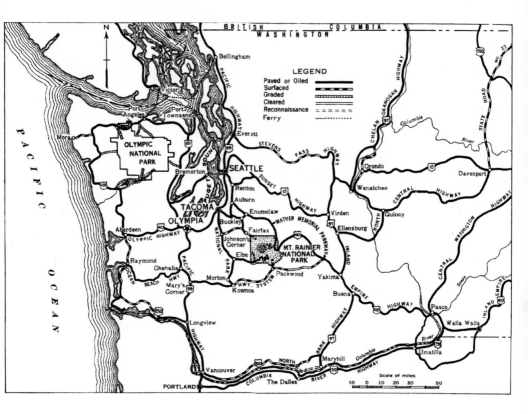

MAP 5. Western Washington's major roads and highways, 1938. By 1938, motorists could drive to and through Mount Rainier as part of a larger highway tour. Meanwhile, no roads traversed the newly established Olympic National Park.

vation. Revisions to road projects at parks like Crater Lake and Mount Rainier not only symbolized this new perspective but also showed the strong influence of Secretary Ickes. Cars were still the primary way that visitors experienced wilderness, but that was changing.

AN ENDURING LEGACY:
PUBLIC ROADS AND PRESERVING NATURE

By the late 1930s, both transpark roads and circle highways were anathema to national parks, especially those dedicated to wilderness like Olympic. Highways and automobiles remained part of encounters with and the preservation of national parks, but the role of cars and roads evolved. As the Hurricane Ridge Road proposal suggests, a new conceptual model was born,

Wilderness with a View 85

one that combined elements of high mountain roads and loop highways. It was a model that built on Albright's vision of Mount Rainier's revised road system, in which the circle road was still intact as part of the larger public highway landscape. Puget Sound residents could experience Mount Rainier on a longer loop drive that took them outside as well as inside the park. And while in the park, they could encounter the mountain's scenic grandeur from the roadside.

In a sense, the completion of the park-to-park highway fostered this broader interpretation of national parks as integral features of highway travel. Not only was Mount Rainier part of this highway landscape, but so too was Olympic. It was serendipitous, perhaps, that the Olympic Highway encircled the new park, connecting tourists from Seattle and Tacoma to the region in a way similar to their connection to Mount Rainier. Although the highway passed through parklands briefly, much of it along the shore of Lake Crescent, it was in effect the "park road," and the spur road to Hurricane Ridge functioned much in the same way as the roads to Paradise or Yakima Park in Mount Rainier. Although criticism of autos in national parks would build, for many Americans, including wilderness advocates, the highway experience continued to provide a powerful means of understanding and appreciating the primitive values of the natural world.

By proposing an Olympic park, Rosalie Edge and her colleagues recognized the permanent protection parks offered under congressional authority, but they also implicitly acknowledged the role of roads in preserving parks as wilderness landscapes. On the one hand, Edge and her cohorts saw themselves as pragmatic. "No one who knows the National Parks is so naive as to believe them wilderness areas," said Edge. After all, she asked rhetorically, "can a wilderness contain a highway?" The naturalist Willard Van Name, an active member in the ECC, added that some road building in national parks was unavoidable. But there would be even more road construction through scenic areas, he asserted, if parks were not created.[38]

On the other hand, park supporters demonstrated that there was something intangible about parks and modern life. As implied by Edge and noted by Van Name, it was important to remember that in parks cars and roads were mostly well restrained; they operated on a different plane than they did outside parks, where few restrictions existed to protect the natural world. Cars traveled at a slower rate of speed in parks, and roads brought visitors into closer contact with nature.[39] Parks, Van Name suggested, were still idealized landscapes for machines and nature.

Wilderness with a View

In the case of Olympic, roads were integral to the conception of the park as wilderness and the shaping of its final boundaries. Contrary to definitions of wilderness as primordial land untouched by mechanized transportation, it was essential not to insist on a park of "absolute roadlessness," Van Name asserted. This approach might gain only a park where roads could not be built, like the rugged peaks of the Olympics. Without question, he wrote, there should be "no through roads, and no roads for people with no interest in nature to speed around on 'to pass the time.'" But if park supporters were willing to accept one or two roads for providing access a short distance into the park, then they stood a greater chance of also preserving the region's lower altitudes: its river valleys and primeval forests.[40]

The park idea for Olympic also revealed that people's impressions of, and desire to preserve, wild landscapes continued to be influenced by their views from the road. In the early twentieth century, part of the allure of the Olympic Peninsula was its reputation as "America's Last Frontier." The region was popularly referred to as the westernmost point in the continental United States that still retained its essential qualities as a remote and wild land. By the late nineteenth century, settlement and resource exploitation had been relatively light and confined to the coastline and river basins, leaving the vast interior relatively unharmed.

But despite its wild character, the Olympic Peninsula was a frontier, an "uncivilized" country, known by automobile. The Olympic Highway, covering more than three hundred miles, was built in stages beginning in the teens. It formed a complete loop around the peninsula; winding along the foot of the Olympics, the highway passed some of the region's most scenic features, such as Hood Canal to the east, the Strait of Juan de Fuca to the north, and Grays Harbor to the southwest. The highway offered occasional glimpses of the Pacific Ocean and brought motorists close to Lake Crescent and Lake Quinault as well as the old-growth forests of the Bogachiel, Hoh, and Queets rivers on the western slopes of the Olympics. When the highway reached west from Port Angeles in the 1920s, the Lake Crescent country and resorts like the Olympic Hot Springs and Sol Duc Hot Springs became popular destinations for tourists getting "back to nature."[41]

The same conditions that contributed to Mount Rainier's popularity with residents of the Puget Sound region during the 1920s and 1930s applied to the Olympic country as well. The peninsula region was not removed from urban centers but was connected to them through a system of highways that was capable, as portrayed by Washington's tourist promoters, of making

auto travel a "wilderness" experience. Photographs in promotional litera-
ture showed touring cars meandering through massive Douglas fir forests
over smooth highways. The Pacific, Sunset, Inland Empire, National Park,
and Olympic highways conducted tourists through rural settings, deep into
mountain ranges and forests, and along winding coastal stretches. Not only
could motorists leave Seattle or Tacoma and within a short period of time
be in the alpine grandeur of Mount Rainier National Park, but they could
also travel the Olympic Highway to access the "last frontier," to enter a land
of untamed mountains, lakes, forests, wildlife, and Indians. When the western and final section of the highway was finished in 1931, motorists were
able to circumnavigate the peninsula, but even then the popular press did
not herald an end of the region's primitive values. Rather, the highway's
"conquest" of the peninsula created a new "vacation land," unlocking its
beauty to auto and driver during an age of "crowded population and extensive travel."[42] More than any other mode of travel, the Olympic Highway
informed people's perceptions of the peninsula's primitive values and enabled
their encounters with it; motoring through nature actually stimulated an
appreciation of the peninsula's wilderness character.

Motoring on the peninsula was also important in fostering the desire to
protect the region as a national park, in part to ensure that auto tourists
could always experience the area's primitive character and in part to respond
to a growing sense that its great forests were disappearing. Assurances that
motorized travel would always beat in vain against the Olympics did little
to assuage wilderness advocates and scenic preservationists. They were concerned not only about the rugged high country but also about the forest
beauty they saw from the roadside. As early as 1914, Grays Harbor County
commissioners suggested protecting an extensive swath of trees along the
Olympic Highway as it traversed the national forest. They wanted to ensure
the "permanent and perpetual reserve" of "big firs" to create a "highway of
great natural beauty."[43] While they were not necessarily proposing a national
park for the region, their interest was consistent with roadside beauty enthusiasts throughout the country and the Pacific Northwest beginning in the
teens and twenties. Many, like the Natural Parks Association, shared Stephen
Mather's interest in preserving scenery along Washington's highways, especially those leading to Mount Rainier. In the 1930s, a similar campaign was
underway for the Olympic Peninsula. As part of their activities to coordi-
nate efforts to protect forested roadsides adjoining parks and forests, the
Forest Service and Park Service attempted to preserve roadside strips of tim-

Wilderness with a View

ber along the Olympic Highway. They were particularly interested in reserving forest fringes leading to the Olympic Primitive Area and to Mount Olympus National Monument.[44]

These endeavors, however, were hardly enough to reverse public opinion about the loss of the peninsula's forests. During the 1930s, fewer and fewer miles of the Olympic Highway wended through "virgin forest." The highway may have made it possible to experience the "last frontier" by automobile, but there were no guarantees that the frontier would survive much longer. In a sense, like other aspects of the frontier myth, the forested land was gone before large numbers of auto tourists ever arrived. And its loss was one of the primary motives behind the ECC's desire to establish a national park. Anyone who believed that the Olympic Peninsula was a "vast region of untouched nature, gigantic trees, and abundant wildlife," wrote the ECC, was "forty or fifty years behind the times." Logging operations had wreaked destruction on most of the peninsula's landscape. "Let no one imagine that a trip around the Olympic highway," one of the committee's brochures stated, traversed "primeval forests of immense trees." Most of the highway crossed recently logged off forests or second-growth timber and in many places a well-settled landscape. Only through the northwestern portion of the circle highway could any "impressive forest growth" still be "seen by one who travels along the road."[45]

By encircling the Olympics, the peninsula highway turned travelers' views inward, toward the untrammeled wilderness, but the landscape of stumps and burns along the highway spurred concerned citizens to seek national park protection. Ironically, roads in this context were not the greatest threat to wilderness, for they revealed to tourists not only the ancient forests of the Olympic country, but also the effects of logging and other forms of environmental "degradation." Perhaps the most poignant moment in this relationship came when President Roosevelt toured the peninsula in 1937. The president was a park supporter and a champion of trees. Needless to say, his impressions were critical to the future of the Olympic campaign. And because of his physical disability, his impressions of the country were shaped largely by what he could see of it from an automobile. Although the president supported a large park, Irving Brant, his closest advisor on the Olympic campaign, knew of his interest in having scenic areas accessible by highway. Upon hearing the park referred to as a "wilderness without roads," Roosevelt asked, "How would I get in?"[46]

By choice more than because of physical limitations, most Americans who traveled to national parks and the peninsula shared the president's perspective. Aware of this, the Forest Service committed a tactical error in the park battle. Forest managers were so concerned about the scenic conditions of the highway that prior to the president's tour they busily placed signs along the highway identifying private land and national forest land. (They asserted that most logging operations seen from the road were on private land.) One sign selectively marked a splendid stand of trees welcoming the presidential party to Olympic National Forest near Lake Quinault. In the same area, however, a farewell sign was moved inside the forest boundary some two miles to a more scenic location, and the sign marking the true boundary was temporarily removed. In between was a blackened waste of logged-off land. When the Forest Service's deception was later exposed, Roosevelt ordered the forest supervisor transferred. Any arguments the agency could marshal to prevent the creation of a park thereafter seemed hollow.[47]

YOU CAN SEE IT FROM HERE: HURRICANE RIDGE AS THE IDEAL WILDERNESS ROAD

Roosevelt's tour of the Olympic Peninsula was only one element deciding the fate of the park, but it illustrates how, despite the wilderness mission of the new park, highways and cars still organized and influenced tourists' perceptions of it. In the late 1930s, the Park Service's plans for Hurricane Ridge perpetuated the notion of a windshield wilderness while adjusting it to portray the park as roadless. The plans represented a new concept in its formative stages, and perhaps one of the agency's greatest challenges was convincing itself and the public that it was capable of shaping the park with this new model.

In the years following the establishment of Olympic National Park, Park Service officials supported the Hurricane Ridge developments because they provided a familiar park experience—a loop drive through a wild landscape. For many, however, managing the park as a wilderness took them into uncharted territory. One outcome was a new metaphor for managing the park. Since all roads were to stay outside or near the edge of the park, managers began to consider the merits of road projects, both planned and proposed by the public, by how they would affect the "heart of the park." The central mission of the park, after all, was the preservation of its wilderness core. Agency officials were able to use this idea both to resist any road proj-

Wilderness with a View

ects that would bisect the park's wilderness center and to justify their decision to build the road to Hurricane Ridge.

Some of the most fundamental questions early in the park's administration emanated from basic concerns about how motorized access—and the extent of improvements for autos—would affect Olympic's wilderness character. In November 1938, for example, park ranger Fred Overly criticized the master plan's overemphasis on wilderness, asserting that it slighted the "general motoring public who have as much interest in the Olympic National Park as anyone else." At the very least, he suggested, the agency should use Mount Rainier's road to Paradise as a model for the proposed Hurricane Ridge loop drive. It would improve the poorly constructed Forest Service truck trail and satisfy the immediate needs of motorists. In the long run, he added, another entrance road should be built to Hurricane Ridge directly out of Port Angeles, up the west side of Mount Angeles from an area known as Heart of the Hills. The Heart of the Hills route would not only eliminate a steep and dangerous approach, but with its easy grade and panoramic views would provide an experience similar to the Paradise road.[48]

Overly's ideas anticipated the development strategy for Hurricane Ridge, but at the time were not readily accepted by his colleagues. The need to preserve the park's "wilderness charm" was foremost in the minds of other officials, and building a road of the same caliber as those in Mount Rainier might destroy "our wilderness values," observed the park's first superintendent, Preston Macy.[49] Biologist Lowell Sumner Jr. noted that any improvements to the Hurricane Ridge truck trail would destroy wildlife habitat. Improving the route would also perpetuate a development paradox. Sumner, who had accused park planners of widening Yosemite's Tioga Pass Road without considering the ecological effects, said that modifying older, steeper roads for modern cars only led to more modifications. If the "ancient cars" of the 1920s could negotiate these roads, he asked, why was it necessary to improve them for newer and more powerful vehicles?[50]

In the late 1930s and early 1940s, Park Service officials seemed to be experiencing a wilderness conversion when it came to Olympic. Rather than suggesting how the road proposals would be integrated into the park's natural landscape, they tended to respond to them by first considering how they might affect the park's wilderness values. When the public expressed interest in a road connecting Sol Duc Hot Springs to Olympic Hot Springs, Regional Director Frank Kittredge acknowledged that the route, part of the

Seven Lakes Basin road proposed by the Forest Service, was popular for its views of the high country and opportunities for skiing. But he doubted the project would be realized. Although a decade earlier as the Park Service's chief engineer he had advocated a high-line route for Mount Rainier's Stevens Canyon Road, Kittredge felt differently now. "I have some rather pronounced ideas against roads," he wrote, especially roads in the high country because they inflicted such heavy scars. He now favored one-way roads at high elevations; they were narrower and caused less scarring on steep slopes. In this sense, it seemed, the circuit road proposed for Hurricane Ridge was the better choice, for it was nearly in place.[51]

While Kittredge's interest in wilderness preservation may have been genuine, it was also politically calculated. Wilderness groups were important allies in the agency's management of Olympic. The Federation of Western Outdoor Clubs, for example, was keeping a close eye on the Park Service's activities. This coalition of conservation organizations opposed any road construction other than what the master plan outlined. The groups specifically opposed any roads that would penetrate the park's interior and its truly wondrous places like the Seven Lakes Basin. The coalition, however, did support the Hurricane Ridge Road project.[52]

Like accommodations for tourists, wilderness values were becoming an integral part of the Park Service's public relations strategy and its policy decisions in the management of Olympic. A dramatic example of this new perspective was the Park Service's plans to delay the construction of a coastal parkway along the newly acquired ocean strip in the 1940s. Along with the Queets River corridor, the Olympic coastal strip was reserved for future additions to the park by Secretary Ickes in 1939. By secretarial order, Ickes used Public Works Administration (PWA) funds to purchase the areas, though they were not officially added to the park until 1953 by presidential proclamation. In order to justify the use of PWA funds, Ickes declared that the purpose of setting aside the coastal strip was to survey and develop a scenic parkway along the ocean from Ruby Beach north to Lake Ozette.[53]

But in 1944, parkways were losing their appeal. They were out of favor with wilderness supporters, expensive to build, and were thought of by a growing body of critics as monotonous and artificial. These criticisms, although leveled at eastern parkways and anticipating the expansion of conventional highways in the postwar era, influenced the Park Service's plans for the coastal parkway. After close study, Thomas Vint recommended that the agency "abandon the thought" of a parkway. The narrow strip, then about

Wilderness with a View

one mile wide and some forty miles long, was a typical north Pacific Ocean headlands in mostly pristine condition. Building an ocean drive was impossible given the unstable soil conditions near the often steep shoreline, and it would destroy the very scenery motorists would want to see. There were other places farther north to develop a parkway, near Cape Flattery and the Makah Indian Reservation, Vint concluded, that would expose tourists to far more of the peninsula's coastal scenery. There was simply no reason to force a road through this unique coast land, a natural feature "worthy of protecting for the values it contains."[54]

While the Park Service shelved plans for a coastal parkway, it did not advocate preserving Olympic as a wilderness for its own sake. With the nation's entrance into World War II, the agency's New Deal programs ended, cutting off funding for the coastal surveys and road development. The war also turned the attention of park officials to protecting the park from pressures to exploit its resources for defense purposes, including the cutting of Sitka spruce for airplane construction. Although some logging occurred in the Queets River valley, which had not yet been added to the park, the war effort caused only minor damage to Olympic.[55]

But the war did expose the wilderness park's weakness. Until the Park Service could provide services to meet the public's expectations for a traditional park experience, popular support for its wilderness mission was in doubt. Created shortly before the nation entered the war, Olympic was poorly funded, and the Hurricane Ridge drive, its main development project, remained on hold. The delay forced the Park Service to contend with proposals that ran counter to the park's wilderness mission. Beginning in the mid-1940s, for example, Congressman Henry M. Jackson urged the Park Service to build a few new stub roads into the park, along with some alpine lodges to provide scenic vistas and winter sports opportunities. He wanted to see such facilities in the Seven Lakes Basin country as well as in the Hurricane Ridge area and was reportedly a "little disappointed" to learn that the Park Service had not requested funding for these projects. Jackson was responding to his peninsula constituents, such as the Port Angeles Chamber of Commerce and the Olympic Ski Club, who believed that in order for the park to be enjoyed by a substantial number of people, "it must have some good roads to the high country and good resorts in the mountains."[56]

By espousing a traditional view of a park, in which an alpine lodge and scenic highway were greater tourist draws than its primitive qualities, Jackson placed Park Service officials in the awkward position of defending their plans. The agency could only try to assure Jackson that Hurricane Ridge would satisfy a broad spectrum of park visitors and that there was no need to extend roads farther into the park's interior. The Park Service also had to respond to peninsula boosters who felt slighted by its selection of Port Angeles as Olympic's gateway city. The decision not only tarnished the over-looked towns but also diminished their ability to reap the "golden harvest from tourists" that the agency had promised during the park campaign.[57]

The desires of peninsula communities also challenged the Park Service's commitment to preserving the park's wilderness heart. In 1949, for exam-ple, the Quilcene Community Association, representing Jefferson County, mounted a campaign for the construction of the Dosewallips-Quinault road over the southern section of the park. Besides this transmountain route's fine scenery, the road's boosters regarded it as superior to the Port Angeles entrance because it was much closer to Seattle and Tacoma, "the metropolitan centers from which the tourists come," wrote Arthur Garrett, the associa-tion's president. It would make up for the considerable loss of tourist rev-enue destined for Port Angeles. Macy denied the proposal because the road would travel too far through dense forest cover and would not provide the "superior panoramic views" only found above an elevation of 4,000 feet (above timberline). Most of all, it would deeply scar the hillsides as it passed through the park's wilderness center.[58]

The Park Service, however, was not against all new road construction, as long as it did not pierce the heart of the Olympics. Its alternative to the transpark road was a shorter loop route across the southern section of the park, linking the Hood Canal with Lake Quinault, from the Staircase Resort to the Quinault River. What made the route so attractive, according to agency planners, was that it was confined to the extreme southern portion of the park, covering some thirty-three miles "rich in virgin forests, water-falls, glaciers and wild life." Almost seven miles of the route lay above tim-berline, affording motorists "superb views of the Olympics." Moreover, this route would better serve auto tourists than the one suggested over Anderson Pass because it would "provide quick access to the high coun-try, the rain forests, and the ocean." It would also reduce travel time to the west side of the peninsula.[59]

Even though the route would provide a more traditional park experi-ence, Garrett and other boosters from the east side of the peninsula were unimpressed. They continued to argue for some road improvement on the Dosewallips River, an "unexcelled" entrance to the park, and they prom-

Wilderness with a View

ised an "unrelenting" series of "gripes and complaints" until the matter was finally resolved. Nevertheless, park administrators held firm and refused to improve the Dosewallips route, claiming any road work would be so damaging to the landscape as to defeat its purpose. They were also concerned that any road extension would fuel arguments to complete the larger project of a transmountain road. If the agency did not plan to build the Staircase-Quinault road, noted Macy, the Park Service would be under constant pressure for a road through the middle of the park.[60]

With its approval of the southern road in March 1949, the Park Service began to shape a road system for Olympic that employed an old yet important park design concept: a circuit road augmented by a series of scenic spur roads and loop drives. Preservation through development remained the management concept. But it soon became apparent that under new circumstances this model of road building was highly problematic. A circuit road might possibly act as a new boundary, making forest lands to its south vulnerable to elimination from the park and open to logging by local timber companies. Further, surveys concluded that a road through the southern portion of the park would require expensive and heavy construction and would significantly mar the country through which it passed.[61]

The road reports presented park managers with a dilemma; any new road into Olympic to open up views would exact a heavy toll on construction budgets and nature. As noted by the associate director of the Park Service, Arthur Demaray, "sacrifices" would be required to build a road in the southern section of the park. Superintendent Macy and other agency officials doubted that the road was worth it, but their alternatives were no better—in part because they believed that the Hurricane Ridge project held the greatest promise. One park employee, for example, thought the Park Service should reconsider plans to build a road through the Seven Lakes Basin. In this way, auto tourists could experience all of the natural wonders the park possessed, its true "grandeur," in one circle trip without "appreciably impairing the wilderness."[62] Regional Director Owen Tomlinson, who oversaw the road development of Mount Rainier as superintendent, suggested another route just outside the south side of the park through Olympic National Forest, with a spur road leading to a scenic vista within the park. He thought this lower-elevation route would be less expensive to build, yet a spur road above timberline would be equally if not more costly than a road through the park. Without the spur road, however, the route "would fail to reveal the many scenic features" of the park. Superintendent Macy added that another possibility would be a shorter loop road in the park's southwestern corner from Highway 101 connecting the North Fork of the Quinault River with the Queets River to the north. Even though it would provide motorists better views of Olympic's glaciers, it would require extensive construction.[63]

Ultimately, these proposals pointed the Park Service back to Hurricane Ridge as the best and only choice for a park road. How important was it, pondered Macy, to run a road through the park's most outstanding natural features so motorists could get better views of glaciers? If the Park Service were to build a road that would provide "the ideal park experience," he wrote, the road would have to pass through the heart of the park. It would travel east to west, ending at the coast, linking together examples of all the park's features. But in doing so, he asserted, "we would destroy the very thing we seek to preserve and present." The wilderness would be gone forever, and the "purpose of the park defeated." To his way of thinking, Hurricane Ridge was the only choice for a new road. The ridge provided the greatest "sample of the park," from glaciers to wildflowers. The road from Heart of the Hills to Hurricane Ridge was the only new road the park would need for a long time. It was widely supported by peninsula communities and accepted by wilderness groups. Other road proposals, while trying to accomplish something similar, paled in comparison.[64]

SOMETHING OLD, SOMETHING NEW: HURRICANE RIDGE AS THE ROAD TO END ALL ROADS

The conception of Olympic as a wilderness park viewed from one great road, augmented perhaps by smaller loop drives, would not be fully realized until the mid-1950s, when in 1956 the Park Service launched its Mission 66 program. Prior to the improvement initiative, national parks languished. The postwar era found parks poorly funded and staffed, significant budgets having faded with the New Deal. Yet the popularity of parks continued to rise and, besieged by the travel boom of the late 1940s and 1950s, parks suffered. Auto tourists swarmed into parks, in many cases exposing the frail condition of public facilities and the need for more. When Olympic was finally "complete" in 1953, for example, Washington residents renewed proposals to build a coastal parkway, part of which would travel through Olympic's ocean strip. Park Service director Conrad L. Wirth responded that while the parkway was still under consideration, his agency had no

Wilderness with a View

immediate plans to complete it. National park roads alone needed more than $197.5 billion for repairs and new construction. In Olympic all available funds were channeled toward building the Hurricane Ridge Road, as well as some minor improvements. Surveys had begun in 1949 and the agency had selected the more direct and scenic Heart of the Hills route from Port Angeles proposed earlier by Fred Overly. The road's projected completion date was 1958.[65]

Besides being a comprehensive planning and development effort, Mission 66 was significant for Olympic because it interpreted the park's wilderness mission of the 1930s within the context of the postwar period. The era was characterized by rapid population growth and suburbanization, resource use and a consumer economy, higher education and greater leisure time, rising interest in outdoor recreation—forests, parks, and wilderness—and a growing awareness that these and other natural areas were not just America's playgrounds but were also essential elements in one's quality of life. These conditions, especially the ideal of preserving nature for its own sake, would spawn the modern wilderness movement. Some of the earliest and most defining battles would involve national parks as preservationists initiated national campaigns to save these treasured landscapes from hydroelectric dams and other industrial intrusions. The postwar period also anticipated another generation of national parks like Redwoods and North Cascades that symbolized the era's views on environmental protection and wilderness preservation. As in the early history of national parks, however, a key element in the conception of national parks as wilderness was still the nation's expanding highway system. It was no coincidence that Mission 66 and the Interstate Highway Act were passed in the same year, while forty years earlier, Congress had also simultaneously enacted the nation's first highway legislation and created the National Park Service.

Understandably, in an age of wide, multilane highways built for high speed, limited access, efficient travel, and national defense rather than scenic beauty, some feared that national park roads would take on new design characteristics. Like other aspects of postwar urban sprawl, interstate highways homogenized the American landscape; they standardized both the modern roadway and roadside by making every region of the country appear the same. And they threatened to do the same to national parks. Sierra Club leaders worried that recent and planned renovations of Yosemite's Tioga Road indicated future changes for all parks. "We don't build public thoroughfares through museums, libraries, art exhibits, or cathedrals," wrote

Richard Leonard, president of the Sierra Club. "Let us not build them through our parks."[66]

While the full ramifications of improved highways and the national park experience would be debated for years to come, the concern over modernizing highways illustrates that with each successive generation national parks were responding to new automobile and highway standards. Even a park like Olympic, which was lightly visited and arguably not a motorists' park, responded to these new conditions simply because automobile travel was everywhere on the rise. Given the park's wilderness mission, the Sierra Club and other organizations were particularly interested in the Park Service's "ambitious plans" for road development in Olympic.[67]

What most likely captured the attention of these groups was the agency's intent to use the Hurricane Ridge Road as a form of wilderness preservation. Under the leadership of Wirth, the project symbolized the rationale of using the new road standards as a way to turn parks into day-use areas. With its ability to accommodate modern cars and its close proximity to an urban center, the ridge road would not only enable tourists to see the park's scenic grandeur but would also allow them to travel outside the park for overnight accommodations and other amenities. There would be no need to develop similar services within the park.

Although Wirth's reasoning echoed plans from the late 1930s, he brought the initial concept of the road and its role in conveying the park's wilderness attributes full circle. Trained as a landscape architect, he headed the Park Service's recreational planning during the New Deal era and understood the concept of roads within the tradition of national park landscape design. At the same time, he was trying to make sense of roads within the context of the times. Even amid mounting skepticism about automobiles in relation to wilderness, Wirth was able to portray them as compatible with parks and thus clarified what the Park Service believed were the essential qualities of national park wilderness.

Like the 1938 master plan, the Mission 66 plan for Olympic described how the Park Service conceived of the wilderness park largely in terms of its relationship to highways and automobiles. Drafted in 1956, the new plan proclaimed the park's purpose as a roadless, unmodified country. The interior of the park, it asserted, was "a living wilderness." It was a large landscape, a complex yet "unified, functioning model of nature" that was "friendly and inviting" to those seeking tranquility as well as adventure, for much of it was "undeveloped, wild and mysterious." But it was also "a sce-

Wilderness with a View

nic wilderness," and in order for visitors to be inspired by the park's natural beauty, the park's trail and road system needed to make Olympic's "most inspiring views and important features" accessible to the public.[68]

While committed to preserving the "wilderness character of the park," agency planners were faced with some staggering figures. They anticipated that within a decade a million visitors would enter the park annually and that the majority of them would see it by automobile. The trend had been growing with every improvement to Highway 101 and with the postwar travel boom. Close to 93,000 people visited Olympic in 1941, prior to World War II. A decade later, 415,000 visitors came to the park, and by 1955 the figure had risen to 775,000. Although "trail users" once dominated the park, "road users" now outnumbered them. Park planners may have been committed to keeping all "future road construction ... to the periphery of the park," but they focused intently on Hurricane Ridge as the main conduit for automobile travel in the park. And since the majority of Olympic's visitors came during the summer months, when the high country was free of snow, it would be the park's scenic "grandstand."[69]

In some ways, Park Service leaders endorsed the Hurricane Ridge Road because they had little choice. The route had been approved and funded since the late 1940s not only to fulfill the original "roadless" concept for the park, but also to appease Congressman Jackson and peninsula boosters who wanted high-country access and overnight lodging. Jackson had helped secure the appropriations for the road and for the construction of a ski lodge at Hurricane Ridge, which opened in 1954. Furthermore, the other proposed routes were too expensive and destructive to build and maintain. And while there was renewed interest in a coastal road, it was another high-priced and controversial project. Its development would happen in the distant future, if at all.[70]

In another way, agency leaders were playing to the park's wilderness constituency. Although the Sierra Club and other park defenders would question the Park Service's commitment to protecting parks as "true" wilderness as the Mission 66 program progressed, they supported certain aspects during its initial stages. They endorsed Wirth's concept of turning the parks into day-use areas as much as possible. In this respect, they were arguing against Jackson and Washington senator Warren Magnuson, who supported the development of overnight facilities. As Fred Packard of the National Parks Association wrote, the fine, large hotels in parks like Yellowstone, Yosemite, and Mount Rainier were used during the early age of auto tourism, but they were outdated and unnecessary. Now visitors could approach parks after spending the night in hotels outside the parks, exemplified by Olympic's Hurricane Ridge Road. As an alternative, though camping was not for everyone, Packard wrote that "camping impresses us as contributing more beneficial enjoyment than viewing scenery entirely through the windows of an automobile."[71]

Packard reflected the main idea embedded in the Mission 66 planning process, but the plan conveyed a complex message. It seemed to offer a new concept of national parks as places that were no longer resorts for auto tourists. At the same time, as Packard suggested, parks were still places for motorists. Only now they slept differently—on the ground instead of in hotel beds. Parks were still places in which automobiles interacted with a wilderness landscape without apparent conflict.

In 1957, Wirth put forth this notion in the brochure, *The National Park Wilderness*. Wirth published it to disarm critics who charged that Mission 66, with its extensive developments and modern architecture, was not only building up the parks but was diminishing their primitive qualities. Rather than the rustic design of the 1920s and 1930s, which harkened back to primitive America, Mission 66 symbolized urban America with its standardized structures, which were cheaper to build and maintain than the log and stone structures of the past. The brochure was timed to allay concerns about the intent of Mission 66 and to respond to the emerging wilderness movement of the postwar generation.[72]

The brochure was especially appropriate for interpreting events at Olympic because it portrayed Mission 66 as a wilderness preservation program. By promoting more visitor use, roads like the one to Hurricane Ridge could protect the park from more development and the persistent attempts of lumbermen and commercial interests to run a road through the heart of the park. Certainly, this had been the justification for the road all along, but now there was an official statement about the meaning of park wilderness to support it.

Wirth's publication was a kind of meditation on wilderness. The brochure continued the discourse agency leaders and landscape architects had begun the late 1930s, in which national parks were a "special kind" of wilderness, containing both "superlative wilderness areas" and "wilderness qualities," wild places you could encounter physically and emotionally. Although centered around human appreciation of nature, the management mission of national parks was "largely a wilderness philosophy," the brochure assured

Wilderness with a View

its readers. This applied to unmodified, primitive landscapes, a single natural feature, or "wilderness values along the roadside." The successful protection of a "roadless wilderness," however, was still dependent upon the existence of more easily accessible and intensively developed and used portions of a park. Like other park development strategies, the Mission 66 program was based on the belief that wilderness preservation and "national park hospitality" were "not irreconcilable." In all instances, the Park Service sought a "sane and practical middle ground" without compromising the "basic and traditional purpose of national parks."[73]

The brochure was also indebted to earlier agency attempts at defining wilderness when it suggested that wilderness was a highly subjective, value-laden term. Pure wilderness was a landscape that existed without human interference. Given the reality of modern life, as Thomas Vint asserted, using *Webster's* definition, there was no wilderness left in America, except perhaps in Alaska. But wilderness could be less than pristine and still be considered vital if human interference lay lightly on the land, as with trails for recreation, and did not affect natural processes. It was possible to employ a flexible concept of wilderness—just as it was possible to treat the national park idea as a flexible concept. Such an adaptive notion recognized the value of a relatively pristine environment as well as a human-modified environment that could be restored to a wilderness condition.[74]

In addition to seeing wilderness as a physical space understood in ecological terms, the brochure suggested that wilderness was a quality defined through personal experience or feelings. It identified five wilderness qualities that national parks perpetuated: a scene or vista of a natural wonder or beautiful landscape unaffected by any obvious human intrusions; an area secluded from the sounds, sights, and odors of motorized transportation; a spot where one could find refuge and solitude from modern life; a place where a person could visualize and sense America's frontier past; and the opportunity to experience nature relying on one's own physical skills and intuition. Considered in this way, wilderness did not have to be narrowly constrained because the "quality of wilderness" could be found in "an expansive roadless area, in a narrow glen, or even close to a major highway, if shielded from the effects of mechanized civilization."[75]

Although the brochure concluded that wilderness was an "ecological condition" as well as "a state of mind," its main concern was with the perception of wilderness as an "essential attribute of a scenic national park." Echoing Frederick Law Olmsted from the mid-nineteenth century, the Park

Service maintained that wilderness was scenery. The primitive country beyond roads was the background—the "atmosphere"—for the park as a whole. But wilderness qualities, those natural elements that gave visitors a wilderness feeling, could be discovered "along park roadsides." While "true wilderness" was important, it was restricted to a specific area, whereas wilderness qualities applied to the entire park. Thus, comparatively few experienced a national park's real wilderness, while millions of visitors benefited— perhaps more—from the qualities of wilderness found near park roads and other developed areas. This was what national park management and the Mission 66 program were about: ensuring that wilderness areas were protected but that above all park visitors were exposed to a park's wilderness essence.[76]

In this light, the role of roads in parks had changed little since the 1920s. Roads provided reasonable access to parks so visitors could enjoy the natural scene. Master plans governed their selection and compatibility with other developments, and thoughtful design still influenced the placement and treatment of park roads so that they blended with the topography and provided intimate roadside encounters with nature. Roads, furthermore, had not diminished the wilderness values of national parks. "Anyone who seeks wilderness," the brochure asserted, "can find it in the national parks." Even those who never ventured far from their cars experienced the quality of wilderness. "For them wilderness might lie but ten minutes' walk from most park roads, or they may sense it" looking out from one of the many great park roads. Even though they may never leave the roadside, "visitors see, sense, and react to wilderness," for this was the legacy not just of park roads but of park conservation. "The wilderness," the brochure ended, was there, and "consciously or unconsciously, people respond to it."[77]

Completed a year after the wilderness brochure was released, the Hurricane Ridge Road represented what the Park Service intended for a park road in the wilderness age. The thirteen-mile road conveyed motorists through a scenic landscape and climaxed at the ridge, the "grandstand" view of the "mountainous wilderness of the interior Olympics." Leading out of Port Angeles, the road ascended through dense Douglas fir forests, then climbed through alpine fir and grass-covered slopes as it rose above timberline and provided sweeping views of the inner Olympics. It revealed to visitors the wilderness qualities of the roadside and the great wilderness background of the park.

In 1959, after the road's first full season of use, the Park Service proclaimed it a success. Park managers based their conclusion on visitor surveys sampled from some of the estimated eighty-six thousand people who stopped at the ridge that year. With few exceptions, managers claimed that park visitors were "extravagant in their praise." As one "typical" visitor comment stated: "The road from Port Angeles to here is the most perfect road I have ever driven over." In their effusiveness, the park's authors overlooked the irony that the most popular pullout, Lookout Point, provided a panoramic view not of the park but of the Puget Sound country. In fact, the road generated more enthusiasm for the northern views of the Strait of Juan de Fuca, Vancouver Island, and Mount Baker than for the southern view into the park. This may have been a minor point, but it suggests that with a road of such a grand scale, motorists might not have comprehended where the park was as they drove to see the wilderness interior.[78]

But the Park Service already knew that Hurricane Ridge was popular, and what the agency really wanted to know was whether it needed to build overnight accommodations there. Agency leaders, given the emphasis of Mission 66, had already decided against further development, but they had to prove their point to congressional leaders such as Henry Jackson, who had been supporting a high country lodge for more than a decade. In order to gauge public opinion about the need for overnight services and slant the results in their favor, park managers modified the original plans for Hurricane Ridge and experimented with a new circulation system. They closed down the original access road from the Elwha Valley. There was really no reason to keep the "steep-pitched, winding road" open for modern drivers in "their low slung automatic transmission cars." Although managers played up the fact that the route was not suitable for the new car models, their views also reflected previous management decisions. In the short term, if they kept the older access road open, travel over it would be slow, fueling the demand for building overnight facilities. And in the long term, keeping the road open would require expensive maintenance, and its continued use might lead to more modernization.[79]

In a sense, the Heart of the Hills route had been designed with these considerations in mind. It was a two-lane road constructed to modern standards. It was not part of the series of one-way drives anticipated in earlier plans, connecting the Deer Park Road with the Obstruction Point Road from Hurricane Ridge to the old Elwha route. Visitors, it seems, never knew what they were missing without the option of entering and leaving from different places. "The great majority," the Park Service reported, drove "back down the road they came up without comment of any kind." And very few people inquired about overnight lodging. Olympic managers deduced from this that a "circulating road," such as the one planned between Deer Park and Hurricane Ridge, would be accepted but was not necessary. They recommended abandoning the Elwha Road, keeping the Heart of the Hills route as the main access route, and reconstructing the old Obstruction Point Road as a two-way, low-standard road, designed as an interpretive drive or auto trail. It would take motorists out to a scenic point and allow them to return the same way. [80]

The road to Hurricane Ridge, whether it was a loop or a spur road, further maintained the park road model employed at Mount Rainier and other older parks; it provided motorists with access to a scenic vantage point. What made Olympic's road system different, what identified it as a transition from an older to a newer way of knowing parks by machines, was that most of the highway encircling the park lay outside the park's boundaries and was not federally owned. Park Service planners attempted to use this situation to their advantage, treating the road system like a wheel from which they could attach short loop drives through the park's periphery. Ostensibly, these were to satisfy motorists' desires to "see" the park from more than one side and to promote the park's protection by enabling more people to view it. But more than justifications for traditional reasons of public access, the spur roads were intended to forestall a transpark road. For a variety of reasons, the loop roads were never built, but they served a more conceptual purpose, because they emphasized the importance of preserving the "heart of the park," its wilderness core.

Olympic was a wilderness park autos would never cross, but the Hurricane Ridge Road allowed motorists to encounter it. In this way, automobiles and roads continued to shape ideas of national parks as wilderness. Even though, in the late 1950s, the road's success could not be adequately measured, it was significant because it embodied what Conrad Wirth and the Park Service meant by wilderness. Wilderness was a physical landscape—the Olympic Mountains—and it was "a state of mind," a quality one could see and sense from a park road. Ultimately, national parks preserved wilderness as scenery, and roads and cars made experiencing wilderness possible. They made it possible to understand Olympic as a national park.

4 / A ROAD RUNS THROUGH IT

A Wilderness Park for the North Cascades

I n the years after World War II, Americans began to understand national
parks in a different way. For many, a wilderness encounter increasingly
meant leaving the car behind and heading into the backcountry on foot
or horseback. Even the Beat writer Jack Kerouac, symbol of life on the road,
felt drawn to mountains like Washington's North Cascades, where he abandoned his car for a summer to contemplate life's deeper meanings.[1] In
Olympic National Park, the Hurricane Ridge Road, completed in 1958, characterized the Park Service's road improvement and construction program
during Mission 66, which Director Conrad Wirth justified as a form of
wilderness preservation. Although this road responded to a growing interest in preserving parks as wilderness undefiled by automobiles, it still promoted the ideal of wilderness as scenery viewed from a car. And thus in the
1950s and 1960s, preservationists greeted the Park Service's management plans
with skepticism. Even though road developments like the one at Olympic
showed some restraint, they doubted that this and other road proposals
would truly protect the wilderness values of national parks. Instead, wilderness advocates believed, these projects would subject the country through
which they passed to more scarring and motorists.

In their disenchantment with Park Service policies, preservationists
began to interpret the meaning of parks within the context of the postwar
wilderness movement. More Americans, motivated by rapid changes in society and the economy, expressed concern over the loss of wild places to
resource production. They campaigned to preserve nature as an amenity

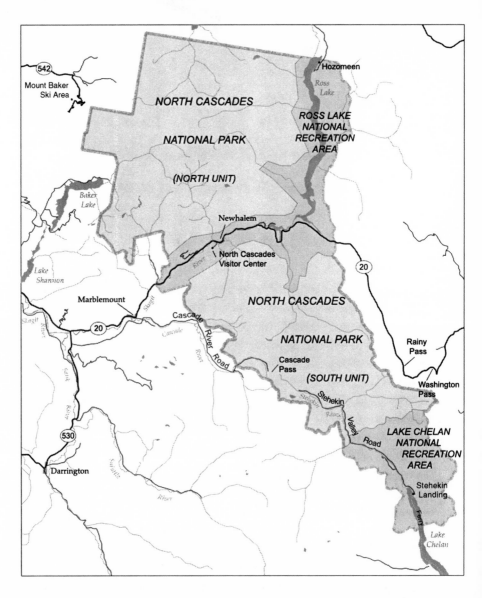

MAP 6. Road system of North Cascades National Park Service Complex

of life rather than as a commodity for the marketplace. Their new attitude was particularly important for national parks; it inspired preservationists to protect Dinosaur National Monument's Echo Park, for example, from being dammed in the mid-1950s. The victory not only launched a national crusade against the damming of the West's rivers and reinvigorated the

A Road Runs Through It

wilderness movement, but it also suggested that national parks were wilderness sanctuaries. Parks deserved the highest form of protection.[2]

Unlike their predecessors, wilderness advocates in the 1960s had more legal and political power at their disposal, and they used it to pressure the Park Service to manage parks as unimpaired reserves, free of roads and cars. Especially significant was the Wilderness Act of 1964. This far-reaching and complex preservation measure established congressionally designated wilderness areas on federal land, including national parks, ensuring their permanent protection as part of a national wilderness system. More importantly, the act legally defined wilderness as a primitive landscape, uninhabited, undeveloped, and roadless. Machines were not allowed. Preservationists urged the Park Service to implement, if not in reality then at least philosophically, the intent of the act. They saw the agency's response to the postwar travel boom, with the flood of motorists it brought to the parks, as flawed. Despite creating parks as "day-use areas," the Mission 66 program seemed intent on expanding visitor facilities.

Other incentives prompted reconsideration of the relationship between autos and nature in national parks. One was the nation's waning love affair with the automobile. Another was a rising ecological awareness. Together, they prompted many to see cars less as vehicles of freedom and a means to retreat to nature's wonders and more as sources of pollution, urban sprawl, and congestion. Beginning in the 1960s, with a broader understanding that population growth, resource depletion, and polluted water and air would directly affect human welfare, wilderness advocates were part of conservation's evolution into environmentalism. People began to consider that no quick technological fix would solve the world's mounting environmental crisis; modern technology could not replace the vast quantities of nonrenewable resources it consumed. There were limits to natural abundance.[3]

From this perspective, the automobile, that potent symbol of twentieth-century technology, was a negative agent of change that would reduce rather than advance one's quality of life. Even national parks, where historically automobiles had carved out a different relationship for people and nature, were not immune from this change in attitude. According to some critics, cars were transforming the natural paradise of parks like Yosemite into urban areas with their negative associations of crime, noise, foul air, and overcrowding. The accord between machines and wild places, it seems, had dissolved.

Although these changing views, expectations, and attitudes marked a major turning point in the way Americans thought about the relationship between national parks and automobiles, parks retained some of their allure as idealized landscapes capable of sustaining automobiles and roads. People may have been looking at parks through a new lens, one that sharpened the meaning of parks as wilderness reserves and biological systems, but their perceptions were still informed by an older way of knowing nature through machines. In fact, it seemed that without access for automobiles and scenery framed in a windshield, national parks would lose their identity.

Olympic's provision for a road to the park's wilderness margin offered one response, but the creation of North Cascades National Park suggests that the story of parks and cars grew more rather than less complicated in postwar America. It was time, it seemed, to eliminate cars from parks altogether, and North Cascades seemed the right park to make this happen. Established on October 2, 1968, the park protected the northern section of Washington's Cascade Range: a formidable landscape of high, angular peaks, glaciers, and steep-sided valleys, filled with dense forests and drained by swift-flowing rivers. But rather than simply creating a national park dedicated solely to wilderness, the legislation established a "park complex" of some seven hundred thousand acres. The complex consisted of a large national park separated into northern and southern units, and two smaller units, the Ross Lake and Lake Chelan national recreation areas. Although the park proper was roadless, State Highway 20, which opened in 1972, crossed the range and provided access. The highway, it was believed, posed no threat to the sanctity of the national park itself. The route was contained entirely within Ross Lake National Recreation Area (NRA), bisecting the northern and southern units of the park. The Park Service considered recreation areas—and other types of park sites such as lakeshores and seashores— to be slightly lower in status and open to a wider range of uses than national parks. Although the agency would determine eventually that all park units deserved the same intense focus on nature preservation, recreation areas served as a kind of supporting cast for parks. In this way, Highway 20 appeared only as a minor intrusion on the park's overall wilderness setting.

Even though the intent of the park complex was to reconcile finally the presence of automobiles in the primitive landscape of national parks, this arrangement suggested that the general public and the Park Service itself never fully abandoned the expectation of viewing splendid scenery from the roadside within a park. The layout of park and recreation area units perpetuated the typical park experience, but in a different way than ever before. Penetrating the heart of a park complex valued for its wilderness character, the highway was how the majority of North Cascades' visitors would encounter the wild country. Although not on the same scale as Highway 20, two other roads—the Stehekin Valley Road and the Cascade River Road—brought visitors to the brink of the park's wilderness and, though they were unimproved, offered a similar experience.

In the late 1950s, wilderness advocates—led by the Sierra Club—decided that the North Cascades deserved to be a national park. The range possessed scenic grandeur and something more impressive. In an era of rapid growth and resource consumption, it was one of the "most untouched primeval regions," a sanctuary from the complicated life of modern society, "one of the country's last [wilderness sanctuaries] and perhaps its greatest," outside of Alaska.[5] Time and again, the region had turned back highway projects and civilization's chugging agent of progress, the automobile. And even well into the twentieth century, the lone settlement of Stehekin, at the head of the fjordlike Lake Chelan, could not be reached by road. By accident of geography, wilderness enthusiasts suggested, the North Cascades had been spared.

Preservationists believed that national park status offered the best form of protection for the region. But the decision to pursue a national park carried considerable baggage, especially about the role roads and cars would play in interpreting wilderness. In order to justify the park, proponents proclaimed that it would be a wilderness park, similar to those created in the late 1930s and early 1940s, such as Olympic and Kings Canyon. Yet in their attempts to rationalize the decision, the Sierra Club and other preservation groups implied that one could not easily escape that parks were places, at some level, where wilderness and roads came together. In making their decision to support a park, these groups had to reconcile their own concept of the real value or essence of wilderness with the traditional—and current—management of national parks.

One of the most important factors in their decision was the legacy of Robert Marshall. Marshall, who perhaps did more for wilderness than anyone of his generation, surveyed the North Cascades in the 1930s.[6] He concluded that it was one of the West's three great wildernesses on national forest lands and the "second largest potential forest wilderness remaining in the

United States," outside of Alaska. He proposed designating as wilderness the entire Cascade Range from Stevens Pass north to the Skagit River valley, a distance of some forty miles north to south and thirty-two miles east to west. Named for its geological centerpiece, the ten-thousand-foot volcanic cone of Glacier Peak, this wilderness would join the newly established North Cascades Primitive Area (801,000 acres) straddling the backbone of the Cascades along the Canada–United States border. All together, the northern Cascades wilderness would total some 1.5 million acres out of a possible 2.8 million acres. Although this mountain wilderness encompassed a vast area, there was no reason, according to Marshall, to build roads or truck trails into it; it posed little fire hazard and possessed little commercial value. Seattle's Skagit River hydroelectric project in its northwestern corner presented the only intrusion. Marshall contended that the Forest Service should prevent all other forms of mechanical development in order "to preserve for wilderness travel one of the most stupendously scenic areas in the United States."[7]

To comply with his recommendation, the Forest Service would have had to block the long-proposed state highway across Cascade Pass, which commercial interests and local communities on either side of the range supported as important for economic development. But in Marshall's opinion, economic prospects such as logging and mining paled compared to the importance of wilderness protection. So did the argument that abandoning the highway project would deprive millions of Americans from seeing the spectacular scenery of the northern Cascades. Here was a classic example of where the desires of the majority—in this case motorists—should not have precedence over those of the minority—wilderness travelers. Wilderness was like art, Marshall suggested. To be fully appreciated it needed to be preserved in its original form. A road through wilderness was like cutting up the *Mona Lisa* into small pieces. In both cases, a masterpiece would be destroyed. Opening up the heart of this wilderness country to motorists would give them an unfair monopoly on the northern Cascades' beautiful landscape. Already those who did not care to, or could not, travel by primitive methods had many "splendid automobile trips" at their disposal on either side of the range, including the volcanic cones of Mount Baker and Mount Rainier. All of this "would certainly give the automobilist an immense variety of Cascade scenery," he concluded, "and a fair break in the allocation of the beauty of this marvelous region."[8]

Although his contemporaries in the nascent wilderness movement of the

A Road Runs Through It

1920s and 1930s, such as Aldo Leopold and Arthur Carhart, shared similar views about wilderness, Marshall perhaps did more to broadcast this message through his life's work and writings than anyone else. Indeed, Marshall's concept of wilderness as a primitive landscape and his arguments for wilderness resonated deeply with many in the postwar generation; his views seemed more relevant than ever in the chaotic atmosphere of the 1950s and 1960s. But they were not necessarily easily adapted to the traditional national park model. For Marshall, wilderness stood as the antithesis of modern life and nothing symbolized modern life more than automobiles and roads. He conceived of wilderness as "a region which contains no permanent inhabitants, possesses no possibility of conveyance by any mechanical means and is sufficiently spacious that a person crossing it must have the experience of sleeping out."[9]

Wilderness protection seemed to be a simple matter of protecting lands that had not yet been transformed or disfigured by road building and automobiles.[10] However, "The Problem of the Wilderness," about which Marshall wrote in his famous 1930 essay of that title, was not so much its impending destruction and need for preservation, as it was its definition. As historian William Cronon argues, "wilderness came to embody the national frontier myth, standing for the wild freedom of America's past and seeming to represent a highly attractive natural alternative to the ugly artificiality of modern civilization. The irony, of course, was that in the process wilderness came to reflect the very civilization its devotees sought to escape." Urban Americans such as Marshall, who grew up in New York City, projected their own image of wilderness as a roadless, untrammeled land onto the American landscape. And thus rather than saving something that already existed, the act of preserving created wilderness as they saw it. Wilderness, in this context, was uninhabited, unworked, and unchanged from its original, pristine state when God created it. Gone were the Indians who had once made their homes in that land. Gone, too, was the contest for survival. For this reason "the wilderness lost its savage image and became safe: a place more of reverie than revulsion and fear."[11] In this way, even though wilderness in Marshall's conception was necessarily unmarred by modern conditions, wilderness did in fact mirror modernity.

This wilderness paradox posed the greatest challenge for wilderness activists in their quest to protect the North Cascades as a park, for national parks were wilderness reserves whose accommodations for America's car culture only reflected modern life in a more visible and obvious way. Still attractive, though, to wilderness supporters as well as to the general public was a national park like Mount Rainier, because it presented a relatively pristine landscape traversed by roads and expressed the potential for harmony between machines and nature within the boundaries of national parks. The times had changed, but perception, as Ralph Waldo Emerson observed in the mid-nineteenth century, was still a crucial aspect of how people interpreted nature—and national parks—as wild.

The concept of a park as a wild landscape compatible with roads was central to understanding how preservationists would justify, at least implicitly, their national park strategy for the North Cascades, but it was not shared by Marshall. He objected to the creation of a park in the region because the Park Service had a long history of developments at the expense of wilderness, especially during the New Deal. Among the projects that drew fire from Marshall and the Wilderness Society was the agency's 1937 proposal to create a park for the entire Cascade Range in Washington, the "Ice Peaks National Park." Marshall argued against the plan, noting that the new park, under current agency practice, "would have roads extended into its heart."[12]

Marshall's wilderness proposal for the North Cascades, as was true of many of his other proposals, was never fully realized. In the North Cascades dispute, the Forest Service employed tactics similar to those it had used in the Olympic battle—using primitive and wilderness designations to fend off park proposals—only with more success. The creation of Olympic National Park raised considerable controversy and caused some Washington residents and resource-dependent communities and industries to become suspicious about the Park Service's intentions elsewhere in the state. They wondered if the agency's interest in such a large park was not really just a land grab directed by Secretary of the Interior Harold L. Ickes, another skirmish in his mission to bring the Forest Service under his control. In the late 1930s, as head of the Forest Service's Division of Recreation and Lands, Marshall optimistically believed that the park issue would persuade regional foresters to show more concern for the recreational rather than the timber values of the national forests. He had helped develop strict regulations for Forest Service wilderness areas. But that agency's leaders decided against wilderness designation for the Glacier Peak country. Classifying the region as wilderness, they believed, would only invite park proposals and would alienate the agency's traditional supporters in the timber and mining industries. Marshall managed only a small measure of success with the creation of the Glac-

A Road Runs Through It

ier Peak Recreation Area in 1938, a relatively small area covering some 275,000 acres. He died suddenly the following year. And with the Ice Peaks proposal fading with the nation's entry into World War II, so too did the idea of wilderness for the North Cascades.[13]

When preservationists turned their attention again to protecting the North Cascades, they realized that fulfilling Marshall's vision for the range was no simple task. At midcentury, the range may have been one of the most unknown and virtually undeveloped sections of the nation outside of Alaska, but it was not the fortress against change they had imagined. An accident of geography had only delayed, not terminated, development plans for the region. Much to the disappointment of wilderness proponents, Marshall's own agency promoted the exploitation of the range. In the 1950s, the Forest Service began to reevaluate the national forests, including the northern Cascades, to meet the demands of the postwar housing boom, the pressures of an expanding population, and a dwindling private timber supply. Its role was to plan for the greatest production and wisest use of the nation's limited supply of natural resources.[14] In doing so, the Forest Service considered a variety of prospective uses and developments for the North Cascades, including timber harvesting, mining, and highway construction, as well as wilderness classification for the Glacier Peak country. While the Forest Service saw itself promoting a number of uses for the region—meeting both economic and recreational demands—preservation groups saw the agency opening the doors of this wilderness stronghold to irreparable harm.

The most startling evidence of this was the Forest Service's flagging commitment to wilderness. As the agency pursued a more aggressive timber management program after the war, it reduced the size of many primitive areas to promote logging, setting off a series of conflicts with preservationists. As Chief Forester Richard A. McArdle observed in 1955, in the spirit of multiple use his agency would designate as wilderness only those areas that had the slightest commercial values and where wilderness represented "the highest form of public use." The policy, as wilderness advocates witnessed, informed the agency's decision to redraw the boundaries around a number of primitive areas, including the Glacier Peak country, leaving only the high country of rocks and ice as wilderness.[15] The Forest Service's plan, released in 1957, recommended 434,000 acres as the Glacier Peak Wilderness Area and included roughly half of the area recommended by Marshall. Its boundaries left out many of the densely forested river valleys draining the range in order to extend roads up the valleys for logging and roadside recreation. The boundaries so deeply indented the range from the east and west that the proposed wilderness looked like a starfish, easily severed at its center by roads.[16]

The agency's proposal ignored the appeals of wilderness supporters, such as the Wilderness Society, the Federation of Western Outdoor Clubs, and Seattle's Mountaineers, who had urged inclusion of the entire area proposed by Marshall. In particular, they wanted the country between Cascade Pass and the Stehekin River protected, which was where the Forest Service was planning its most controversial projects: timber sales in the Stehekin River valley, often likened to Yosemite, and a road to link the valley to the future cross-mountain highway over Cascade Pass.[17]

Even after the Sierra Club mounted a national campaign, similar in scale and kind to its successful defense of Echo Park in Dinosaur National Monument, the Forest Service made few concessions.[18] In 1960, the secretary of agriculture designated a slightly larger Glacier Peak Wilderness Area, but only directed that the Cascade Pass–Stehekin River country be managed for recreation—not as wilderness. "Where are the blazes with which Bob Marshall marked the trail toward wilderness?" asked Sierra Club leader David Brower. Farther and farther beyond the end of a logging road, it seemed. A new path to wilderness protection, many concluded, could only be found by preserving the North Cascades as a national park.[19]

ROAD TO NOWHERE: STEHEKIN AND THE SHAPING
OF A NEW WILDERNESS PARK

Forest Service actions made the decision to support a park a relatively easy one for preservationists. Even though Bob Marshall had opposed national park designation, preservationists could remain true to his legacy by keeping wilderness as their objective. Still, the route to national park preservation was paved by roads and traveled by autos. In their reevaluation of national parks as wilderness reserves, preservationists seemed to concede that trackless wilderness was not necessarily without the influence of roads and cars. The village of Stehekin, for example, played a key role in defining the range's wilderness caliber, and when threatened, it was a rallying point for the defense of wilderness and ultimately the range's protection as a national park.

Since its establishment in the late nineteenth century, Stehekin had been

A Road Runs Through It

a small village at the head of the twisting, narrow canyon of Lake Chelan. Originally serving miners and homesteaders seeking their fortunes and futures in the region, the settlement functioned as a gateway to the peaks and glaciers that lay beyond the valley. Hunters and tourists also flocked to Stehekin seeking out its wildlife and its renowned scenery of high, glacier-chiseled mountains that rose some seven thousand feet above the lake to elevations just under nine thousand feet. At one time, small supply businesses, hotels, and other establishments lined the Stehekin landing, where the daily arrival of the *Lady of the Lake* signaled the only communication with the outside world, bringing people, goods, and news from the city of Chelan, fifty-five miles downlake. Like many places in the West, tourism became one of the isolated village's primary draws, as mining and other extractive industries declined. As early as 1892, boosters proclaimed the picturesque scenery of the upper lake country and surrounding mountains worthy of protection as a national park. Although only the promise of mining, logging, and other commercial developments existed in the late nineteenth and early twentieth centuries, these were enough to defeat park proposals. Nevertheless, Stehekin appeared in 1950 much as it had sixty years earlier. Some thirty year-round residents inhabited the lower ten miles of the U-shaped valley, with its fortress of peaks and open forests of ponderosa pine. Residents lived mostly subsistence lifestyles, hunting, gardening, and bartering. Some supplemented this by working for the Forest Service, which managed the national forest lands in the Stehekin watershed. Others provided services such as lodging and transportation for the tourists who continued to seek out the region's scenery.[20]

Stehekin retained its isolated character, its supporters argued, because of its most distinguishing quality: no road reached the valley. Although there was a short road in the valley, you could not drive to Stehekin even in the age of superhighways, and this made it "unique and beautiful." It was, as Grant McConnell observed, how "most places of the earth once were, but known only to a few." McConnell, a political scientist, Stehekin resident, and conservationist, noted that for decades Washington State officials and various "outside" groups had schemed to build a road up the shore of Lake Chelan. They had also started another from the west, which would go up the Skagit River, over Cascade Pass, and down the Stehekin River valley. But the formidable country rendered road plans impracticable; in the case of the Cascade Pass road, heavy snows and flooding reclaimed what progress had been made. In McConnell's eyes, nature seemed in force here, its inhabitants in accord with it, and for this reason Stehekin remained beyond the modern highway, the automobile, and thus "the currents of American life racing past the mountain barriers around it."[21]

For McConnell, one of Stehekin's most eloquent spokesmen, Stehekin was a place where wilderness and automobiles appeared to be mutually beneficial. The valley road symbolized how the northern Cascades somehow contained and limited the modern world. It was the road to nowhere; Stehekin, after all, was on the way to nowhere. There was no industry to speak of in the valley. Mining ventures repeatedly failed, thanks to the harsh climate, thinly veined minerals, and distance from market. The Forest Service, at least until recently, considered the region's forests of ponderosa pine, grand fir, and aspen to hold little marketable value. Finally, without a local government, no one clamored for improvements. The road itself had evolved almost organically. True, various government entities—the county, Forest Service, state—had influenced its development, each with the intent of aiding in transportation through or management of the North Cascades. But the road developed through human use over time and only then because people followed the natural corridor of travel along the river, through the woods, up the U-shaped valley until it narrowed and steepened, and ended some twenty miles later in the glacial cirque of Horseshoe Basin. Travel over the road was always subject to weather and the changing conditions of the mountains. All of this gave the road, McConnell noted, "a quality of perfection: it is complete, whole in itself and unconnected with other roads. It goes nowhere because to do otherwise would be pointless."[22]

The Stehekin ideal described by McConnell resembled in many ways the national park ideal. It suggested that members of an industrial society could live in harmony with the natural world. As scholar Leo Marx so astutely said of the nineteenth century, Americans imagined that the machines of progress could have a positive influence on their relationship with nature. Locomotives (and later automobiles) not only aided in the settlement of the nation, but they also helped foster an appreciation of wild nature by conveying Americans to and through it in relative safety and comfort. Although Marx was referring to the pastoral in American life, his formula can help explain the continued attraction of automobiles in primitive settings like national parks in postwar America. Despite being symbols of the nation's complex industrial order, and thus a source for the destruction of the natural world, automobiles still enabled people to experience nature in the parks by bringing them to the parks. Roads in effect created "middle landscapes," where the machine and nature existed in a seemingly balanced state. This state was contradictory and fleeting, of course, because progress never stopped. The more relevant point for national parks, however, was that roads and cars helped shape the landscape people thought of as wild.[23]

McConnell and other wilderness supporters, then, were able to think of the valley as a national park because it was already like a park. Stehekin was removed from the outside world but was very much a part of it. Many residents, for example, related to their surroundings in a familiar fashion; they owned cars and trucks, which they had barged uplake. Moreover, though physically isolated from mainstream society, Stehekin residents behaved much as their counterparts did in the world beyond the valley. Their daily lives revolved around driving the valley road to greet the boat from Chelan, which carried their supplies and mail. In a region without electricity or telephones, the boat served as their connection to mainstream society, and more than ever, this connection was represented by an increasing number of tourists after the war. Visitors toured the Stehekin country in open-air cars or modified school buses, and the experience was essential to their conception of the valley as one of the nation's last wild places—a place worth saving. When threatened with resource and highway development, Stehekin served as a rallying point for a national park for the North Cascades.[24]

In their desire to preserve the North Cascades, wilderness supporters never strayed too far from the windshield. Wilderness for the environmental movement and the postwar generation was not simply about the intrinsic values of unmodified nature set aside to improve or sustain one's quality of life— or life in general. It was also about perpetuating a wilderness experience, or perhaps crafting a wilderness or outdoor lifestyle, that was part of a larger turn toward consumerism for the postwar generation. Americans of the 1950s and 1960s may have expressed a love for hiking and climbing, but many were also comfortable in station wagons. Like an earlier generation of tourists, they had greater amounts of leisure time and higher incomes, and they expected cars to take them to nature. Only now they headed outdoors in much greater numbers and traveled over smooth, regional highways. Even with the chaotic pace of two-week summer vacations, the auto still promised freedom and an authentic experience with the natural world for postwar middle-class Americans.[25]

At the same time, the idea that autos could be a positive force in American life, including national parks, was problematic. In the 1950s, as the defenders of Olympic National Park understood, the car was transforming the American landscape at a brisk pace. An estimated fifty-two million automobiles were on the road in the middle of the decade. With the passage of the Interstate Highway Act of 1956, the federal government assured the construction of a forty-one-thousand-mile superhighway system.[26] Moreover, the automobile encouraged expansion of suburbs on the outskirts of American cities and an entirely new architecture of shopping malls, drive-in restaurants and theaters, motels, multilevel parking garages, and freeways. In a time when cities were feeling the strains of the nation's population explosion, suburbs held out the emotional appeal of rural life's closeness to the natural world. Suburbs offered a connection to open space and quiet, achieved, ironically, by cutting down trees and turning fields into asphalt streets.[27] As the social critic Lewis Mumford observed, the automobile made this retreat possible, but its popularity was its downfall. The "sense of freedom and power" associated with the auto was only possible so long as there remained open country into which urban dwellers could flee. And as suburbs filled the countryside, that prospect grew more and more remote.[28]

Mumford's indictment of the auto suggests why preservationists thought a national park could protect the North Cascades: a park would be removed from the negative effects of urban sprawl. Cars may have given residents of western cities greater freedom and mobility to live, work, and play where they wished, but cars also were the source of isolation, congestion, and air pollution. Unchecked urban growth, led by automobiles, and forecasts that the nation's population would double by the end of the century, made this outlook even more alarming. For the Pacific Northwest, this meant that the entire corridor between Eugene, Oregon, and the Canadian border would be transformed into "one continuous urban and suburban area," wrote Supreme Court justice and noted conservationist William O. Douglas. Douglas, who also campaigned to protect Olympic's wild coastline, believed that areas like the North Cascades were essential to the nation's "physical and spiritual therapy." Without wild places like this to build strength and character, we would become lazy and dependent, Douglas claimed, a "race of apartment-born people . . . coddled and protected, utterly dependent on machines for its existence."[29]

Meanwhile, the postwar travel boom placed the automobile more at the center of the national park experience than ever before. The Echo Park victory may have "resoundingly reaffirmed" the sanctity of the national park system and firmly associated the protection of the nation's parks with wilderness preservation in the public mind, but in the wake of that victory, the popularity of parks among auto tourists soared. In 1946, Americans hit the highways by the millions, freed up from gas and rubber rationing and ready to take long-delayed vacations. They could afford to travel long distances from home, and they headed to the national parks in record numbers. That year alone, nearly twenty-three million tourists visited the national park system, up nearly 40 percent from before the war. By the mid-1950s, that figure had almost doubled, with nearly all park visitors entering parks in automobiles.[30]

Although conservation groups saw some promise in the Park Service's response to this deluge of motorists with the Mission 66 program, they roundly criticized as artificial Director Wirth's vision of wilderness as something viewed from a road. They thought this vision would diminish the wilderness values of an area like North Cascades, should the region become a national park. David Brower blasted Wirth's wilderness message as propaganda aimed at justifying Mission 66 development; the Park Service was blurring the line between easily accessible natural areas and true wilderness country by promoting "roadside wilderness" for automobile tourists.[31]

But wilderness activists' responses were complex, because their objections also revealed a fondness for roads and nature in national parks. Like McConnell's vision of the Stehekin road, Brower and others pined for roadways that summoned images of a slower-paced, less complicated life. They disliked the latest phase of park developments, it seems, because it departed from the familiar rustic style of the 1920s and 1930s with its use of logs and stone materials—reminiscent of pioneer America. The more contemporary style appeared sterile by comparison in its use of concrete and masonry building materials. The visitor center, a new building type in national parks, expressed one of the major tenets of modernism. It was designed for changes parks were experiencing, especially the postwar surge in visitation, by centralizing visitor and administrative services in one facility. To build as many visitor centers as quickly and economically as possible, the Park Service expressed another aspect of modernism, the use of relatively inexpensive materials such as steel, concrete, and glass. Thus, the Mission 66 program gave the appearance that the Park Service was mass producing these and other park structures.[32] This shift in architectural style was compounded when the agency adopted modern highway standards. New park roads, many without log or stone guard rails, seemed to force their way through the landscape; they were too wide and, like the nation's expanding interstate highway system did for the country as a whole, invited travel through parks by greater numbers at higher speeds.

Perhaps the best example of the conflict over new construction standards was the Sierra Club's continued opposition to the Park Service's improvement of the Tioga Road in Yosemite.[33] Deeply troubled by the renovated road, the photographer Ansel Adams lamented the loss, not of the wild country through which it traveled alone, but of the old Tioga Road. Like a trail, the old road had been part of the natural scene, Adams wrote. It slowly meandered through the high Sierra, taking the driver to the pleasing solitude of Tuolumne Meadows and Tenaya Lake and the shining glacial polish along its shoreline. The road conformed to the landscape; it did not impose itself upon it. Unfortunately, the Park Service destroyed this. "I am an artist," Adams wrote, aware that "we can't keep everything in a glass case—with the keys given only to a privileged few. Nevertheless, I want people to experience the magic of wildness; there is no use fooling ourselves that nature with a slick highway running through it is any longer wild. We need balance; our 'progress' has ruined much of it, and unless we all stand and be counted to speak in solemn protest, no one can foresee the end."[34]

Wilderness advocates did not necessarily believe that all road development detracted from their perception of Yosemite as a primitive landscape, but they wanted assurances that parks would not become excessively modernized. They worried that the agency's cool reception to the national wilderness bill signaled bureaucratic arrogance. They also worried that the agency's management philosophy of wilderness preservation through development was flawed; and that its faith in master plans instead of a federal law to protect parks would lead to another incident like the Tioga Road or produce another park like Mount Rainier for the North Cascades.[35]

Like park supporters of an earlier generation, conservation organizations expressed optimism about the potential for creating a wilderness park open to machines. They imagined a place like Stehekin. In this way, they shared views more similar to those of Wirth and the Park Service than they realized. In 1958, McConnell endorsed a park for the North Cascades because, as he declared, parks were dedicated to scenic preservation rather than to commercial development. But more importantly, the park concept could embrace wilderness in a slightly modified form, thus providing protection for his beloved Stehekin Valley with its primitive road. The Park Service could manage the valley to preserve its unspoiled beauty by incorporating this scenic gateway into the park's larger wilderness setting. To accomplish this,

A Road Runs Through It

McConnell noted, the agency would—as it always had—employ landscape architects to plan appropriate recreational and visitor developments and to design roads with scenery and not clear-cuts in mind.[36]

McConnell and others envisioned a national park for the North Cascades as a place where wilderness and roads maintained a delicate balance. Stehekin, in this respect, was central to their vision of the park, and their interest in preserving the valley and its "wilderness" road softened their stance on Mission 66. Even the outspoken David Brower acknowledged that the Stehekin road treaded softly on the earth, beginning near the busy lakeshore and ending in "paradise." Brower believed that the Park Service, despite its current focus, offered the best opportunity for retaining Stehekin's primitive character. His earlier criticism of Mission 66, he told McConnell, was "an honest difference of opinion between groups of people working for the same goal—preservation of national parks and their primary asset of wilderness." True, he acknowledged, Mission 66 was about construction in the parks, and its road standards were too modern in places. But, echoing Wirth, Brower stressed that "the NPS [National Park Service] constructs to preserve—just as the National Gallery had to be constructed to preserve." Like museums, parks protected natural scenery, which admirers saw from a road corridor.[37]

THE WILDERNESS WAY: ROADS AND CARS
IN A NORTH CASCADES NATIONAL PARK

In their efforts to create a wilderness park in the North Cascades, preservationists abandoned their original quest to fulfill Bob Marshall's legacy. Instead, they shaped their own concept of a park that could, at some level, be understood from and protected by roads and cars. In 1959, for example, the Sierra Club led a number of outdoor organizations in calling for a national park of some 1.3 million acres. Their vision was similar in size to Marshall's wilderness proposal and was based on the Park Service's Ice Peaks study of the late 1930s. Preservationists, ironically, were now trying to protect the wilderness Marshall had wanted to save using the same Park Service study he had opposed.[38]

In 1963, the North Cascades Conservation Council formally proposed a wilderness park with roads as one of its central themes.[39] Although the council, which had become the main force behind the park campaign, maintained that its primary mission was to preserve as much of the North Cascades in as wild a state as possible, its prospectus emphasized that national parks preserved wilderness in such a way that everyone could get "a taste of it." Stephen Mather's vision of a seamless landscape of wild beauty, composed of roads, cars, and primeval nature, resonated throughout the group's proposal. It was the "undeveloped wild land beyond the roads," the plan declared, that provided the "setting and the background" for the entire park atmosphere. National parks, then, were large reserves where roads and wilderness existed in relation to each other, and where automobiles conveyed wilderness-seeking tourists into and through park landscapes.[40]

In presenting a proposal for a large wilderness park, the council seemed unfazed that its notion of wilderness harkened back to Mather. Autos and driving in nature were important justifications for creating the new park. Forest Service protection contrasted to national parks, as council member John Warth wrote, because "the boundaries of dedicated wilderness areas [in national forests] are almost invariably set several miles back from the main roads. This practice excludes the bulk of the commercial timber and other commercial resources." In short, the Forest Service defined wilderness boundaries by chain saw. A typical Forest Service wilderness area boundary was located on a distant ridge, and "the motorist seldom has the feel," as in a national park, "of driving through a vast wilderness." Instead, drivers encountered logged and bulldozed slopes and sights of other "wilderness-destroying activities." These practices, moreover, often rendered the wilderness itself "relatively inaccessible—hence the prevalent misconception that wilderness is only for the hardy or wealthy minority."[41]

Besides suggesting that wilderness was also for the majority, the council's vision of a wilderness park took some of its inspiration from Mount Rainier. There, roads harmonized with the surrounding landscape, not only because landscape architects designed them for this purpose, but also because they intended the road system as an ideal means for motorists to see the park in a peaceful and quiet atmosphere and at a leisurely pace. In the new wilderness park, roads would lead unobtrusively to "a scenic panorama, a waterfall, a grove of big trees," and provide "a pleasant driving experience with stop-offs along the way."[42]

The council's proposal also employed the concept of a circle road, or parkway, used at Mount Rainier and later at Olympic to incorporate the park into the region and nation's larger highway geography. Tourists, for example, sped up State Highway 99 into Canada without seeing even "a remnant of the tall timber" that once covered the western half of the state, and scenic drives into the mountains were equally impoverished, since the major-

A Road Runs Through It

ity were dusty, washboard logging roads traversing acres of forest devastation. In an age when interstate highways were forcing their way "through the landscape," a series of scenic roads could encircle the wilderness park in the North Cascades—preserving the primitive but also furnishing much of the state and nation's "need for scenic roads." Thus, the council proposed renovating existing roads in the vicinity of the proposed park to conform to national park standards and contemplated creating an extended scenic drive around the North Cascades known as the Round-the-Park Loop, a roadway that would be "unexcelled in the United States for variety and beauty."[43]

Like the road system serving Olympic, the North Cascades loop road would stay on the proposed park's perimeter as much as possible, defining boundaries and creating tourists' impressions of the park. Visitors' visions of the park would be of a distant mountain range complemented by scenes of rural Washington. Only when the loop drive entered the proposed park's northern margin over the projected North Cross-State Highway, between Mazama and the Skagit River, would park visitors come closest to the park. Along this stretch of road, they would encounter snow-mantled mountains, deep-cut valleys, forests, and what conservationists considered the region's true essence, "a wild land of rugged peaks." The council also asserted that the Park Service should manage this section of highway to maintain it always as "a way through wilderness," and in doing so, they struck the familiar theme of compatibility between wilderness and roads. National parks preserved wilderness in a unique way; they allowed access into it for all Americans, especially Americans behind the wheel, without any apparent harm.[44]

FROM HIGHWAYS TO TRAMWAYS: A PARK WITH ROADS LESS TRAVELED?

Although by 1965 the council's prospectus had won the endorsement of all conservation groups involved in the North Cascades campaign, it seemed to contradict the general consensus at the time: there were simply too many cars in the national parks.[45] National parks, especially Yosemite, were choked with them. Mission 66, apparently, had worked too well; too many visitors were able to visit national parks in the late 1960s, and roads and cars were causing serious damage to the natural systems of the nation's parks. Worse yet, they were giving parks an urban ambiance. As a *Wall Street Journal* headline announced in 1966, "Ah, Wilderness: Severe Overcrowding Brings Ills of City to Scenic Yosemite." More densely populated by three times than Los

Angeles County on a summer day, Yosemite Valley rang with the sounds of urban life—radios, children playing, and revving engines. Except for trailers and tents squeezed into camping areas, it could have been "any city after dark."[46] According to writer and wilderness advocate Edward Abbey, there should be "no more cars in national parks. Let the people walk."[47]

Changing the way Americans visited and experienced—and thus conceptualized—national parks, however, was a tricky prospect, and one the federal government tried to resolve with its proposal for a park for the North Cascades. In January 1966, the North Cascades Study Team, an interagency group composed of Park Service and Forest Service representatives, offered its own answer for shaping a wilderness park. The team, made up of two feuding federal bureaus, proposed a park (smaller and different from the one proposed by conservationists) from the Canadian border south to several miles below the head of Lake Chelan. The park's boundaries would embrace Mount Shuksan to the west, Ross and Diablo lakes to the east and south (along with Seattle City Light's associated hydroelectric facilities), the Picket Range and Eldorado Peaks country, as well as the Stehekin Valley. And running roughly through its center would be the North Cross-State Highway, also known as Highway 20.[48]

The proposal operated on at least two levels. On one level, it was a political compromise meant to soften the blow to the Forest Service by not turning more of the North Cascades into a national park. The Forest Service opposed a park and the loss (once again) of any of its land to the Park Service. The proposal would satisfy demands for more permanent protection of the range while not completely alienating the Forest Service. On another level, however, the proposal suggested that the Park Service could not envision a park—even one as rugged and wild as the North Cascades—without access for automobiles. Park Service director George B. Hartzog Jr., a member of the study team, had even grander plans for a road system than the one proposed by the North Cascades Conservation Council. In the face of rising opposition to automobiles and roads in national parks, the rather brash Park Service leader proposed to develop a scenic road system in the North Cascades, including a road along the eastern shore of Ross Lake from Canada to connect to Highway 20.[49]

Conrad Wirth's successor, Hartzog came from a background in politics, not landscape architecture, and his rationalization for new parks and highways as a promotional tool sounded a note of alarm for preservationists. Hartzog appreciated wilderness from the comfort of a backcountry chalet, and throughout his tenure he claimed that designating wilderness in national parks, as called for by the Wilderness Act, would not provide parklands with more protection, but actually "would jeopardize the whole national park concept." Wilderness under the law, it seemed to him, was not compatible with national parks. Evidently, the Wilderness Act's criteria— its prohibition of roads and other permanent man-made features—would lower the standard of national park wilderness or "compromise its integrity."[50] Hartzog believed, as perhaps did many tradition-minded Park Service employees, that wilderness in parks was different than on other federal lands. Wilderness was an aspect and not the sole purpose of national parks, and its management should be governed by the Organic Act of 1916 (which established the Park Service's mission). While this perception had deeper philosophical roots in the meaning of national parks, Hartzog likely believed that the Wilderness Act threatened his agency's bureaucratic autonomy. The law restricted the Park Service's administrative discretion; it added a separate set of management directives for wilderness in parks by prohibiting the use of motorized equipment and means of access in backcountry management. Moreover, formal wilderness designation would limit the agency's ability to expand visitor facilities and other developments within the parks.

Hartzog expressed a fairly traditional vision of national parks. They were more products of human design than of nature, and the Wilderness Act might limit parks from reaching their full potential. His vision, in this regard, more closely paralleled that of Stephen Mather than the views of the burgeoning environmental movement, with its emphasis on protecting ecological relationships. Hartzog seemed reluctant to give up the notion of wilderness as a scenic quality and the ideal of park roads as positive rather than negative forces in the national park experience. He appeared immune to worries about the dramatic changes in visitation and developments in the five decades since Mather had taken over the agency. In Hartzog's view, more road projects would enable more Americans to see the national parks, even though the new highways would bring streams of heavy traffic through the very places that needed protection from the cars and people coming to see the parks. Hartzog, even at this late date, thought it necessary to maintain the political support for parks from the millions of Americans who toured them in cars.

At the same time, Hartzog shared Mather's political acumen and knew that the rising concerns surrounding autos and roads in parks could not be ignored. Ironically, by attempting to say what people wanted to hear, that there were substitutes for autos in parks, he inspired one of the major debates during the park's congressional hearings. The issue focused on other forms of transportation—helicopters or tramways—that could move visitors into and through this mountainous country, provide them an intimate experience with it, and convey a sense that their presence was not an artificial intrusion in an otherwise pristine landscape. Hartzog asserted that these "imaginative and creative" transportation proposals were intended as a means to enter and see this new national park, to move swiftly to the heart of its alpine zone, with less damage than roads and without the controversy associated with roads and cars.[51]

During the congressional hearings on the park's legislation, held in 1967 and 1968, agency leaders, congressional representatives, and the general public tried to come to terms with the access and transportation issue. Was substituting one form of mechanized transportation really the answer? If so, what kind of access was appropriate for this new park dedicated to wilderness—and by association all national parks? Was it possible to replace autos and have the same experience of knowing nature through machines? Secretary of the Interior Stewart L. Udall, like Hartzog, believed that tramways offered the best solution to these questions. (Hartzog's helicopter proposal was shelved after considerable protest from conservation groups such as the North Cascades Conservation Council and the Sierra Club during the North Cascades study. They opposed it, among other reasons, because of the noise and the development of heliports in the range's most isolated areas.) Udall, who at the time directed one of the most ambitious programs to preserve wilderness and expand the park system, told Nevada senator Alan Bible that tramways presented a serious "attempt to solve some of the old [park access] problems in a new way and to show that we can provide transportation in parks by means other than the automobile."[52]

Although the idea of installing cable-car systems in national parks was not new, support for them by the Park Service was. Schemes to build cableways connecting the rims of Grand Canyon, carrying visitors to Glacier Point in Yosemite, or taking them up Mount Rainier had arisen during the first decades of the Park Service's existence. Their proponents often presented such systems as better ways to see the scenic wonders of the parks, but the agency had dismissed them as unsightly and inappropriate for national parks. Trams and the like intruded on the natural scene, no matter their perceived benefits for transportation or convenience.[53] But in the late 1960s, the agency revised its position and offered tramways as a form of wilderness protection—

similar to Conrad Wirth's concept of park roads—and thus as an effective "substitute for automobiles and a highway."[54]

Hartzog's proposal made him appear as a kind of transportation visionary. Both the nation and national parks, the director testified, were at a crossroads in their relationship with the automobile. In the past, "we have taken the view that access to the great national parks should be by roads," but with a rising population and thus rising visitation, "we are simply strangling to death in roads," and "I don't believe that we can continue to build roads to take care of the people who want to see these parks by automobile."[55] The concept of automobiles as one of the primary means of seeing a national park had become "obsolete," and there must be "some other access or we will destroy the very values that we are trying to save."[56]

The tramway idea also reflected the Park Service's response to the popular interest in ecology and the growing awareness of the need to preserve the natural values of parks. The clearest statement of this new approach was the so-called Leopold Report of 1963. Produced by an advisory committee of scientists, selected by Secretary Udall and chaired by A. Starker Leopold (Aldo Leopold's son), the report served as a blueprint for the agency's resource management goals. The report's guiding principle was that all parks should be managed for their "original conditions" as witnessed by the first white settlers. The agency should not only strive to protect parks as "vignettes of primitive America" but should also restore nature to its original state whenever possible. One way to achieve this was to leave park wilderness roadless, and rather than expand the road systems in parks, it would be better to limit visitors.[57]

The scientists who wrote the Leopold Report, however, made their own culturally informed assumptions about what constituted "original conditions," assumptions that shaped ideas about how to measure disruptions in park ecosystems and thus how to repair them. The ideal natural world, as depicted by the authors of the report and shared by many, was one without a human presence, one in which nature existed in a wild, undisturbed, and balanced state. Within this framework, inventions such as autos were obviously intruders, since they did not exist in the early nineteenth century. Eliminating cars from parks would help restore these landscapes to their pristine, presettlement state. Yet this vision was selective, for it did not propose to restore the Indian tribes who lived in, used the resources of, and shaped the "wild" landscapes that early white explorers had encountered.

The Leopold Report proposed, then, to re-create park landscapes within a historical context, America's preindustrial past.[58]

In this framework, North Cascades offered a way to repair the mistakes of past park management: national parks could begin anew as wilderness reserves in which automobiles would have little or no presence. "I think," Secretary Udall informed the Senate subcommittee in his support of the Park Service's tramway plans, that Mather and other early agency officials "were a bit too much addicted to the idea of roads and we think, looking at some national parks . . . that there are probably too many roads today." It was time to get people out of their cars, Udall claimed, but it was not necessarily time to limit the number of people who were in them from entering the parks. Were Yosemite, one of the nation's oldest and most treasured parks, to come into the park system today, he continued, we might not "plan to put a road right in the heart of the valley. We might very well decide that we would have people park at the edge of the park and have electric trains run into the heart of the valley and keep the automobile with all of its noises and odors out of the center of the national park."[59]

Udall, however optimistic, still conceived of parks as places where machines and nature were in accord. By attempting to find a "nonautomotive means of modern transportation," Udall and Park Service officials were ultimately searching for cars and roads by another name. Park Service policy, as the secretary stated, "has not been to keep machines out of national parks because we build roads in most of our national parks." Roads furnished an integral part of the national park experience; they gave visitors a territorial view of the park landscape and led them to the rim of the Grand Canyon or through the ethereal heights of the Rocky Mountains. And tramways in the North Cascades would continue this practice.[60]

Building a road to experience the "overpowering view" of the North Cascades, like the road proposed for the northern slopes of Mount Rainier in the 1920s, was nearly an impossible thing. It would have been exceedingly difficult and expensive to construct from an engineering and, more importantly, from an environmental standpoint. Even the contemplated road along Ross Lake, Hartzog declared, sounding like an environmentalist, would have desecrated the range's alpine scenery. It would have blasted away so much of the narrow canyon that it would have looked like any interstate highway. "What is the attraction," he asked, of traveling all that way "to see the same thing?"[61]

Hartzog's confidence that roads and cars were "just not relevant in the

A Road Runs Through It

North Cascades" convinced few members of Congress, however, to abandon them as the primary means of access to North Cascades or other national parks. Committee members such as Senator Clifford P. Hansen of Wyoming found the idea of tramways in parks appalling; they would deface the very natural wonders they were supposed to be bringing visitors to see. "We had one proposed on top of the Grand Teton," Hansen stated. "Everybody in Wyoming . . . was up in arms about it." Were the Park Service to reverse its policy and build tramways in one national park, he concluded, where would it stop?[62]

The tramway proposals nearly backfired on Hartzog, for the ensuing debate forced the Park Service to defend the very presence of roads and cars in national parks. Colorado congressman Wayne N. Aspinall, for example, wanted to know if park roads, like the famous Trail Ridge Road in his state's Rocky Mountain National Park, desecrated all mountainsides—"just the sight of it?" Would Hartzog, if he could, replace it with a tramway? Hartzog's response was ambiguous. Trail Ridge Road, he suggested, was "perfectly proper" because, built in the early 1930s, it conformed to Park Service design principles of that period; it lay on the ground in "a manner that does not defy and desecrate that great range." It reflected a certain time and place in American life in which that kind of development seemed to mediate between humans and nature in national parks; it seemed to reconcile the presence of machines in primordial nature. It would not be built again, however. The director had denied recent plans to widen the road to accommodate larger numbers of automobiles. This kind of renovation, Hartzog felt certain, would have harmed the ecologically sensitive alpine tundra, because the fifty-mile scenic drive traveled above tree line, along the "roof of the Rockies," taking motorists to more than twelve thousand feet above sea level. In the nearly forty years since the road's completion, the tundra along the roadside had still not fully recovered. Left undisturbed, ecologists estimated it might heal in another one hundred years; more road construction might scar the landscape for centuries.[63]

The director's response, though it recognized the environmental damage caused by the road, suggested that landscape architecture still provided a powerful rationalization for the presence of autos and roads in parks—and now for the development of tramways. In the sensitive high country of the North Cascades, Hartzog proposed to construct the tramways using the same design principles employed in the construction of Trail Ridge and other park roads during the 1920s and 1930s. Typically, ski lifts or European tramways, such as those found in Switzerland or West Germany, were built in wide-open spaces with high-tension cables cutting a swath through a forest or across the horizon like power lines. Instead, Park Service planners had carefully chosen the routes of the Price Lake, Colonial Peak, Ruby Mountain, and Arctic Creek trams in North Cascades so that they would be screened from the park's wilderness high country or popular hiking trails up the valleys of Big and Little Beaver creeks adjacent to Ross Lake. The Arctic Creek tram, for example, would fit inside the valley's "compressed and compact" terrain, and as Udall elaborated, the agency planned to blend and hide it in "the natural setting to the highest degree possible." Like park roads, tramways would provide visitors the "magnificent views" of the North Cascades and conform to topographical features as much as possible. Seemingly, they, too, would not intrude on the park landscape.[64]

AN OLD NOTION, A NEW PARK MODEL

In the late 1960s, wilderness activists and park supporters howled against the tramway proposals. Tramways, they argued, were uniformly bad innovations, poorly conceived concessions to win the support of the local tourist industry, and "entirely contrary to the whole idea of parks as natural preserves." Yet wilderness groups continued to conceptualize national parks in their traditional form: as places where "true" wilderness and automobiles were intimately related. Preservationists, for example, objected to the elimination of Granite Creek valley from the proposed park. Located on the eastern side of the northern Cascades, Granite Creek was the last unfinished section of Highway 20. Originally, the study team's park boundaries embraced this highly scenic valley, but as a concession to the state of Washington, Secretary Udall removed it from the park. In doing so, the valley remained under national forest management and the highway under state control. Udall thought the revision would please wilderness supporters because now the highway would traverse only the recreation area, not the national park. But during the Senate hearings, park advocates argued to retain Granite Creek within the park—not as an intrusion on the wilderness scene but as an integral component of its protection and enjoyment. For similar reasons, preservationists wanted the park's boundaries to embrace the Cascade River valley on the west side of the range. The valley's unimproved dirt road led motorists to the base of Cascade Pass, one of the few places easily reached by car, where they were rewarded with close views of the range's subalpine terrain and

A Road Runs Through It

Matterhorn-like peaks. Having both drainages under Park Service control would prevent the Forest Service from scarring the valleys with clear-cuts and turning the drive to the park's border into a wasteland.

Park supporters were operating on a model similar to the one fashioned for Mount Rainier and Olympic, in which a highway formed the main organizational feature. As Patrick Goldsworthy, president of the North Cascades Conservation Council, asserted, the "highway environment in Granite Creek and the scenic climax at Washington Pass are undeniably of national park caliber and as such need maximum scenic protection." The group renewed its proposal to have the Granite Creek section of the new park managed as a parkway, similar perhaps to Mount Rainier's Mather Memorial Parkway.[65] Moreover, Brock Evans, who testified on behalf of the Federation of Western Outdoor Clubs, noted that having a section of highway within the park would satisfy the historical need for access to parks by automobile, providing the "opportunity for visitors from other parts of the country to drive through the park." At the same time, with a road already running through the park, the Park Service would not be pressured to construct its own roads (for visitor and interpretive services) "into the existing wilderness which is the prime glory of the North Cascades."[66]

Wilderness defenders thought of a park road ultimately in terms of how it would shape the park and provide for its protection as wilderness, and they returned their argument to where it began, the Stehekin Valley. With Granite Creek in the proposed park, they believed, the Park Service would have no reason to build a spur road down Bridge Creek—another project the Forest Service had planned. And for similar reasons, the Park Service would have no incentive to link Cascade Pass with the Stehekin Valley Road if the Cascade River were added to the park. Finally, it seemed, with these measures accomplished, the future of Stehekin would be secure and this remnant of early America saved. During the park campaign, the Stehekin country had drawn a national audience and had come to symbolize the romanticized wilderness experience for ordinary, middle-class Americans. As one writer observed, Stehekin represented a place where people still lived in "an intelligent harmony with nature." In this place Americans could seek renewal with an idyllic past: "the wild, unspoiled valley of the Stehekin" presented "a modern-day version of Walden on a grand scale."[67]

Stehekin was perhaps the best model for a national park of its time. Like parks of the past, it assured members of an industrial society that they could live in relative accord with nature. They could reshape it to meet their needs, especially to accommodate modern forms of conveyance, while retaining the illusion that they were driving their twentieth-century cars into a seemingly unbounded wilderness. As preservationists contended, should a road enter the valley it too would become crowded with automobiles. Stehekin would become as "ordinary" as Yosemite, and the ideal would end.[68] If protected properly, though, Stehekin would help sustain a landscape in which cars and wilderness seemed in accord.

The Stehekin ideal, more than any notion of roadless wilderness, shaped North Cascades as a national park. The park's legislation, though it did not include Granite Creek or the Cascade River drainage, proclaimed that no new roads would enter this park, specifically to Stehekin from Highway 20 or over Cascade Pass. To further accommodate Stehekin, the Senate committee created the Lake Chelan National Recreation Area (NRA), covering some sixty-two thousand acres and embracing the upper Lake Chelan country and lower Stehekin River valley—the inhabited and developed areas. Under the recreation area category, hunting and other historic uses of the land, not permissible in a national park, could continue. These provisions thus guaranteed that the "pioneer" community would carry on much as it always had. Moreover, Stehekin would remain a landscape that the automobile would not defile. Visitors would encounter nature here much as they would in any other national park. Nearly half of the Stehekin Road remained in the park proper, so visitors as well as residents could travel back and forth over it into the heart of the North Cascades.

Besides Stehekin, the legislation made provisions for automobiles and roads through the heart of the new park. Granted, by leaving the Granite Creek valley out of the park, the legislation accomplished a number of political compromises. It appeased the Forest Service, by allowing it to retain this scenic country as national forest. And it met a goal of wilderness defenders and government officials: no highway would run into this new national park. Yet the legislation provided the park with highway access. Also, because the state owned the road, the Park Service could not be accused of resorting to its old road-building practices. A similar rationale was used for excluding the Cascade River drainage from the park's legislation. All told, the agency would be absolved of the sins of its road-building past.

In the end, the legislation seemed to have solved the most important issue of all: the paradox of windshield wilderness. The way to have a wilderness park with a road running through it was not to create a national park at all but a park "complex." The Park Service had promoted the mixture of national park and recreation areas in order to sidestep many of the nagging issues revolving around access and visitor services in national parks. Under the guidance of Senator Henry M. Jackson, the legislation divided the park into two units of 570,000 acres to be managed as roadless wilderness. This eliminated Seattle City Light's hydroelectric projects on the Skagit River and avoided setting what preservationists considered a "wretched precedent" for national parks.[69] Ross Lake National Recreation Area, located between the two park units, encompassed Ross Lake and the sections of the Skagit River containing all of City Light's operations—Gorge, Diablo, and Ross dams and lakes. Like the recreation area in the Stehekin country, Ross Lake NRA would not interfere substantially with existing land use. The most important aspect of the boundaries, however, was that the Ross Lake NRA enclosed the highway corridor as well as City Light's dams; the northern and southern units of the park were only a short distance away from the recreation area and some—not all—of their spectacular scenery was visible from the road.[70]

What made Ross Lake and Lake Chelan recreation areas so special, agency officials contended, was that they buffered the "true" park wilderness from modern intrusions. And a new term entered the agency vocabulary, "wilderness threshold," to describe the recreation areas and their relationship to the larger park landscape. As wilderness thresholds, the recreation areas would bear the weight of providing traditional national park services and accommodations for windshield tourists. The first of its kind, the park complex offered another version of the national park ideal; it would preserve the North Cascades' primary asset of wilderness while allowing a place for autos and roads in an otherwise wild setting.

The law creating North Cascades National Park, which President Lyndon Johnson signed on October 2, 1968, may not have been perfect from anyone's perspective, but it was creative. It modified the national park concept in a way that recognized wilderness as the most significant resource, yet still held the door open for America's motoring masses. Only now that opening seemed much smaller. It remained to be seen, however, how the Park Service would manage "a true wilderness" with tramway proposals still in the planning stages, with roads that led into or to the brink of the park's backcountry, and with the long-awaited Highway 20 on the verge of becoming the main corridor of travel for thousands of park visitors seeking a wilderness experience.

5 / WILDERNESS THRESHOLD

North Cascades and a New Concept of National Parks

I n the late 1960s, the establishment of North Cascades offered a varia-
tion on national parks as wilderness reserves open to automobiles. Like
Yellowstone, Yosemite, and Mount Rainier, North Cascades possessed
unique natural wonders of grand proportions. The park also reflected more
contemporary visions of wild nature. Its mission was the total preservation of primordial nature, a nature so defined by its absence of roads and
cars. As an early National Park Service planning document stated, "The
visitor's early contact with the area will probably be through the windshield
of a car, [but] the real . . . experience begins only when he has been separated from his car."[1] A new conception of national parks, influenced by
the burgeoning environmental movement of the 1960s, was partly responsible for this change in emphasis. Yet while traditional park uses, such as
windshield tourism, disappeared from the park itself, they reappeared in
the adjacent recreation areas. Ross Lake and Lake Chelan national recreation areas contained roads and provided auto tourists the opportunity to
drive through the new parkland. Ideally, the roads serving the new park
complex made visitors feel as though they were driving through a national
park renowned for wilderness.

Even though the park itself lay well beyond the roads, Congress had created a kind of virtual national park. Motorists could glimpse it from a distance, but they were never actually in it: Highway 20 traveled through the
Ross Lake NRA, always outside the park itself. Wedged between the northern and southern units of the park, the recreation area afforded motorists
impressive views of some but not all of the North Cascades. But, except for

a sign on the highway, visitors would find it difficult to know whether they were in a park or a recreation area. It was not clear where the boundaries of the recreation area ended and those of the national park began. Their only clues were the highway over which their cars carried them and the chain of emerald-colored reservoirs behind Seattle City Light's dams along the road. Otherwise, park visitors found themselves driving through a relatively undisturbed setting of mountains, glaciers, and rivers.

The relationship between park and recreation areas seemed to resolve the dilemma of cars in a wilderness setting. This solution was timely for the Park Service because in the late 1960s and early 1970s the agency began to emphasize the importance of natural regulation in park management. North Cascades and Redwood national parks, established at the same time, symbolized the new direction because their respective missions were wilderness preservation and ecological restoration. Even in the system's oldest parks, Yellowstone and Yosemite, the agency reconsidered the need to build more services for motorists and declared that the guiding principles of park management should be the preservation and maintenance of the natural values for which these and all national parks were established. Park planners considered ways to curtail the use of automobiles, envisioning a time when some form of public transportation would convey the majority of visitors through the parks. In 1970, Yosemite closed a section of the valley to automobiles. As one Park Service critic so aptly observed, in the wake of Mission 66 and with the rising tide of environmental awareness, "Motoring was out and protection was in."[2]

At the same time, the Park Service was not about to close the gates of parks to automobiles. Agency leaders beginning with Stephen Mather had helped craft the popular image of national parks as primitive landscapes visited by Americans in cars, and public expectation in this regard had changed little over the years, despite a heightened environmental awareness. What the arrangement at North Cascades suggested, though, was a conceptual departure for the agency. It did not reverse past practice, but rather offered another way of thinking about national parks within the context of the motor age. Parks were still products of human design, but in North Cascades that design was not evident in the "naturalization" of park roads or in the attempt by a park master plan to harmonize roads and nature. Instead, the Park Service relied on a new management metaphor—wilderness threshold—to convey the compatibility of machines and nature.

By designating the recreation areas as wilderness thresholds, the Park Service was able to provide services to motorists, similar to older national parks, and at the same time protect the park as wilderness. The agency, for example, returned to the idea of tramways in the recreation areas as an alternative way to see the park's scenery and attempted to curb new road improvements and limit the use of existing roads for the entire park complex. The wilderness threshold designation, though intended to distinguish between the park and recreation areas, suggested a mental image of the park complex in which their borders were blurred. In the end, park managers determined that the best way to interpret North Cascades' wilderness values was from the road running through the greatest portion of the park complex, Highway 20. As with the roads designed at Mount Rainier some seventy years earlier, the lines between pristine nature and modified nature were not readily apparent. At North Cascades, park planners relied on traditional roadside interpretation of the park beyond the road; they also employed an alternative means of impressing visitors with the park's wilderness setting through a film shown at the park's newly constructed visitor center. In this respect, it seems, the virtual park had been realized. What visitors could not see from a car, they could see through another kind of window.

A PARK BY ANOTHER NAME

The concept of wilderness threshold suggested that the Park Service was engaged in a kind of semantic strategy at North Cascades. By defining areas with roads (as well as reservoirs) as something other than wilderness, the agency would avoid the apparent contradiction of parks in wilderness. At both Mount Rainier and Olympic, the agency had addressed these contradictions by formulating a landscape design philosophy that embraced wilderness preservation through developments for windshield tourists. The idea of wilderness thresholds carried forward the notion that national parks, though modified for motoring Americans, were seamless landscapes of wild beauty. The main difference was that the agency developed the idea of wilderness thresholds in response to the Wilderness Act of 1964. A reluctant supporter of the act, the agency argued for buffer zones, and similar classifications, around and within the designated wilderness of national parks, monuments, and other areas under its charge. The policy reflected the need for transition zones between "intensively developed portions" and the wilderness areas of the parks. These zones, or thresholds, were deemed to have high natural values but were not eligible for wilderness status. Their value, as some critics argued, was to allow the Park Service to reserve sections of the park for further development that would otherwise have received stricter protection. The agency, however, asserted that wilderness thresholds held great promise; they afforded the newcomer an opportunity to experience "the mood and temper of the wild country before venturing into the wilderness beyond." These buffer zones, the agency believed, offered "an unequaled opportunity" not for allowing visitors to experience wilderness firsthand but for interpreting to them the "meaning of wilderness."[3]

Conveying the meaning of wilderness to visitors, few of whom would actually ever set foot in it, was as optimistic as it was problematic. Most park visitors would spend their time in the recreation areas, which historically the Park Service had not considered to be of the same caliber as a national park. The recreation areas were open to a wider range of uses and, because the Park Service envisioned them as staging sites for entering the "true" wilderness of the park, these areas became the scene of traditional park developments for auto tourists. They became what people perceived to be "the park" and were the most commonly "experienced" aspect of North Cascades. Through its use of the wilderness threshold concept, the Park Service appeared to have resolved the issue of autos in national parks, but it merely transferred the debate to another setting. In the recreation areas, as in national parks, the same questions about access, scenic views, and accommodations for windshield tourists prevailed.

The agency's willingness to embrace the wilderness threshold idea, despite its flaws, suggests that the Park Service was experiencing something of an identity crisis. While managing national parks as biological reserves rather than resorts for auto tourists was a major theme in the agency's mission in the late 1960s and 1970s, park visitation continued to climb. In 1966, annual visitation to the park system reached 133 million, up from more than 62 million visits a decade earlier, when the Mission 66 program began. By 1972, total annual visits reached 212 million. With few exceptions visitors still saw the parks by automobile, and thus those managing parks as natural reserves needed to address their presence. One response to the rise in visitation and motorists, and another aspect of the agency's management approach, was to expand the national park system to embrace the nation's increasing urban population. Between 1961 and 1972, a total of eighty-seven units joined the system, constituting nearly 3.7 million acres. The majority of these new areas came in under the leadership of George Hartzog, as part of his "Parkscape U.S.A." program, an agenda launched to succeed Mission 66 and to enlarge the park system by 1972, Yellowstone's centennial year. Although Hartzog had championed the establishment of a large natural park like North Cascades, he also pursued the addition of numerous nontraditional parks. These were mainly recreation areas that featured reservoirs, seashores, lakeshores, parkways, trails, performing arts facilities, and major urban recreation complexes. This latter type of park area had perhaps the greatest consequence for the system. With the acquisition of Gateway and Golden Gate national recreation areas in the crowded metropolitan areas of New York City and San Francisco, the Park Service entered the business of urban mass recreation.[4]

In the past, urban residents had sought out national parks; now national parks were moving to the cities. Although the departure was controversial and stressful for an agency with a popular image and self-conception as the protector of natural wonders like Yellowstone, it also was important because it meant that what people thought of as "national parks" had broadened. And while preserving North Cascades as "wilderness" was still important for the Park Service and its supporters, it was also important for the agency to consider the nation's rising population and increasingly urban character in the management of national parks.

SEEING IS BELIEVING: PLANNING A WILDERNESS PARK IN THE ENVIRONMENTAL AGE

At North Cascades, the Park Service attempted to take into account the changing expectations about and new pressures on national parks, and to redefine the popular meaning of parks as places in which automobiles had little influence. In 1970, the agency released its master plan and wilderness proposal for North Cascades, declaring that its mission was the preservation of the park's "spectacular wilderness qualities." It recommended some 516,000 acres for wilderness designation. With few exceptions, the Park Service would classify the entire national park as wilderness, and to a much smaller extent some selected lands within the recreation areas. But in order for visitors to appreciate this wild country, they would have to encounter it first (and for many, entirely) from outside the park. So that the agency could manage the national park as a wilderness reserve, the park complex's two recreation areas would serve the needs of the park visitors. These areas would not only be managed and developed to supply services for the general public and "their great recreational potential," they would also function as "wilderness thresholds."[5] They would be the places from which park tourists would see, or at least sense, the wilderness park closed to roads and cars.

The plan seemed a bold declaration suited to an environmental age, but it also set up a strange situation for national parks: a park in which automobiles were not welcome. And while the park complex's first superintendent, Roger J. Contor, assured visitors that they would soon find facilities familiar to national parks, such as lodges and campgrounds, they would not find these amenities in the park proper. The recreation areas would accommodate such development, bringing all types of visitors to the periphery of wilderness while ensuring that the national park would remain in "a wilderness state." "We only want to introduce" the park to the public, Contor stated, by bringing people to "the doorway in a comfortable and pleasant manner."[6]

But Contor, like an earlier generation of Park Service officials, believed that it would be unfair to deny mainstream Americans—those whose summer vacations were spent driving across the nation to see their national parks—a way to see and experience the grandeur of the North Cascades. It would be undemocratic to make them hike deep valleys or climb the high peaks of this rugged area as their only options for seeing the park. The new park presented unfamiliar challenges for the average national park tourist accustomed to viewing nature from behind a wheel, the superintendent noted. North Cascades possessed the "classic attributes" of wilderness: it was remote and inaccessible to motorized travel. Although accessible to hikers, climbers, and people on horseback, its steep terrain, dense vegetation, and "unforgiving weather" conspired "against the wilderness traveler," Contor concluded.[7] The relationship between park and recreation areas, then, was essential because it would allow windshield tourists to drive to the brink of wildness, giving them at least the sense of driving through the park's wilderness setting.

The idea of using the recreation areas as park substitutes reveals more than the Park Service's struggles to break with the past. It also shows how the agency imagined the park within the context of modern realities. North Cascades could not be managed as a wilderness without considering its close relationship with the urban and industrial centers of Washington. Since the first cars entered parks like Mount Rainier around 1910, it had become possible for people to think of national parks as wilderness known because of, not apart from, progress. Granted, Americans gained an appreciation of wilderness in urban settings and were inclined to imagine cities and wilderness as often distant places in the nation's physical as well as mental geography. But in the latter twentieth century, it was all too apparent that the two were growing closer together in space and time as well as on the mental maps of Americans.

In the thirty years after World War II, cities in the far West epitomized this trend; they expanded quickly on a horizontal rather than vertical scale. The process enabled them to integrate the larger landscape of mountains, lakes, rivers, farmland, and scenery into their borders. In doing so, western communities identified themselves with the "'natural' West," whether in their backyards or national parks, and saw their homes "as gateways to the special environs of the region."[8] Such an expansive character and attachment to the natural setting would not have been possible without autos. Untethered from city centers, urban dwellers could live farther from downtowns and motor freely through the country beyond their homes.

In order to manage North Cascades for its primitive qualities, agency planners had to consider the park's proximity to cities as one of its most distinguishing characteristics. It was a situation, they believed, that "exists nowhere else in the United States." In 1970, nearly 75 percent of Washington's population resided in the Seattle-Tacoma metropolitan area. With the recent completion of Interstate 5 in the mid-1960s, some two million people were within a two-hour drive of the Skagit Valley and the heart of the park complex. Residents from those cities who had enjoyed easy access to Mount Rainier, and later Olympic, would have another nearby national park. Furthermore, Interstate 5 placed other urban centers within "reasonable driving distance" from North Cascades, so that managers expected to draw visitors from a wide range of cities in Washington, Oregon, California, and British Columbia. From its inception, then, North Cascades served an expansive and influential urban-industrial population that increasingly sought out unspoiled lands and recreational opportunities within its reach.[9]

Planners also conceived of the park as a wilderness landscape, like other parks of Washington and the nation, within the country's highway geography. They anticipated that Highway 20 would "revolutionize" vacation travel patterns, linking the interior of the northern Cascades with the interstate highway system and other state highways on the east and west sides of Washington. They assumed that the park complex would be used extensively by day or weekend visitors and perhaps to a lesser extent by those seeking out lengthier encounters with the area's wild alpine country. Moreover, what park supporters and agency officials considered the most distinguishing fea-

Wilderness Threshold

ture of the park, its knife-edged waves of peaks, would be hidden from most visitors. In order to convey the significance of "this resource to the Nation and the region," the master plan concluded, the Park Service would have to provide some opportunity for people to experience its true essence, "if only briefly, and from a distance."[10]

At North Cascades, the Park Service focused its energy on improving the new park area as a wilderness threshold and paid less attention to its main attraction of wilderness. The agency had acted similarly in parks like Yellowstone, where it planned wilderness threshold communities within the park as portals to the surrounding park wilderness. By concentrating visitor services in central locations and removing them from popular scenic attractions, agency leaders envisioned transforming parts of Yellowstone and other parks into wilderness islands. To encourage park patrons to leave their cars behind, Park Service planners proposed a mass transit system—possibly monorail service—to serve Yellowstone from gateway towns outside the park. It was one thing, though, to return parks like Yellowstone or Yosemite to a wilderness condition by creating enclaves of development within them.[11] It was quite another to create a wilderness park such as North Cascades and not let anyone see it. A park without easy access and visitor services seemed foreign to the general public. As one newspaper noted, "The park's destiny cannot be realized until both the highway and mass-recreation facilities are completed." A wilderness park inaccessible to the American people "is only an exercise in futility."[12]

At North Cascades, tramways still seemed the best way for visitors to see the park. By using tramways in the steep terrain, the Park Service could reveal the range's wonders to tourists while avoiding costly and environmentally destructive highway construction. Tramways at North Cascades were more likely to be accepted since, as a new area, the park lacked well-established patterns of use, and driving had not become central to experiencing the region. At the same time, tramways would provide a windshield experience of a national park similar to that offered by auto travel. If successful at parks like North Cascades, Secretary of the Interior Walter J. Hickel implied in 1969, tramways had the potential to replace roads and cars in all national parks. Tramways not only would bring people into parks, but they would also protect park resources. The impression conveyed by Hickel and others was that tramways would enable people to look at but not disturb park landscapes.[13] At a time when automobiles and not the people driving them were considered the main problem for national parks, tramways offered a convenient substitute. Using the same logic their predecessors had employed to rationalize the presence of cars in parks, agency leaders suggested that tramways could be integrated with the natural world.

More than roads, however, tramways were still anathema to the national park ideal. In the early 1970s, for example, the Park Service proposed constructing a tramway from the valley floor to Glacier Point as part of its larger proposal to close off all of Yosemite Valley to automobiles. Although the agency argued that this form of public transportation would relieve pressure from the car-congested park, it set off a firestorm of protest. Preservationists supported removing private autos from the valley, but they fought and killed the tramway alternative. They argued that the Glacier Point tramway was not a serious effort toward dealing with overcrowding but a poorly veiled attempt to increase development in the park, the primary beneficiary of which would have been the park concessionaire. However attractive abolishing cars from the park appeared, each car meant less business for the Yosemite Park and Curry Company; an aerial cableway would have helped offset company losses.[14]

Wilderness supporters, such as the Wilderness Society and the North Cascades Conservation Council, reacted similarly to the tramways proposed for North Cascades. As they had argued during the park campaign, tramways were an invasion of the range's wilderness scene, and they urged the agency to eliminate them from its plans. Three of the four considered, the Arctic Creek, Price Lake, and Colonial Peak trams, entered proposed wilderness through creative boundary adjustments, known as enclaves. By reserving areas of the park (as well as Ross Lake NRA) from wilderness classification, agency planners were promoting the installation of permanent structures in some of the park's most remote areas. The tramways were also unnecessary because the impressive panoramic views they offered could be found elsewhere, in most cases outside of the park.[15] The National Parks and Conservation Association called on the agency to adhere to past policy. It historically had prohibited these "devices" in parks because they were scenic impairments. Now it was in danger of installing them as transportation to view or enter "into the wilderness," and in doing so it would preclude both. Tramways destroyed the character of wilderness.[16]

Even though the Park Service argued that the proposed tramways were not technically in the park and that most were within a recreation area, this mattered little to wilderness activists. They were concerned that tramways would not provide a suitable alternative to automobiles in national parks.

Wilderness Threshold

The tramways, like roads and cars, would diminish a wilderness experience by bringing people to its edge. The contraptions would also insulate people from having any elemental contact with nature, wilderness advocates believed, further alienating visitors from, rather than striking a closer bond with, wilderness. In this respect, tramways would only serve as a convenient solution for most park visitors who wanted a wilderness experience but had neither the time nor the ability to hike into a park's backcountry. Like cars, tramways would transport visitors to the top of a mountain, giving them a truly "wilderness threshold experience," as the Park Service promoted. "Peering at a wilderness from a tramway station, however," as lawyer-critic Joseph L. Sax suggests, "is *not* a wilderness experience; the sense of wilderness is not achieved by standing at its threshold, but by engaging it from within." Tramways or similar devices only "falsified or domesticated" the experience of "true wilderness," and by building them, the Park Service would be doing a great disservice to the American public and the natural world.[17]

Although preservationists displayed similar ideas in the North Cascades, they were more willing to accept at least one of the four proposed tramways, the Ruby Mountain tram, primarily because its route lay entirely within Ross Lake NRA. In this regard, they supported the Park Service's plan for concentrating developments in the recreation areas. They also believed that without the tramway, "visitors would not get to appreciate the vast, breathtaking, storm-tossed sea of peaks through which they were passing." In their minds, wrote Patrick Goldsworthy from the North Cascades Conservation Council, the tramway would be "the counterpart of Hurricane Ridge in Olympic National Park" and its "panoramic view out into the Park's . . . wilderness, with its great forests, peaks, and glaciers." While still controversial, a tramway's presence in the recreation area at least would not desecrate a national park or penetrate any lands recommended to Congress as wilderness. Renowned mountaineer James Whittaker went so far as to endorse this and other tramways in the North Cascades as one of the best ways to view scenery "not excelled anywhere in the world." A tramway would enable everyone, "not just mountain climbers," to see the range.[18]

The Park Service retained the Ruby Mountain tram in its final master plan, in part because outdoor organizations did not oppose it outright. Although the agency also planned to construct a tram up Arctic Creek, only the Ruby Mountain tram proved to be viable in the long term. Located in a largely inaccessible area on the north end of Ross Lake, some of which would be flooded if Seattle City Light raised Ross Dam, the Arctic Creek tram would never be built. The Ruby Mountain tram stood a greater chance of being constructed. It was slated for installation in Ross Lake NRA, like the Arctic Creek tram, except its route lay close to Highway 20, making its construction seem more realistic.

Another reason the Park Service retained the Ruby Mountain tram was political necessity. Although no tramway had ever been built in a national park area, traditional Park Service management beliefs held that people needed to see a park through some convenient means of conveyance. Otherwise, they were not likely to appreciate its value. Without popular appeal and approval, the new park complex would become a political liability. To make certain this did not happen, Senator Henry Jackson and Congressman Lloyd Meeds from Washington State's congressional delegation pressed for the project. Meeds was especially active in supporting the tramway's construction, among other improvement programs, because Meeds wanted North Cascades to be "pro people."[19]

Gaining the support of the American people was central to the future of North Cascades, as it was in all new parks. Meeds feared that thousands of visitors would travel through the park complex over Highway 20 with no place to stop and nothing to see. With its lower terminal near Ross Dam, the Ruby Mountain tram would alleviate this problem. The facility would serve as the hub for visitor services along the highway. More importantly, it would lift windshield tourists a mile above the highway to the top of Ruby Mountain, an elevation of 7,200 feet. Floating over trees and snowfields for three and half miles, the aerial tram would operate only in the summer and in two stages, with gondolas carrying people up and down the mountain at the same time. Nature trails awaited visitors in the subalpine zone, snowfields at the upper terminal awaited advanced skiers, and a striking panorama of peaks awaited all. With these attractions, the tramway, Park Service planners anticipated, would be fully loaded all summer and serve more visitors than any other site in the park complex.[20]

In the early 1970s, however, it only appeared that North Cascades was poised to offer Americans a new way to experience the scenic grandeur of national parks. A number of events coalesced to doom the Ruby Mountain tram. The most widely reported reason was skyrocketing cost. Because of inflation, the cost of building the tram and related facilities—from planning to finished product—rose so high that the Park Service made the project a low priority. Estimates that hovered around $8 million in 1972 zoomed to more than $13 million (one account reached $20 million) several years later. Even Congressman Meeds, whose zeal for seeking appropriations for the park complex often exceeded the needs of the Park Service, could not overcome such a dramatic increase.[21]

Less widely known reasons for delaying the tramway came from within the agency itself. Publicly, agency leaders such as Regional Director Charles Odegaard proclaimed their desire to follow through with the proposal. Without the aerial tram, Odegaard said in 1980, visitors "can't truly appreciate the grandeur of the park." Although the tramway was still a "viable project," the "key" to its completion was money.[22] Privately, Odegaard and others knew the money would probably never materialize as congressional budgets tightened. What funds were available would not be earmarked for such an expensive and controversial project. The tramway proposal faced an even greater challenge if it was to comply with the National Environmental Policy Act of 1969. The legislation required that the agency conduct environmental reviews of its proposals. Since the tramway had been proposed prior to the review process, the Park Service would have to revisit the plan and consider its potential environmental damage in a public forum. Even with Meeds as its political ally, the agency apparently did not want to battle environmentalists over the damage the tramway's installation would cause. Upper-level officials within the agency, it seems, shared similar concerns over the project's environmental impact. There was also the question of containment. Once in place, the tramway would lead to more development pressures, particularly for a ski area on Ruby Mountain.[23]

Criticism of the wilderness threshold concept also led Park Service leaders to reconsider the project. Wilderness activists were beginning to argue against the wilderness threshold philosophy because it allowed national recreation areas to be treated as second-class sites.[24] Groups such as the North Cascades Conservation Council, for example, asserted that "wilderness threshold" was really a euphemism for development. Building up the recreation areas in North Cascades with visitor services would seriously compromise their use as wilderness buffers for the park. Granted, legislation for Ross Lake NRA sanctioned tramways and similar projects by stating that the recreation area's purpose was to provide for public outdoor recreational use and enjoyment of portions of the Skagit River, Gorge, Diablo, and Ross lakes, and surrounding lands. Protection of the area's "other values," namely wilderness, was important only insofar as it contributed "to the public enjoyment of such lands and waters." As Secretary Udall declared during the 1967 Senate hearings on the North Cascades bill, one of the main reasons for creating Ross Lake NRA was to provide more "intense recreational use than is normally the custom within a national park." Park Service officials, critics asserted, were too quick to interpret this statement as an approval for developments on the scale of those found in older parks in the name of wilderness protection.[25]

In their arguments against wilderness thresholds, environmental organizations were really expressing a desire to treat recreation areas, like Ross Lake, as wilderness. More revealing in this regard than their aversion to tramways was their opposition to Seattle City Light's High Ross Dam project. Environmental groups acknowledged that Congress authorized raising the dam in the North Cascades legislation and drew the boundaries of the recreation area to accommodate the enlarged reservoir. But they fought the project because, as they asserted, at full pool the reservoir would needlessly flood wilderness valleys forever (including some in British Columbia) as a short-term solution to increased power demands. Members of the Sierra Club and the North Cascades Conservation Council described Ross Lake as a place where wilderness persisted even around a reservoir. They contended that the isolated, man-made lake—set in a jumble of precipitous, glacier-clad peaks—possessed the scenic qualities and unique natural wonders of a national park and deserved to be treated as one.[26]

Although preservation interests helped stop the dam project, which was resolved by an international treaty in 1984, they muddied the distinction between the protection of nature undisturbed by humans and of nature remade by humans, and thus the distinction between park and recreation area, as well as wilderness and wilderness threshold. By suggesting that the recreation area had wilderness values, they took some of the attention away from the park that lay "beyond" the recreation area and focused it on the management of the recreation area itself. Preservationists underscored that developments for motorized entry into the recreation area deserved the same scrutiny as they would within the national park. And whether they fully realized it, they implied that for most park tourists, including members of outdoor groups, what they saw from their cars would form their understanding of North Cascades—as a national park. As wilderness gateways, with roads running through them or to them, Ross Lake and Lake Chelan national recreation areas were key elements in exposing windshield tourists to the North Cascades. They were, in effect, "the park."

By turning the Park Service's strategy back on itself, wilderness activists forced agency managers to justify their manipulation of the natural environment, whether in the park or recreation areas. The Park Service was not an altogether unwilling participant. As the 1970s came to a close, environmental laws and changes in agency policies mandated that the Park Service change its ways. The central message of these laws and policy revisions was that the protection of natural systems was a universal and not a selective mission of the agency; it applied to all park units, including recreation areas. In this regard, the agency's subdivision of the park system into management categories (historical, recreational, natural) ran counter to Congress's conception of the system as an integrated whole and weakened rather than strengthened parks in the face of internal and external threats. Abandoning the separate management categories in the late 1970s, the Park Service began to treat, at least in theory, Ross Lake and Lake Chelan national recreation areas as if they were part of North Cascades National Park.[27] The change in management approach, however, tended to obscure the intent of the wilderness threshold concept. It also focused attention on what the Park Service had hoped to downplay: how integral roads and cars still were to experiencing national parks. Several projects and management strategies employed by the Park Service illustrate the agency's attempts to restrict the use of automobiles in national parks like North Cascades, where automobiles seemed to be the only way of reaching visitors with the park's wilderness message.

The first of these vignettes was the proposed Roland Point Road. The Roland Point Road was the only new road planned in the North Cascades complex, and the agency's treatment of the project suggests that it was serious about limiting services for cars in North Cascades. Initially, though, the agency touted the road as a kind of ideal park development, a true wilderness threshold experience. Without a tramway to take people to the wilderness, park planners seemed ready to let the spur road accomplish something similar. The road would lie within Ross Lake NRA and connect Highway 20 with a development on Roland Point, which included an overnight lodge, marina, and campground along the eastern shore of Ross Lake. It would be the entry point for a trip to the wilderness of the park. Once at Roland Point, visitors would leave their cars, explore the lake and its surroundings by boat or foot, and enjoy a modicum of solitude, freedom, and comfort. (One element of the plan even included a ferry for lake travel.) When they were uplake, visitors could use shoreline campgrounds and backcountry hostels to launch extended outings into the park's mountainous interior.[28]

Anxious about providing services for the traveling public, Congressman Meeds pressured the Park Service to complete the road and lakeshore development for the multitude of automobile tourists destined to travel through the park complex along Highway 20. To the congressman's way of thinking, the project was not only practical; it was essential. "The facilities to accommodate more than a handful of the people who want to visit this magnificent park," Meeds observed, "just don't exist." There was no road access to the southern end of Ross Lake, and he wanted the road built to open up this section to motorists and boaters. Otherwise the only way to reach Ross Lake by car was over a long, rough road from Hope, British Columbia. Without the road, he implied, mostly Canadians would enjoy this American parkland. Moreover, in the minds of park boosters and politicians alike, it was imperative to construct the facilities at Roland Point for mass recreation. For Meeds, as well as for Senator Jackson, a project like Roland Point would increase the new area's popularity and, more importantly, bring the economic prosperity that they had promised to local communities through tourism. The Roland Point Road would also make the remote park more "people friendly," as Meeds desired. It would give the new park's visitors something to see and do, letting them know they were in a "park."[29]

Such an extensive development, modeled after those in earlier national parks, and the idea that it would be part of a transition into real wilderness, did not sit well with preservationists. The North Cascades Conservation Council opposed the project, for reasons similar to those it used against the High Ross Dam. The council argued that the project would not promote but would actually diminish the *wilderness* experience visitors would find *on* Ross Lake. The Roland Point development would bring a high concentration of automobiles and motor boats, the group contended, to the southern end of the lake, ruining the serenity of this fjordlike setting, damaging fisheries, and polluting the aquatic environment with gas, oil, and sewage.[30]

Evidently, some Park Service leaders shared these feelings. At least in this instance, responding to agency directives and expressing a greater interest in protecting natural values, they were not convinced that developments for motorized recreation would convey to visitors the park's wilderness qualities. They only kept the project in the complex's master plan as a concession to Meeds. According to Superintendent Lowell White, the road would have been an environmental disaster. Preliminary assessments indicated that the five-mile access road would have significantly damaged the natural landscape, causing serious erosion in steep terrain that received heavy snowfall. Visually, it would have created a long, ugly scar across the southern and western slopes of Jack Mountain, visible from both the highway and the lake. Finally, as with the Ruby Mountain tramway, construction costs were prohibitive, ranging from $6.5 million to $10 million.[31]

Early in 1972, when it became apparent that Roland Point might go undeveloped, Meeds asked a far-reaching question. Where, he demanded to know from Director Hartzog, "are the people going to go?"[32] For the congressman, it was difficult to imagine national parks, even new ones dedicated to wilderness, without developments for motor tourists. Granted, Meeds stood to bear the brunt of his constituents' dissatisfaction if they found little to entertain them in the new parkland. But on a deeper level, the congressman was asking what place automobiles—and their drivers and passengers—still had in national parks. The people about whom he was speaking were not those "hardy enough to carry a pack," but the thousands who would stream across the range in the summer season looking at the wild Cascades through their windshields. For many, the drive and brief stop would be their only encounter with this wilderness park.[33]

Park managers would have difficulty answering Meeds. By the late 1970s, they had convinced the congressman that the Roland Point project was not feasible, primarily because the proposed High Ross Dam would flood Roland Point. And then they shelved plans for the project. Still, Meeds's concern about allowing visitors to gain a sense of appreciation for the wild land beyond the recreation area remained unaddressed. This suggested that the Park Service's concept of a wilderness threshold was purposefully deceptive; it was about neither wilderness nor a transition to wilderness.

Times had changed in national park management. In the age of the National Environmental Policy Act, the agency could not exercise the same control over road projects as it once had in the 1920s. Park managers could not fall back on the promise of landscape architecture to blend the road with nature. Their projects were now subjected to environmental analysis and public review to determine whether the damage caused by construction and use was worth the precious price of wilderness. The notion, it seems, of creating an ideal park experience in which a road appeared to belong in nature had been supplanted not only by the concept of wilderness as road-less, but also by the measure of a road's effects on the health of nature. These concerns quite often scuttled plans for new roads.

Ironically, the situation did not lessen the demand for automobile access to remote park settings like North Cascades. What tended to happen was that existing roads were forced to shoulder the burden of the traditional park experience, as demonstrated in the cases of three other roads in the park complex. While park managers wanted to limit auto use by encouraging vis-itors to leave behind the "sensory deprivation of the automobile" for wilder-ness recreation, they also had to satisfy the desire of motorists to drive into a primitive landscape.[34] Americans may have become more ecologically savvy, but they were not abandoning their cars. Complicating matters further, the Park Service had cultivated this expectation, leading the agency to face its past. In some instances it broke with tradition, but more often it modified the ideal of knowing nature through machines in a new setting.

Tourists often seemed more interested in the new park as windshield wilderness than as a wilderness threshold. In the early 1970s, for example, when North Cascades managers attempted to break with the past and decided to close the upper section of the Cascade River Road to private autos, they met with stiff resistance. Park superintendents such as Roger Contor and Lowell White wanted to comply with agency initiatives to find alternative means of access to national parks and to protect the fragile subalpine envi-ronment of Cascade Pass. Cascade Pass was one of the most popular attrac-tions in the national park, and the Cascade River Road led to its base, just a short distance within the park's boundaries. Since the turn of the century, highway builders and Washington drivers had fantasized about building a road over Cascade Pass not only to complete a transmountain road, but also to open to motorists the wonders of Lake Chelan and "some of the wildest and most beautiful" areas of the state. Although the road never crossed the pass, it made the pass one of the only places to which the casual visitor could drive to see the park's famous scenery. Motorists who dared to drive the twenty-five-mile, mostly washboard road were rewarded with views of the range's impressive relief, chiseled peaks, and hanging glaciers as they neared the pass. They were able to glimpse what were popularly known as "Amer-ica's Alps."[35]

By the early 1970s, though, the paradox of autos in nature was written clearly on the subalpine terrain of Cascade Pass. Reached with relative ease by car, especially by residents of the Puget Sound region, the pass was pop-

Wilderness Threshold

ular with, and overused by, people on horseback, hikers, and campers. These activities had severely eroded and gullied the pass and its surroundings over the years under Forest Service management. And with the so-called backpacking revolution in full swing, the abuse might continue. At peak periods in the summer, an estimated one thousand people a day drove to the foot of the pass.[36] Many of them walked from there to the summit, a distance of about three miles. People, as the Park Service wanted, may have been leaving their cars behind, but in doing so they were also furthering the decline of the natural world they were visiting.

In 1974, Superintendent White revealed a plan to restore the pass's fragile environment in which controlling auto access was critical. Like other aspects of the Park Service's approach to preservation during the Mission 66 program, promoting the area for day-use activities, such as hiking and sightseeing, was central to the plan. The agency needed to limit how long people stayed in the area, especially if new policies prohibiting camping, banning horses, rehabilitating trails, and initiating a long-term revegetation program were to succeed. White proposed closing the Cascade River Road to private cars several miles below the foot of the pass and initiating a shuttle bus service that would take visitors the rest of the way.[37] This would allow the pass to retain its popularity for sightseers. It would also be used, as it had been for generations of native peoples, as "the way through" the North Cascades into the Stehekin Valley or the park's backcountry.

But not everyone agreed with the Park Service's attempts to grant visitors "the privilege of walking" to see scenery. At public meetings held to review the plan, people protested restrictions to their "equal access rights." For many, even when faced with the cause of wilderness preservation and ecological restoration, their image of national parks was still influenced by the legacy of Stephen Mather, and his vision of parks as places for the highway in nature.[38]

Protesters represented a cross-section of the general public who, for one reason or another, were opposed to the idea of taking public transportation—and walking—into the park. The car was still an icon of American freedom, it seems, and mass transit a symbol of anti-individualism. Mountain climbers, who professed a close relationship with nature here and in parks like Mount Rainier and Yosemite, protested the use of shuttles because they might be inconvenienced by bus schedules that did not match their own. They might have to walk an additional three miles to their cars, quite possibly at night and in inclement weather. Others observed that restricting access was a form of discrimination. They argued that the road offered the only motorized access to one of the park's most scenic places. To close it would unfairly deny the experience to those for whom walking this last section of road was difficult, namely the elderly, physically challenged, and families with young children. Though the shuttles would stop only a short distance before the end of the road, it was a rugged and steep section. The most impressive view of the pass and surrounding alpine scenery lay where the road ended, not before it. As Kenneth Schell, a spokesman for Washington's International Trailer Clubs of America, proclaimed, the plan was really about controlling backpackers and hikers to the detriment of windshield tourists. "We merely want the ability to look, not invade," Schell stated. In fact, the "ecological problem" at the pass resulted not from day users driving to the area but from backpackers, according to Don Johnson, a local landowner. Therefore, the Park Service should implement the shuttle bus system for backpackers and allow day visitors to drive to the end of the road. "North Cascades National Park" was "far too large to not have at least one viewpoint accessible by private automobile."[39]

When the Park Service issued the Cascade Pass plan later that summer, it omitted the road closure proposal. In one respect, political realities led to the plan's revision. Skagit County owned the road, and based on the public hearings, the county commissioners opposed closing it to cars. In another respect, however, agency officials revised the plan because automobiles continued to be an integral part of the national park experience. For almost seventy years, Americans had been able to motor to canyon rims and mountainsides for panoramic views of nature's grandeur. And now they were being told they could not. Certainly, agency managers could point to wilderness preservation and ecological restoration as powerful and popular reasons for the road closure. But in order to find success for its proposal, park managers faced an even greater obstacle: overcoming the popular impression of national parks as wilderness landscapes through which automobiles traveled.

In their management of the Stehekin Valley Road, park managers attempted to create a new impression: in national parks autos could be driven to but not through a pristine landscape. The Stehekin Road had occupied a central role in the North Cascades campaign. This "road to nowhere" traveled through a picturesque country, often compared to Yosemite, and demonstrated that roads and autos could exist in a primitive landscape without destroying it. The road symbolized that North Cascades was a national park. By forbidding the construction of any outside roads to the valley, the North Cascades legislation assured that this middle landscape would never be threatened. It would never become part of the larger public landscape of highways and nature that shaped other national parks.

This quality, perhaps more than any other, made Stehekin a wilderness threshold in the minds of park supporters such as Grant McConnell as well as Park Service officials. The valley road was an integral part of their conception of Stehekin. To them, the Stehekin Road was a road to wilderness, allowing people to experience the park's wilderness qualities. The road connected the lower valley, where visitors arrived at the head of the lake by boat and where residents lived, to the wilds of Horseshoe Basin, a glacial cirque several miles east of Cascade Pass. There, at the headwaters of the Stehekin River, the road turned into a rugged, two-track path until it disappeared altogether. The road also provided visitors with the experience of going to wilderness as a destination, a real place. Its lower section was contained in Lake Chelan NRA, while its upper section lay within North Cascades National Park. In theory, park visitors could drive a short distance into the North Cascades; they could feel as though they were driving into wilderness.

In the 1970s, the Park Service tried to preserve this quality; it designated the road as an enclave in the park complex's wilderness proposal, by drawing the wilderness boundary to within two hundred feet of the road corridor. In this way, the road's presence in the park, both real and imagined, would not conflict with the legal definition of wilderness set down in the Wilderness Act.[40] Although preservationists such as McConnell argued that the section of the road within the park should be closed and returned to a wilderness state, Park Service officials relied on agency tradition to rationalize their decision.[41] Superintendent Contor observed, echoing Conrad Wirth, that keeping the road open would serve as a preservation measure. Since the road ended a few miles from the eastern side of Cascade Pass, it would promote day use of this fragile area and would contribute to its restoration. Hikers, starting from either side of the pass, would be less inclined to camp if they could ride to and from the trailhead.[42]

But Contor's other reason generated more controversy. With the road open, park visitors could encounter this new parkland as they would in any parkland, by driving. And judging from the debate over the attempted closure of the Cascade River Road, it was an experience they were not likely to relinquish quietly. Contor's reasoning also revealed that the Park Service was more comfortable with wilderness as a scenic quality viewed from a car.

As he asserted, all people, including the nonhiker and elderly visitor, should see the park. The decision to keep the road open, while arousing a "divergence of opinion," was a fair compromise, he argued, especially in a park that had "fewer roads than any other major park in the system."[43]

The Park Service also favored automobile use over strict nature preservation because the conditions in the Stehekin country differed from those in most other national parks. Managers like Contor shared the views of preservationists who valued Stehekin as a place where the potential for regulating the relationship between machines and nature appeared real. There were only a limited number of cars in the valley and there always would be, it seemed. Since the valley was unconnected to the rest of the nation by road, visitors arrived not by car but mostly by boat. The situation provided a rare opportunity to control transportation in a national park area. Initially, visitors relied on private taxis and rental cars owned by residents to tour the valley. Shortly after the park complex's creation, these were all but replaced by a popular shuttle bus service, operated both by the Park Service and a concession. For a small sum, visitors, many of whom spent less than a day in the Stehekin country because of the boat schedule, could ride the shuttles the entire length of the valley road, stopping at popular scenic sites, trailheads, campgrounds, and other places.

Although the shuttle system's popularity had implications for the entire park system, as a way to remove the strain of autos from overcrowded parks, the Park Service also intended the shuttle to allay the concerns of McConnell and others. The agency planned to use the shuttle to limit traffic on the valley road and would make only necessary improvements. "In other words," Contor observed, the road "will be managed as a motor nature trail. . . . *A la* street car!"[44] The shuttle system, like the justification for keeping the Stehekin Road open, would help protect the upper valley from overuse because the Park Service allowed only shuttles over the last section of rather treacherous road. The road to wilderness may have been open to vehicles, but by regulating travel over it, park managers appeared to have met both the popular need for motorized access to primitive landscapes in national parks and their obligation to protect them.[45]

But regulated access really could not be implemented elsewhere, except perhaps in park areas in Alaska that were far from any highway, and the situation led the Park Service to engage in some contradictory practices. On the one hand, the agency wanted to convey to the public that America's car culture had little influence on the Stehekin landscape. In 1969, Contor went so far as to clean up the valley's image—barging out the "eyesore" of its many junked cars visible all too frequently from the road—to help shape this impression. On the other hand, although fairly innocuous and welcomed by valley residents, the car removal program did not diminish the Park Service's focus on automobiles and roads. Instead, that focus increased. The agency expended considerable sums of money—more than on any other area of the park complex in early stages of management—to improve and maintain the entire road. The agency's desire to present nature's beauty from the road, it seems, never diminished. Nature annually wanted to reclaim the road, but the Park Service resisted. Every season, it repaired the road in order to preserve Cascade Pass and the visitor's windshield wilderness experience.[46]

In its efforts to maintain the road as a way to wilderness, though, the agency was replacing more than the physical road. It was restoring the notion of a road as compatible with a wilderness setting. Convincing everyone, especially preservationists, of its intent was difficult for the Park Service. Although he had sung the praises of the valley and its road during the park campaign, and had even touted the agency's ability to design roads in harmony with nature, McConnell expressed dismay at the Park Service's road management. Improvements, such as paving a section of the lower valley road, altered not only the road's physical character, but also his perception of its "natural" character. By association, the character of valley life—as symbolized by its rural values, self-reliance, and close relationship to the natural world—was also changed. The old, largely unimproved road "necessitated low speeds . . . by cars driven with a respect for the country." Paving may have kept the dust down on the lower road and made sightseeing more enjoyable. But a wider and smoother road invited travel at higher speeds, spurred residents to bring more cars into the valley, and encouraged demands for continued improvements, all accelerating Stehekin's slow-paced, backwoods lifestyle. The Park Service's actions were therefore inappropriate, in McConnell's opinion. It had gone too far, using technology to build roads as they were "built elsewhere—for the benefit of machines, not of the country." The balance between machine and wild nature in the valley—and thus in a national park setting—had shifted in the wrong direction.[47]

Although the ideal of Stehekin Valley Road was problematic and subject to interpretation, as a model it was essential to understanding the Park Service's concept of a wilderness threshold. Highway 20, however, would convey a similar message to a much broader audience. Running "through" rather than into North Cascades, and connected to the larger public highway system, the highway gave tourists visual access to the park without allowing their automobiles to physically enter the wilderness. Roads like Highway 20, even in the opinion of national park critic Joseph Sax, made North Cascades look enticing to "as wide a spectrum of the public as possible." Newcomers especially, he observed, "need a taste of the opportunities the land offers," and therefore, "it makes sense to have—as we do in many parks—a highway designed to provide an introduction for those who are deciding whether they want to come back for more."[48]

Highway 20 would serve in this capacity; it would be the park's wilderness threshold. With large-scale visitor developments and alternative means of transportation eliminated from the Park Service's plans for the recreation area, the agency decided that the only option for interpreting the park's wilderness values was from the road itself. The agency wrestled with how to impress upon visitors the value of the park if they could neither drive into it nor easily view it from the road. In other ways, though, agency leaders were on familiar ground. The idea of introducing visitors to a wilderness landscape from their automobiles had long been an integral part of managing the nation's parks. Even in the environmental age, when cars seemed anathema to one's quality of life, automobiles continued to be not only a mode of travel into national parks, but also part of the process of knowing them. Agency leaders decided to use Highway 20 as they would have any other national park road: to provide motorists with an unfolding scenic narrative of the park. As one popular account noted, with its "spectacular and absorbing scenery," Highway 20 was similar to one of the nation's most impressive mountain highways, Glacier's Going-to-the-Sun Road—what some considered the quintessential national park road.[49]

As with most management decisions, visitation statistics motivated the emphasis on Highway 20. As anticipated, the majority of North Cascades visitors traveled the highway and a relative handful strayed from their cars. Prior to the highway's opening in the fall of 1972, the park complex's visitation was 250,000; in 1973 it climbed to 690,000 and more than tripled to 830,000 in 1974.[50] Heeding the call of Congressman Meeds to make this "magnificent park" available to "more than a handful of people," the Park Service busied itself over the next decade with increasing services for motorists, primarily by expanding existing, and installing new, drive-in campgrounds.[51]

The main problem for the agency was that it needed to accomplish with

Highway 20, a road it did not own, what it was able to do with most national park roads: create the illusion for tourists that they were immersed, however fleetingly, within primal nature. In the past, agency managers would have relied on the skills of landscape architects to convey this impression. But the state's ownership of the highway complicated this approach, and while many came to view Highway 20 as a wilderness road, the Park Service was only partly responsible for this outcome.

To a large extent, the agency benefited from the highway's popularity, especially its evolution from a commercial route into one of the state's premier scenic highways. Initially, highway boosters had promoted this northerly road, which was conceived at the turn of the twentieth century, as a key link in Washington's economic development; they wanted to exploit mining and timber harvesting opportunities in the northern Cascades.[52] But in the late 1960s, as the road neared completion, Washington senator Henry Jackson urged highway supporters to envision the new parklands and wilderness areas proposed for the North Cascades as the main sources for the region's economic growth. Both the national attention cast on the North Cascades and the completion of the state highway would "attract thousands of visitors and permanent residents" to the area. Recreational development represented "a vast economic potential," Jackson wrote. Conservative projections suggested that "tourism and recreation in the North Cascades will create over 1000 new jobs, generating annual salaries of over $5.5 million, to serve from one to two million visitors who will annually spend an estimated $20–25 million." Largely to gain the support of the highway lobby and northwestern Washington communities, Jackson inserted language into the North Cascades legislation that authorized the state's jurisdiction over the highway and restricted the Park Service's ability to control the highway's use.[53]

The state's control over the highway was not necessarily a disadvantage for the Park Service. State control may have retained the route's commercial promise, but the highway traversed some sixty miles of national forest and national parklands, and the agencies managing those lands could restrict commercial development. The highway was also open only during the summer months, when the range was free of snow and avalanche danger, further limiting resource exploitation while adding to the highway's appeal as a scenic drive. Moreover, because the establishment of the North Cascades complex and the completion of Highway 20 occurred close together, the highway's reputation as a scenic byway grew. Instead of influencing the development of natural resources along the highway corridor, the reputation encouraged the consumption of the area's scenic wonders. This trend reflected the emergence of tourism as a dominant economic force in the latter decades of the twentieth century; tourism, especially in rural areas, competed with and in some cases replaced altogether resource production as the economic mainstay. Tourism enabled Americans to acquire something other than the physical products of the marketplace; it allowed them to purchase certain kinds of "intangibles," such as the experience of motoring through the North Cascades.[54] The popular press described Highway 20, for example, as "Lump-in-the-Throat Beautiful" and a lure for "Wilderness Lovers to Alpine 'Heidi Country.'" Meanwhile, heeding the advice of Senator Jackson, communities like Marblemount on the west side and Winthrop on the east side of the range began to exploit their new roles as the last major service centers for tourists heading through the North Cascades.[55]

The main advantage for the Park Service was that North Cascades became associated with Highway 20, and Highway 20 came to be associated with national park roads. Describing the "epic struggle" to finish the highway, for example, the engineering press used language similar to that of an earlier generation of Park Service leaders and landscape architects. Through their "ingenuity," engineers had opened the "cathedral of nature" to "hundreds of thousands of visitors each year" who never would have been able "to enjoy this beautiful section of Washington otherwise." As the centerpiece of the highway experience, the new national park demonstrated that "man and nature have combined in a cooperative venture to provide America forever with an unsurpassed natural scenic wonderland."[56] In a time of mounting environmental problems, it seemed possible to achieve a balance between roads and primal nature; it seemed possible to create a road that appeared to belong in its natural setting. As the editor of the *Pacific Builder and Engineer* declared, "Good highways and good environment are compatible." More importantly, like other national park roads, Highway 20 created a sense of scenic grandeur. The road made the range "more beautiful than ever." By making that beauty accessible, the road made it real.[57]

The engineers' portrayal of the road as a creative force, as something that enhanced rather than detracted from a wild landscape, suggested a further association with national parks. Without a road and an automobile to travel over it, a national park did not exist—at least as Americans had come to know it in the twentieth century. In other words, not until "first nature" (original, nonhuman nature) became "second nature" (the artificial nature people layer over first nature) did it have an intrinsic value that touched the lives of ordinary people. However much wilderness advocates or highway builders stressed the rights of nature or their commitment to environmental protection, they ultimately lived in a world in which their very presence altered the natural environment. In the case of the engineering press, Highway 20 and its surroundings were the product of their own ideas; one could not exist without the other. Highway builders expressed less concern about respecting nature's rhythms and the destructive effects of construction than they did about reproducing what appeared natural to them: a wilderness landscape modified to meet human needs.[58]

This notion arguably owed a great deal to the way Seattle City Light had remade the larger landscape of the upper Skagit River basin with its hydroelectric project, a landscape that won praise from environmental activists for its "wilderness" character. In City Light's opinion, the Skagit project symbolized the ability to blend the artificial and the natural, to transform a wild and potentially destructive river flowing "wastefully" to the sea into three lakes that became the centerpiece of the recreation area. The utility preferred engineered nature over wild nature and liked to boast that it had made wilderness "usable." As City Light informed readers, it had "created Ross Lake in 1949," and since then more than half a million visitors had enjoyed this quiet place for outdoor recreation and spiritual renewal. With the completion of Highway 20, the entire project became part of a national park area, another roadside attraction.[59]

The Park Service was also intent on using Highway 20 to construct an impression of the park's wilderness qualities. The agency may not have built or owned the road, but as caretaker of the land through which it traveled, the agency controlled the natural setting. To a certain extent, it could regulate what people saw and experienced; it could present nature to motoring Americans as it had in other national parks. Its approach relied largely on negotiation. In a special-use permit issued to Washington State allowing the highway to cross federal land, the Park Service established the highway's right-of-way boundaries through Ross Lake NRA and struck an agreement specifying acceptable maintenance activities within the highway corridor. On a much broader scale, shortly after the highway's completion the Park Service entered into an agreement with the state and the Forest Service to prohibit major developments along the highway's center section, especially ski areas, effectively making Highway 20 a scenic road.[60]

Seeking to expand the highway's function as a wilderness threshold, the

Park Service looked beyond the boundaries of public lands to the gateway communities bordering the park complex. The agency's interest in controlling developments along the highway leading to and through the parkland reflected those of Stephen Mather in the 1920s. Through his participation in the North Cascades Reconnaissance Task Force, an interagency committee, Superintendent Contor convinced members that the drive leading into the parkland should retain its rural character. In the late 1960s the last thing the Park Service wanted, Contor recalled, "was another West Yellowstone or Estes Park," with a congested commercial strip interrupting the gradual transition from a rural western valley to the ethereal realm of craggy peaks. Okanogan and Skagit county commissioners, convinced perhaps of the future of tourism, complied with Contor's request. They agreed to limit commercial development along the highway corridor near the entrances of the park by zoning these sections for residential, agricultural, and recreational uses.[61] Park officials also used their presence on interagency committees to influence the public's perception of Highway 20 as the official park road. In order to associate the road with the park itself, they successfully had its name changed from the North Cross-State Highway to the North Cascades Highway by 1972.[62] And they participated with the highway department in the design and location of viewpoints and pullouts so that motorists could glimpse the wilderness country.

Although they may have effectively created a "national park" road, park managers were really engaged in constructing a kind of virtual park experience. The idea of the road as a wilderness threshold required that they somehow interpret the meaning of wilderness to an audience in automobiles. According to a visitor survey in the mid-1980s, the majority of the visitors to North Cascades drove over the North Cascades Highway and stayed in the parkland less than a day.[63] Few ventured far from their cars. It was unlikely, then, that visitors would leave the road and climb a steep trail from Ross Lake NRA into the park's backcountry or hike high enough to see and, as agency leaders hoped, admire the park's grandeur. Ironically, once Congress passed the wilderness legislation for North Cascades in 1988, "official" wilderness, like the park itself, was within sight of the North Cascades Highway, but for most park tourists was indistinguishable from the rest of the country around them.

Moreover, for more than twenty miles up the Skagit Gorge, windshield tourists enjoyed only glimpses of the Picket Range, a prolonged exposure to Pyramid and Colonial Peaks as they rounded Diablo Lake, and an overlook of Ross Lake. Otherwise, the high summits of the range's sharp-edged peaks, its signature features, remained hidden from view. Only once motorists left the park and reached Rainy Pass (4,900 feet) and Washington Pass (5,500 feet) were they rewarded with a territorial view of the northern Cascades. Only then could they see into the park. Even though the Park Service influenced the location and design of highway viewpoints and pullouts in an attempt to compensate for this reality, most turnouts afforded better views of City Light's hydroelectric project, especially the necklace of emerald lakes behind its dams, than of the Pickets.[64]

For agency officials, it was not enough to concede that the parkland's wilderness significance spoke for itself and that it was up to the traveling public to find it for themselves. In the mid-1980s, Superintendent John Reynolds, a staunch proponent of the park's wilderness values, spearheaded an intensive planning effort to use the highway to communicate those "values to visitors."[65] While Reynolds made this statement in order to strengthen his case for funding highway maintenance and improving Park Service facilities, he was also expressing a deeper point of view—that the highway was more than a transportation corridor. He was suggesting that it was an important space within a wild country. As the cultural geographer J. B. Jackson observed, in our contemporary world roads like Highway 20 can "no longer be identified solely with movement from one place to another. . . . Indeed, they have often become for many the last resort for privacy and solitude and contact with nature. Roads no longer merely lead to places; they *are* places."[66]

Conceptually, then, park managers' treatment of Highway 20 advanced the notion of a wilderness threshold as a space that united the wild with the physical features of the roadway. Through education and interpretation, they attempted to construct a set of visitor opportunities by providing "complementary facilities" and services for park visitors at appropriate activity sites. Park managers would literally compose a mental image of the park's wilderness for visitors, using things like waysides at key points along the highway, for example, to explain to visitors the natural history of the park landscape. Because the narrow geography of the Skagit River valley restricted extensive developments for interpretation to the Diablo Lake overlook, park planners looked for other ways to create an impression of this wilderness parkland. They decided to introduce at waysides and other interpretive sites "a representative environment of the North Cascades." They would provide information about, or views of, everything from the self-evident jagged

topography to the less evident diversity of vegetation and the ecological relationships between the different natural systems. Recreational opportunities, such as trails near the highway, would also play a key part in the park
plan. The intended goal was systematically to create an impression of the
wilderness qualities of North Cascades. Yet as the plan acknowledged, any
appreciation and enjoyment visitors experienced in this country would most
likely be brief and "from a distant vantage point."[67]

Ultimately, the distinction between the road and the primal country
beyond seemed to grow less rather than more distinct. True, the highway
was a conduit of travel, conveying visitors to their destinations within the
park complex as well as affording them spectacular scenery, however limited. But the highway took on its own special significance as wilderness space.
By the early 1990s, the agency had modified its earlier goal of removing visitors from the "sensory deprivation" of the automobile; instead vista points,
campgrounds, and trailheads, among other improvements, lined the roadway and catered to auto tourists. These features helped shape the general
public's experience of this mountain country.

Because many tourists never set off on foot into the park, information
about the park would come via different means. One important vehicle was
the North Cascades Visitor Center near Newhalem. Completed in 1993 and
located close to the highway at the western edge of Ross Lake NRA and near
a rare viewpoint of the Pickets, it offered motorists a comprehensive introduction to the park complex. Visitors could tour a small museum, learn of
the natural and cultural history of the North Cascades, and watch a film
about the range's wilderness essence. Although visitor centers were common to national parks, the one at North Cascades was significant because
without it, park officials believed, tourists would have difficulty locating the
park in physical as well as mental space. The film at the visitor center served
this function and acted as another kind of wilderness threshold.

The film, *A Meditation on Wilderness,* bore a strong resemblance to the
first movie proposed for the park at the valley terminal of the Ruby Mountain tram, more than twenty years earlier. The idea behind that film was to
make sense of what people were seeing on a "more abstract and philosophical
level" by concentrating on "man's timeless and often mystical relationship
with mountains, both real and symbolic, as well as his ties with all things
natural." The visitor center's film accomplished this goal, but not without
controversy. It combined traditional American ideas of nature with a New
Age spiritual perspective. It exposed viewers to a montage of industrial pol-

lution in an urban setting—the human world—alienated from nature. At the same time, it underscored the preciousness of the nonhuman world of nature with images (within the park) that included everything from serene forest floors and plant and animal life to serrated edges of snow-crusted peaks set against an ethereal deep blue sky. Viewers with a strong Christian faith disliked the film the most. Perhaps more than the cascading imagery, the soundtrack offended these viewers with its whispering tones of Native American chants and quotations from environmental thinkers, punctuated throughout by the sounds of drumming and meditation bells. In the late 1990s, the Park Service produced another film, *Return to Wildness*, for North Cascades, which considerably toned down the New Age message.[68]

In the end, both films transported visitors to where a road could never take them, into the heart of North Cascades National Park and its primeval mountains. The films also cast a mental image of the park landscape before visitors as they drove.[69] After nearly thirty years of managing North Cascades as a wilderness park, and nearly a century of automobiles bringing people into the wild landscapes of national parks, the Park Service's ability to resolve the presence of automobiles in national parks—even through the medium of film—seemed elusive. Initially, agency officials identified cars as a source of the problem and proposed tramways as an alternative to highways and auto travel. They also decided to limit accommodations for motorists. These proposals, however, met with mixed results. Tramways fell out of favor for environmental, economic, and political reasons. And even though the Park Service prevented the construction of a road to the shores of Ross Lake, it kept other roads open, namely the Cascade River and Stehekin Valley roads, because visitors still expected to see a park from their cars. Ultimately, the agency fell back on traditional rationalizations for park roads by focusing its greatest attention on Highway 20, adding film as a kind of window to a wilderness park, one visitors would never see from a car.

EPILOGUE

Cars have been in national parks for more than a century, and it would be hard to imagine parks, with the exception of Alaska's reserves, without cars. But what does this really tell us? For one thing, it tells us what we already seem to know: that cars dominate the national park experience. Automobiles provide access to parks, ensuring that most Americans can visit places like Yellowstone, Yosemite, and Mount Rainier. Although fulfilling the democratic promise of national parks, cars appear to overwhelm them at times with long lines at entrances, congested roads, and overflowing parking lots and campgrounds. Within parks, cars are in constant motion (sometimes slow motion), reminders of the nation's mobility and consumer culture, as they motor through forests, along rivers, and over mountains. The hum of engine noise and whine of tires on pavement compete with the roar of falling water and wind and most of all with silence. In parks, cars are integral to an ever-changing mosaic of industry and nature.

But having automobiles in parks also tells us something more subtle—that national parks have been spaces, both real and imagined, for machines in nature. We cannot understand parks without recognizing that cars have been central to shaping how people experience and interpret the meaning of national parks, especially how they perceive them as wild places. But there are different ways of telling this story of parks as wilderness. As the historian Paul Sutter so powerfully suggests, cars have altered the genuine "wildness" of national parks, for wilderness, Sutter argues, is intrinsically roadless. With their accommodations for auto tourists and motorized recreation, national parks have lost their original purpose—the preservation of the natural world in its primeval state. The launching of the modern wilderness movement, in fact, traces its origins to the interwar years, when the National Park Service was developing parks for the new motoring masses. Groups such as the Wilderness Society heralded roadlessness as a quality essential to the definition of wilderness and national parks, making parks important alternatives to modern ideas of recreation and leisure, and thus symbols of the significance of wilderness in American life.

The history of Washington's parks, however, suggests another way to tell the story of cars and their influence, one that touches on the experience of many traveling Americans. In this narrative, rather than working to exclude automobiles altogether, park managers and patrons attempted to reconcile cars with nature in these parks. In doing so, they blurred the boundaries between the natural world and modern life, transforming these (and by association all) national parks into windshield wilderness, places where the relationship between automobiles and nature seemed to be mutually beneficial. However hopeful or paradoxical, the notion suggests that national parks are products of this relationship with automobiles and people and that our reactions to cars reveal how ideas of nature, wilderness, and culture are complex and historically contingent. For many motoring Americans, who appreciate wild nature protected in national parks, "wilderness" is something they encounter while driving. To say that cars destroyed the primitive values that national parks were intended to protect, then, overlooks this equally essential meaning of national parks in the twentieth century.

Responses to autos in parks, however, like expectations about nature and the importance of wilderness, have changed over time. At the turn of the century, the arrival of automobiles in national parks like Mount Rainier received a positive response, albeit with a few misgivings about the future of the machine in the garden. The introduction of cars signaled a new way of thinking about and appreciating parks not just within the context of modern life but within the context of the motor age. Auto tourism—getting back to nature in a car—became the most common way of encountering national parks. As automobiles grew more reliable and affordable for middle-class Americans, ownership rose, exposing more people than ever before to these natural wonders. Prior to the advent of the motorcar, touring national parks was primarily an activity for those who had both time and money, mostly eastern elites, to travel to parks by train, stay in hotels, and tour these nature reserves by horse and wagon. After Henry Ford mass produced his Model T in 1910 and roads leading to and through national parks improved, all of this changed. Cars reordered both time and space and made possible an entirely new set of experiences with, and expectations about, national parks and other western landscapes.

Mount Rainier's biggest supporters, the residents of Seattle and Tacoma, expressed this shift well. They viewed Mount Rainier not only as a symbol of their region's and cities' scenic beauty and a source of tourist revenue, but they also thought of the park in terms of their new mobility. Cars brought the park closer to them physically and altered how they thought of it conceptually. City residents endorsed the use of autos in the park and the development of park roads for auto touring largely as economic and recreational enhancements. But they did so in a way that integrated the park into, rather than separated it from, their urban centers. Mount Rainier, in this respect, was part of a larger highway geography in which national parks were connected by roads and cars and thus were extensions of daily life. Moreover, with its early road to Paradise designed to present scenery to those who traveled it, Mount Rainier offered motorists a chance to encounter the natural world in a setting that did not seem affected by their presence. These conditions added to Mount Rainier's popularity and nurtured the belief that it might be possible to harmonize machines and nature within the boundaries of national parks. In the years 1910–1920, such optimism fostered the notion that people could engage wilderness—could know nature—through machines.

These initial reactions to cars in parks matured with the establishment of the National Park Service, which embraced the harmony of autos and nature as one of its basic management principles. Throughout the 1920s and 1930s, the Park Service shaped parks for automobiles and their drivers, creating idealized representations of the natural world in which technology—symbolized by the automobile—could produce something positive: a middle ground between the human and nonhuman worlds. As an enabling technology, the automobile would not overwhelm the garden. Park Service leaders such as Stephen Mather could envision parks this way because they hewed to the principles of nineteenth-century park design. They thought of parks as wilderness reserves that had a human presence. Wilderness was a visual experience made possible or enhanced by automobiles and the roads they traveled.

Although agency leaders developed parks to curry political support in an age of rising consumerism, recreation, and auto tourism, they shared the optimism of early park patrons. They expanded upon knowing nature through machines with highways that were built as a part of the natural world. They relied on landscape architects and engineers to design roads that would conform to the landscape, order scenic views and, through the principles of rustic architecture, would appear anchored in the earth. Landscape architecture brought together both the physical park, as witnessed in its visitor developments, and the park of the imagination, as portrayed on park master plans. In this way, nature and artifice would be difficult to distinguish, and thus the primitive landscapes of national parks could not be seen as spoiled. Rather, parks would seem to be ideal expressions— authentic representations of the natural world—to a mobile audience accustomed to viewing nature through a windshield. Parks and the wild nature they protected were products of human design; they were created for the motor age.

Or so it seemed. A growing coalition of wilderness advocates who believed that parks should preserve unmodified nature, or at least unmechanized nature, challenged the Park Service. In the 1930s, the establishment of Olympic as a roadless wilderness made the agency pay closer attention to these concerns. It forced the agency to focus on the real meaning of national parks, as reservoirs of the primitive, and to protect them from further decline. Even so, Park Service leaders adjusted but did not abandon their earlier management ideal. Roads, whatever one thought of them, had informed the Olympic movement, in part because a drive along Highway 101 exposed tourists and conservationists alike to the peninsula's expanse of old-growth forests; the drive also exposed them to the signs of forest destruction, logged-off lands. Calls for a park to preserve the Olympic country in fact led the Forest Service to counter with its own proposals for transmountain roads through the region, a mistake from which it would not recover. In the 1930s, roads may have influenced the creation of Olympic, but road building in parks, including parkways, had reached its zenith and had become anathema to wilderness preservation. Rather than integrating a road system with the primitive territory of the park, which was the case at Mount Rainier, Park Service managers decided to bring motorists to its edge—for a view of Olympic's wild interior. In doing so, they retained the illusion that cars could enter national parks without defiling them.

Highway 101 played an important role in creating this impression, for it functioned as the "park" road but lay mostly outside the park boundaries. More importantly, the road to Hurricane Ridge distinguished the road system at Olympic from an earlier generation of national parks like Mount Rainier. Designed during the Park Service's Mission 66 program, which held as one of its main tenets wilderness preservation *through* development, the road brought visitors to a vantage point from which they could gaze into the wilderness without driving across it. In keeping with Mission 66 goals, the road established viewing the park as a day-use activity, thereby eliminating the need for new facilities in the park, further advancing the wilderness preservation ideal of the program. Although tourists could gain access, often on dirt or secondary roads, to other areas of Olympic, they traveled only a short distance within the park's boundaries and would not encounter the same panoramic views. In these ways, the Hurricane Ridge Road departed from past practices while still leaving room for autos and roads to influence ideas of parks as wilderness.

In the late 1960s, the establishment of North Cascades, a product of the postwar environmental movement, seemed to be the final stage in literally pushing cars to the margins of park management. Although North Cascades was created with wilderness as its primary mission, Congress had other things in mind. It created a "park complex" of national park units and recreation areas that essentially tried to please everyone, for the legislation prohibited roads and cars in the new park, while allowing them and other traditional park uses in the adjoining recreation areas. Moreover, when given the task of managing North Cascades, the Park Service continued to focus on interpreting the park—which no roads would enter—from the roadside. Over the next thirty years, Park Service leaders explored alternative means of transportation, like tramways, but discovered that while innovative, they were highly problematic and would not replace cars as the main mode of travel in the park. Most likely, agency leaders recognized that the park's primary audience—even at a time when backpacking, mountaineering, and other forms of outdoor recreation were popular—was still people in cars who expected to see the park from their cars. Thus, the agency focused its efforts to convey the wilderness mission of the park along the state highway, Highway 20, running through the park complex. This highway served the majority of park visitors and provided an introduction by automobile to an otherwise wild and impenetrable mountain country few would ever see.

The story of cars and parks in Washington shares one important similarity with all national parks: cars have been central to our understanding of national parks as wild places. At the turn of the twenty-first century, however, there is a strong desire to reduce the number of cars in parks, or in some cases to eliminate them altogether. After another round of public criticism and introspection, the Park Service has again recommitted itself to protecting the natural values of parks. Cars, not people, are the parks' greatest problem. As a result, the Park Service has raised park entrance fees to maintain park roads and other facilities used by cars. The agency has also explored alternative means of transportation to and into national parks in an attempt to curb the use of cars. In some parks, such as Yosemite, public transit has been in place for years in an effort to reduce the pressure of privately owned autos in the valley. There are also proposals to close roads and force tourists to leave their cars at the edge of the park and get on the bus and, as in the case of Grand Canyon, possibly light rail. Already two national parks—Acadia and Zion, both formerly beset by traffic gridlock—can claim to be practically "carless."[1]

Not all parks, however, lend themselves easily to public transit or transportation restriction, for many, such as Mount Rainier, are closely connected to the nation's web of highways. Roads run through them. Park patrons also may not be so willing to give up their private autos. Or as the current fascination with sport-utility vehicles suggests, people may not be so willing to give up the means of their escape from modern everyday life to a natural world they see as separate. The main theme behind these changes is less an indictment of the role automobiles play in allowing people to visit national parks and more a recognition that there are limits to the amount of use that national parks can withstand.

Park managers are seeking new ways to accommodate cars by determining the "carrying capacity" of parks for machines. Although more than twenty years old, the carrying capacity concept has not been standardized, and has been recently applied to only a handful of parks, because it is an expensive and complicated process. It requires that park managers attempt to determine the social and ecological carrying capacity of national parks, especially those areas within the parks popular with tourists. Managers want to limit the number of autos and people allowed in any given place and at any given time to ensure that visitors enjoy the park to the fullest and that they do not inflict undue damage on the park's natural systems. At Mount Rainier, for example, the Park Service has begun planning for ways to reduce the congestion at Paradise and Sunrise, among other favorite areas, on sunny summer weekends—when 75 percent of the park's nearly 1.5 million annual tourists visit the park. Visitors are drawn to the park from the surrounding region as they always have been: they can see the mountain on a clear day and drive to it in a short period of time.[2]

Perhaps someday the Park Service will close Paradise, or at least restrict the flow of traffic to it. It remains to be seen, however, how Americans will adjust to this kind of change. The agency's attempts to restore some of the natural conditions in Yosemite Valley after the powerful flood of 1997 provide some insights—since Yosemite has long been the park most closely associated with the problems of autos in parks. The Yosemite Valley plan involves, among other things, the removal of several campgrounds in biologically sensitive areas, the expansion of the valley shuttle bus service, and the reduction and centralization of day-use parking. The Park Service saw the flood recovery program as an opportunity to address some long-term issues in the valley, such as the growing problem of automobile congestion and gridlock. Although the higher goals of preserving nature and the national park experience were essential elements of the valley plan— elements endorsed by preservationists—it seemed to many that the Park Service was intent on curbing public access, especially opportunities for camping and auto tourism. Apparently, some feared that unless you were assured of a parking space or had a campground reservation, you would not be able to drive your car into the valley. Although some local community leaders worried about how this would affect tourist revenues, more seemed concerned about being able to "be" in Yosemite. Critics like Allan Abshez, a self-identified "typical Yosemite camper and enthusiast," argued that while the Park Service maintained there would be no net loss in camping in the park, there would be considerable change. "Half of those historically able to experience an overnight stay in the Valley," he concluded, "will be shut out and reduced to the status of 'bus tourists.'"[3]

The conditions affecting the management of Mount Rainier and Yosemite do not necessarily apply to every national park, yet the Park Service's use of the carrying capacity concept and alternative transportation have implications for all parks. These approaches suggest that the attempt to reconcile automobiles and nature in national parks has continued to change. But this change has been about more than separating people from their cars and cars from wild nature. It has also been about the way autos, roads, and wilderness have evolved together in national parks, and thus are deeply entwined with our understanding of parks. Untangling them, as the history of Mount Rainier, Olympic, and North Cascades suggests, can create another set of relationships between automobiles and the natural world. In the end, this story reminds us that cars, like the people who drive them, have a role in shaping how we think of national parks as wilderness reserves, and in the place they all have in nature.

NOTES

INTRODUCTION: NATURE AS WE SEE IT

1. See, for example, Mark Spence, *Dispossessing the Wilderness: Indian Removal and the Making of the National Parks* (New York: Oxford University Press, 1999); Theodore Catton, *Inhabited Wilderness: Indians, Eskimos, and National Parks in Alaska* (Albuquerque: University of New Mexico Press, 1997); William Cronon, "The Trouble with Wilderness; or, Getting Back to the Wrong Nature," in *Uncommon Ground: Toward Reinventing Nature*, William Cronon, ed. (New York: W. W. Norton and Company, 1995), 69–90; Richard White, "'Are You an Environmentalist or Do You Work for a Living?': Work and Nature," in Cronon, *Uncommon Ground*, 171–85; Paul S. Sutter, *Driven Wild: How the Fight Against Automobiles Launched the Modern Wilderness Movement* (Seattle: University of Washington Press, 2002).

2. For the most recent influential critique of the wilderness idea, see Cronon, "The Trouble with Wilderness," 69–90. For challenges to Cronon's views, see *Environmental History* 1 (January 1996): 29–55; the issue contains responses to the essay by Samuel Hays, Thomas Dunlap, and Michael Cohen, along with Cronon's rebuttal. Paul Sutter adds to the debate on the wilderness idea with a perceptive analysis of Aldo Leopold's use of the term "wilderness" to describe a form of preservation; see Sutter, "'A Blank Spot on the Map': Aldo Leopold, Wilderness, and U.S. Forest Service Recreational Policy, 1909–1924," *Western Historical Quarterly* 29 (Summer 1998): 187–214. A more comprehensive treatment of the wilderness idea can be found in J. Baird Callicott and Michael P. Nelson, eds., *The Great New Wilderness Debate* (Athens: University of Georgia Press, 1998). For the views of scholars who question postmodern interpretations of wilderness and nature as "ideas" or "cultural," see

Michael E. Soule and Gary Lease, eds., *Reinventing Nature? Responses to Postmodern Deconstruction* (Washington, D.C.: Island Press, 1995). In addition to Spence, *Dispossessing the Wilderness*, and Catton, *Inhabited Wilderness*, see Karl Jacoby, *Crimes Against Nature: Squatters, Poachers, Thieves, and the Hidden History of American Conservation* (Berkeley: University of California Press, 2001) for an insightful account of the relationship of natives and country people with early national parks.

3. Sutter, *Driven Wild*, 1–53.

4. White, "'Are You an Environmentalist or Do You Work for a Living?'" 183.

5. Spence, *Dispossessing the Wilderness*, 5.

6. For scholars who advance this idea, see, for example, Justin Reich, "Re-Creating the Wilderness: Shaping Narratives and Landscapes in Shenandoah National Park," *Environmental History* 6 (January 2001): 95–112; and James Feldman, "Beyond the Wilderness Boundary: Nature and History at Apostle Islands National Lakeshore," March 18, 2003, essay in author's possession. Feldman, in this and his forthcoming dissertation, suggests the concept of "rewilding" as a way to understand this process. William Cronon touches on this idea as well in his recent essay, "The Riddle of the Apostles," *Orion* (May-June 2003), http://www.oriononline.org/pages/om/03–30m/Cronon.html.

7. Alfred Runte, *National Parks: The American Experience*, 2nd ed., rev. (Lincoln: University of Nebraska Press, 1987); Runte, *Yosemite: The Embattled Wilderness* (Lincoln: University of Nebraska Press, 1990). See also Alston Chase, *Playing God in Yellowstone: The Destruction of America's First National Park* (Boston: Atlantic Monthly Press, 1986).

8. Richard W. Sellars, *Preserving Nature in the National Parks: A History* (New Haven: Yale University Press, 1997). Although Sellars offers an honest and critical portrayal of park management, other scholars have departed from the theme of nature in decline. See, for example, Hal K. Rothman, *Preserving Different Pasts: The American National Monuments* (Urbana: University of Illinois Press, 1989); and more recently, Mark Daniel Barringer, *Selling Yellowstone: Capitalism and the Construction of Nature* (Lawrence: University Press of Kansas, 2002).

9. Two recent studies have enriched our understanding of the built environment of parks and of parks as designed landscapes. See Linda Flint McClelland, *Building the National Parks: Historic Landscape Design and Construction* (Baltimore: Johns Hopkins University Press, 1998); and Ethan Carr, *Wilderness by Design: Landscape Architecture and the National Park Service* (Lincoln: University of Nebraska Press, 1998). The work of cultural geographers also has significant value for thinking of national parks in terms of time and space, interpreting the relationships between people and nature in and around parks (including the spatial organization in and

174   *Notes to Introduction*

around parks), and conceptualizing parks as landscapes both real and imagined: as spaces for humans and nature. See, for example, J. B. Jackson and D. W. Meinig, eds., *The Interpretation of Ordinary Landscapes* (New York: Oxford University Press, 1979); J. B. Jackson, *Discovering the Vernacular Landscape* (New Haven: Yale University Press, 1984); Michael P. Conzen, ed., *The Making of an American Landscape* (Boston: Unwin Hyman, 1990); and Denis E. Cosgrove, *Social Formation and Symbolic Landscape* (1984; Madison: University of Wisconsin Press, 1998).

10. Leo Marx, *The Machine in the Garden: Technology and the Pastoral Ideal in America* (New York: Oxford University Press, 1964); Jennifer Price, *Flight Maps: Adventures with Nature in Modern America* (New York: Basic Books, 1999), 255.

1 / GLACIERS AND GASOLINE: MOUNT RAINIER AS A WINDSHIELD WILDERNESS

1. C. G. Thomson, *The Rim Road—A Wonder Drive* (Portland, OR: Scenic America Company, c. 1924), no pagination.

2. Frederick Law Olmsted, "The Yosemite Valley and the Mariposa Big Trees," reprinted in Lary M. Dilsaver, ed., *America's National Park System: The Critical Documents* (Lanham, MD: Rowman and Littlefield Publishers, Inc., 1994), 22–26; Alfred Runte, *Yosemite: The Embattled Wilderness* (Lincoln: University of Nebraska Press, 1990), 31; Laura Wood Roper, *FLO: A Biography of Frederick Law Olmsted* (Baltimore: Johns Hopkins University Press, 1973), 70, 137–38; Ethan Carr, *Wilderness by Design: Landscape Architecture and the National Park Service* (Lincoln: University of Nebraska Press, 1998), 29; Linda Flint McClelland, *Building the National Parks: Historic Landscape Design and Construction* (Baltimore: Johns Hopkins University Press, 1998), 18–47; Barbara Novak, *Nature and Culture: American Landscape Painting, 1825–1875* (New York: Oxford University Press, 1980); Mary Shivers Culpin, *The History of the Construction of the Road System in Yellowstone National Park, 1872–1966: Historic Resource Volume I* (Denver: National Park Service, 1994), 26–27. David E. Nye, *American Technological Sublime* (Cambridge: MIT Press, 1994), xiii, 70–78, describes the presence of the transcontinental railroad in the western landscape in the late nineteenth century as a dramatic contrast, and I have adapted his observations to illustrate my argument. See also Henri Lefebvre, *The Production of Space*, trans. Donald Nicholson-Smith (Oxford: Blackwell, 1991), 77–78, 94. Lefebvre argues that "space" reflects a set of historical social relationships. This is not to say that the natural forces preserved within the political boundaries of Mount Rainier National Park do not exist outside of human knowledge and experience, but that we conceptualize those forces and the park itself through culture.

3. Alfred Runte, *National Parks: The American Experience*, 2nd ed., rev. (Lincoln: University of Nebraska Press, 1987), 11–47.

4. John Muir, "The Wild Parks and Forest Reservations of the West," *Atlantic Monthly* 81 (January 1898): 26.

5. John A. Millis, "Road into Mount Rainier National Park," in U.S. Army, *Annual Report of the Chief of Engineers, U.S. Army*, Appendix KKK (Washington, D.C.: Government Printing Office, 1904), 4204; Eugene Ricksecker to John Millis, May 14, 1904, box 12, file D30, Mount Rainier National Park Archives, Tahoma Woods, Washington (hereafter MORA Archives).

6. Hiram M. Chittenden, *Yellowstone National Park* (1895; Stanford: Stanford University Press, 1933), 240–43. See also Culpin, *Construction of the Road System in Yellowstone*, 26–53.

7. Ricksecker to Millis, May 14, 1904. Since the road was completed in 1910, the Nisqually Glacier has retreated.

8. Ibid.

9. Ibid.

10. Ibid.

11. Nye, *Technological Sublime*, 76–78.

12. Ricksecker to Millis, May 2, 1903, box 12, file D30, MORA Archives.

13. "Road into Mount Rainier National Park," in *House Doc. No. 283*, 58th Cong., 3rd sess., 1905, 1–9; Ricksecker to Millis, December 26, 1904, box 12, file D30, MORA Archives.

14. Army engineers expressed similar concerns in their plans for the road around the rim of Crater Lake in Crater Lake National Park several years later. Major Jay J. Morrow to Chief of Engineers, December 6, 1911, RG 77, Office of the Chief Engineers, box 406, file CLP 100, National Archives–Pacific Alaska Region.

15. See, for example, John Ise, *Our National Park Policy: A Critical History* (Baltimore: Johns Hopkins University Press, 1961), 123.

16. Major Hiram M. Chittenden to Brigadier General A. Mackenzie, July 30, 1906, box 12, file D30, MORA Archives. For a comprehensive history of the road to Paradise, see Richard H. Quin, "Nisqually Road (Government Road), Mount Rainier National Park," Historic American Engineering Record No. WA-119, Library of Congress, Washington, D.C., 1992, 1–54.

17. "Report of the Superintendent to the Mount Rainier National Park, 1910," in *House Doc. No. 1006, Annual Report of the Secretary of the Interior, 1910*, 61st Cong., 3rd sess., 1910, 507.

18. Visitation statistics can be found in "Report of the Secretary of the Interior, 1917," in Department of the Interior, *Annual Reports of the Department of the Inte-*

rior, 1917, vol. 1 (Washington, D.C.: Government Printing Office, 1918), 79. See also Department of the Interior, *Report of the Director of the National Park Service, 1920* (Washington, D.C.: Government Printing Office, 1920), 350.

19. Warren James Belasco, *Americans on the Road: From Autocamp to Motel, 1910–1945* (Boston: MIT Press, 1979); John A. Jakle, *The Tourist: Travel in Twentieth-Century North America* (Lincoln: University of Nebraska Press, 1985); John A. Jakle, "Landscapes Redesigned for the Automobile," in *The Making of an American Landscape*, Michael P. Conzen, ed. (Boston: Unwin Hyman, Inc., 1990), 293–310; John B. Rae, *The Road and Car in American Life* (Cambridge, MA: MIT Press, 1981); T. J. Jackson Lears, *No Place of Grace: Antimodernism and the Transformation of American Culture, 1880–1920* (New York: Pantheon Books, 1981); T. J. Jackson Lears and Richard W. Fox, eds., *The Culture of Consumption: Critical Essays in American History, 1880–1980* (New York: Pantheon Books, 1983); Hal K. Rothman, *Devil's Bargains: Tourism in the Twentieth-Century American West* (Lawrence: University Press of Kansas, 1998), 50–112; Marguerite S. Shaffer, *See America First: Tourism and National Identity, 1880–1940* (Washington, D.C.: Smithsonian Institution Press, 2001), 263, for quotation.

20. James J. Flink, *The Automobile Age* (Cambridge, MA: MIT Press, 1988), 37–39; Warren James Belasco, "Commercialized Nostalgia: The Origins of the Roadside Strip," in *The Automobile and American Culture*, David L. Lewis and Laurence Goldstein, eds. (Ann Arbor: The University of Michigan Press, 1980), 105–22.

21. Enos A. Mills, "Touring in Our National Parks," *Country Life* 23 (January 1913): 36.

22. Belasco, "Commercialized Nostalgia." For a new interpretation of the introduction and environmental impact of the automobile, see Tom McCarthy, "The Coming Wonder?: Foresight and Early Concerns About the Automobile," *Environmental History* 6 (January 2001): 46–74.

23. Paul S. Sutter, *Driven Wild: How the Fight Against Automobiles Launched the Modern Wilderness Movement* (Seattle: University of Washington Press, 2002), argues that knowing nature through leisure rather than labor characterized the interwar years and the development of the wilderness area as a management ideal.

24. Richard G. Lillard, "The Siege and Conquest of a National Park," *American West* 5 (January 1968): 28–32, 67–72, quotation from 72.

25. Robert Shankland, *Steve Mather of the National Parks*, 2nd ed. (New York: Albert A. Knopf, 1954), 146–47. For more scholarly treatment of autos in parks, see Neil Maher, "Auto Tourism, Wilderness, and the Development of Great Smoky Mountains National Park," in *Making Protection Work: Proceedings of the Ninth Conference on Research and Resource Management in Parks and on Public Lands*, David Harmon,

ed. (Hancock, MI: The George Wright Society, 1997), 47–54. For a standard treatment of automobiles as a political necessity now out of control, see Runte, *National Parks*, 156–61, 167–68, 170–77. Richard W. Sellars, *Preserving Nature in the National Parks: A History* (New Haven: Yale University Press, 1997), provides a broad overview of the ways in which autos and roads have shaped Park Service culture and management.

26. John Jakle refers to roads as containers for automobiles in "Landscapes Redesigned for the Automobile," 293–310.

27. Anne F. Hyde, "From Stagecoach to Packard Twin Six: Yosemite and the Changing Face of Tourism, 1880–1930," *California History* 65 (Summer 1990): 164. See also Shaffer, *See America First*, 133–37, for a broader context for auto tourism; "Report of the Superintendent of the Mount Rainier National Park, 1911," in Department of the Interior, *Annual Reports of the Department of the Interior, 1911*, vol. 1 (Washington, D.C.: Government Printing Office, 1912), 625–27; and Theodore Catton, *Wonderland: An Administrative History of Mount Rainier National Park* (Seattle: National Park Service, 1996), 122.

28. Chester Thorne to Secretary of the Interior, April 8, 1907, RG 79, Entry 1–Records of the Secretary of the Interior, box 38, National Archives, Washington, D.C. (hereafter NA); "Annual Report of the Acting Superintendent of the Mount Rainier National Park, 1908," in Department of the Interior, *Annual Reports of the Secretary of the Interior, 1908* (Washington, D.C.: Government Printing Office, 1908), 477–78; See also Paul Sadin, "Demon, Distraction, or Deliverer?: The Impact of Automobile Tourism on the Development, Management, and Use of Mount Rainier National Park, 1907–1966" (master's thesis, University of Idaho, 2000). In 1908, 117 auto permits were issued and more than 2,800 people visited the park.

29. "Report of the Acting Superintendent of the Mount Rainier National Park [1906]," in *House Doc. No. 5, Annual Report of the Secretary of the Interior*, 59th Cong., 2nd sess., 1906–1907, 679; Department of the Interior, *Annual Reports of the Secretary of the Interior, 1908*, 471.

30. Virginia Scharff, *Taking the Wheel: Women and the Coming of the Motor Age* (New York: Free Press, 1991); Jakle, *The Tourist*; Jakle, "Landscapes Redesigned for the Automobile"; Joseph Interrante, "A Movable Feast: The Automobile and the Spatial Transformation of American Culture, 1890–1940" (PhD diss., Harvard University, 1983); Interrante, "You Can't Go to Town in a Bathtub: Automobile Movement and the Reorganization of Rural American Space, 1900–1930," *Radical History Review* 21 (Fall 1979): 151–68.

31. Department of the Interior, *Proceedings of the National Park Conference Held at Yellowstone, 1911* (Washington, D.C.: Government Printing Office, 1911), 30. Hill's comments, however, anticipated the park-to-park highway dedicated within a decade.

32. See, for example, Runte, *National Parks*, 75, 94; and Runte, "Pragmatic Alliance: Western Railroads and the National Parks," *National Parks and Conservation Magazine* 48 (April 1974): 15–21.

33. James Bryce, "National Parks—The Need and the Future," in *University and Historical Addresses* (New York: Macmillan, 1913), 393–94, 397–401, reprinted in *Mirror of America: Literary Encounters with the National Parks*, David Harmon, ed. (Boulder, CO: Roberts Rinehart, Inc., 1989), 126–27.

34. Department of the Interior, *Proceedings of the National Park Conference Held at Yellowstone, 1911*, 34.

35. Department of the Interior, *Proceedings of the National Park Conference, 1912* (Washington, D.C.: Government Printing Office, 1912), 61. For population statistics, see http://www.census.gov/population/cencounts/ca190090.txt (accessed October 11, 2004).

36. Shankland, *Steve Mather*, 6–7; Lane quoted in Lillard, "Siege and Conquest," 69.

37. Stephen Fox, *John Muir and His Legacy: The American Conservation Movement* (Boston: Little, Brown, and Company, 1981), 139–47; Roderick Nash, *Wilderness and the American Mind*, 3rd ed. (New Haven: Yale University Press, 1982), 161–81. The Hetch Hetchy decision is reprinted in "Report of the Secretary of the Interior, 1913," in Department of the Interior, *Annual Reports of the Department of the Interior, 1913*, vol. 1 (Washington, D.C.: Government Printing Office, 1914), 90–93.

38. Department of the Interior, *Proceedings of the National Park Conference, 1912*, 137–39.

39. Fox, *John Muir and His Legacy*, 127–28, 352; Robert Athearn, *The Mythic West in Twentieth-Century America* (Lawrence: University Press of Kansas, 1986), 196–98. See also William H. Goetzmann and Kay Sloan, *Looking Far North: The Harriman Expedition to Alaska, 1899* (New York: Viking, 1982), and Michael L. Smith, *Pacific Visions: California Scientists and the Environment* (New Haven: Yale University Press, 1987), for insights into the complex social and professional composition of the scientific community around the turn of the twentieth century and how that community influenced perceptions of the natural world and technology. For insights on Muir's debt to Emerson and Transcendentalism, see Leo Marx, *The Machine in the Garden: Technology and the Pastoral Ideal in America* (New York: Oxford University Press, 1964), 227–42, esp. 242.

40. Hyde, "From Stagecoach to Packard Twin Six," 164. This is not to say that the railroads did not play any role in Yosemite's history. The Southern Pacific was somewhat influential in the creation of the park in 1890 and its expansion in 1906. And the Yosemite Valley Railroad, with its terminus at El Portal, brought tourists

closer to the park in 1907. But with the advent of the automobile and better roads, rail traffic declined markedly by the mid-1920s. See Runte, *Yosemite*, 54–55, 120–21.

41. "Report of the Superintendent to the Mount Rainier National Park, 1910," 7–9. Cars brought 4,413 visitors compared to 2,620 who came by stage. See also Theodore Catton, "The Campaign to Establish Mount Rainier National Park, 1893–1899," *Pacific Northwest Quarterly* 88 (Spring 1997): 70–81; and Michael Sullivan, "The Tacoma Eastern Railroad—Linking Puget Sound and Mount Rainier National Park," *Columbia* 13 (Winter 1999–2000): 34–39.

42. Asahel Curtis to Enos Mills, July 3, 1912, Asahel Curtis Papers, box 1, file 23, University of Washington Libraries, Seattle. Note that in the early years of the twentieth century conservationists advocated utilitarian use of natural areas while preservationists wanted to limit human use of those areas; the terms "conservationist" and "preservationist" have shifted over time, becoming more interchangeable.

43. William H. Wilson, *The City Beautiful Movement* (Baltimore: Johns Hopkins University Press, 1989); Arthur D. Martinson, "Mount Rainier or Mount Tacoma? The Controversy that Refused to Die," *Columbia* 3 (Summer 1989): 10–16; Genevieve E. McCoy, "'Call It Mount Tacoma': A History of the Controversy over the Name of Mount Rainier" (master's thesis, University of Washington, 1984); Edward S. Hall to Secretary of the Interior, February 28, 1913, RG 79, entry 6, box 135, file 12–7–2, "Roads, Trails, and Bridges," NA.

44. "Report of the Supervisor of the Yosemite National Park, 1915," and "Report of the Supervisor of the Mount Rainier National Park, 1915," in Department of the Interior, *Annual Reports of the Department of the Interior, 1915*, vol. 1 (Washington, D.C.: Government Printing Office, 1916), 916–19, 963–64, 966–67. Thomas H. Martin, in the "Report of the Rainier National Park Committee of the Tacoma Chamber of Commerce," September 13, 1924, recalled that the California expositions brought considerable numbers of tourists to the region and increased park travel. Records of Mount Rainier National Park, box 7, file D22, MORA Archives.

45. Shankland, *Steve Mather*, 78–79.

46. Rothman, *Devil's Bargains*, 143–67. For an extensive history of Mount Rainier and its relationship with the Puget Sound cities, see Catton, *Wonderland*.

47. Department of the Interior, *Proceedings of the National Park Conference Held at Yellowstone, 1911*, 33.

48. "Favors Road up Mountain," *Spokane Review*, December 7, 1911.

49. Milnor Roberts, "A Wonderland of Glaciers and Snow," *National Geographic* 20 (June 1909): 530, 534.

50. A. Woodruff McCully, "The Rainier Forest Reserve," *The Overland Monthly* 55 (June 1910): 553–54.

51. "Glaciers and Gasoline: Motoring in Mt. Rainier National Park," *Sunset* 28 (January 1912): 41–47.

52. Carpenter Kendall, "Motoring on Mount Rainier," *Sunset* 31 (August 1913): 304–7.

53. Enos A. Mills, "Touring in Our National Parks," *Country Life* 23 (January 1913): 33–36. For a more extensive treatment of urbanites, nature, and parks, see Matthew William Klingle, "Urban by Nature: An Environmental History of Seattle, 1880–1970" (PhD diss., University of Washington, 2001), 164–217.

54. John H. Williams, *The Mountain That Was "God"* (New York: G. P. Putnam's Sons, 1911), 62–64.

55. Asahel Curtis and T. H. Martin to Walter L. Fisher, April 15, 1912, RG 79, entry 6, box 135, file 12–7–2, "Roads, Trails, and Bridges," NA.

56. See, for example, Hal K. Rothman, *On Rims and Ridges: The Los Alamos Area Since 1880* (Lincoln: University of Nebraska Press, 1992), on the relationship between the federal government and private interests in the management of public lands.

57. See, for example, "Mount Rainier National Park," in Department of the Interior, *Annual Reports of the Secretary of the Interior, 1903* (Washington, D.C.: Government Printing Office, 1903), 161–62; "Report of the Acting Superintendent of the Mount Rainier National Park, 1909," in Department of the Interior, *Annual Reports of the Secretary of the Interior, 1909* (Washington, D.C.: Government Printing Office, 1910), 459–60; "Report of the Superintendent of the Mount Rainier National Park, 1911," 623; "Report of the Superintendent of the Mount Rainier National Park, 1912," in Department of the Interior, *Annual Reports of the Department of the Interior, 1912*, vol. 1 (Washington, D.C.: Government Printing Office, 1913), 693–94; and "Report of the Superintendent of the Mount Rainier National Park, 1913," in *Annual Reports of the Department of the Interior, 1913* (Washington, D.C.: Government Printing Office, 1914), 767–69. Of course, park administrators did not stop reporting mountain ascents altogether; the practice continued in later reports, but visitation by auto tourists figured prominently in the reports.

58. "Report of the Superintendent of the Mount Rainier National Park, 1913," 776. In his testimony at the 1915 conference on national parks, Thomas H. Martin described "a great highway crossing from Puget Sound to the southern border of Mount Rainier National Park," and from there to the fruit valleys of Yakima. It would be an unforgettable drive, he noted. In the morning one could drive "through those heights, always with this magnificent dome in sight," and that evening dine in Yakima. Department of the Interior, *Proceedings of the National Park Conference Held at Berkeley, California, March 11, 12, and 13, 1915* (Washington, D.C.: Government Printing Office, 1915), 160.

59. Department of the Interior, *Proceedings of the National Park Conference Held at Yellowstone, 1911*, 34.

60. Francois E. Matthes to Clement S. Ucker, January 6, 1913, RG 79, entry 6, box 135, file 12–7–2, "Roads, Trails, and Bridges," NA.

61. DeWitt L. Reaburn to Stephen T. Mather, November 1, 1915, box 7, file D22, MORA Archives; "Report of the Superintendent of the Mount Rainier National Park, 1916," in Department of the Interior, *Annual Reports of the Department of the Interior, 1916*, vol. 1 (Washington, D.C.: Government Printing Office, 1916), 803.

2 / THE HIGHWAY IN NATURE:
MOUNT RAINIER AND THE NATIONAL PARK SERVICE

1. This is the main argument of Richard W. Sellars in *Preserving Nature in the National Parks: A History* (New Haven: Yale University Press, 1997).

2. Hal K. Rothman, "'A Regular Ding-Dong Fight': Agency Culture and Evolution in the NPS-USFS Dispute, 1916–1937," *Western Historical Quarterly* 20 (May 1989): 141–61; Robert Shankland, *Steve Mather of the National Parks*, 2nd ed. (New York: Alfred A. Knopf, 1954), 83–99.

3. Although much has been written about the National Park Service, Brian Balogh's "Reorganizing the Organizational Synthesis: Federal Professional Relations in Modern America," *Studies in American Political Development* 5 (Spring 1991): 119–47, provides a valuable perspective for understanding the agency within a broader context.

4. Stephen T. Mather, "The National Parks on a Business Basis," *The American Review of Reviews* 51 (April 1915): 429–31.

5. The National Park Service Act can be found in Lary M. Dilsaver, ed., *America's National Park System: The Critical Documents* (Lanham, MD: Rowman and Littlefield Publishers, Inc., 1994), 46–47.

6. Sellars, *Preserving Nature in the National Parks*, 29–33.

7. James J. Flink, *The Automobile Age* (Cambridge, MA: MIT Press, 1988), 37–38; Frederick L. Paxson, "The Highway Movement, 1916–1935," *American Historical Review* 51 (January 1946): 248.

8. "Report of the Secretary of the Interior," in Department of the Interior, *Annual Reports of the Department of the Interior, 1917*, vol. 1 (Washington, D.C.: Government Printing Office, 1918), 80; Department of the Interior, *Report of the Director of the National Park Service, 1929* (Washington, D.C.: Government Printing Office, 1929), 50–52. Mather quotation is from Department of the Interior, *Report of the Director of the National Park Service, 1922* (Washington, D.C.: Government Printing Office, 1922), 15.

9. Paxson, "The Highway Movement," 236–53; John A. Jakle, "Landscapes Redesigned for the Automobile," in *The Making of an American Landscape*, Michael P. Conzen, ed. (Boston: Unwin Hyman, Inc., 1990), 293–97. See also Peirce F. Lewis, "America Between the Wars: The Engineering of a New Geography," in *North America: The Historical Geography of a Changing Continent*, Robert D. Mitchell and Paul A. Groves, eds. (Totowa, NJ: Rowman and Littlefield, 1987), 411–14; and Marguerite S. Shaffer, *See America First: Tourism and National Identity, 1880–1940* (Washington, D.C.: Smithsonian Institution Press, 2001).

10. Charles W. Eliot II, "The Influence of the Automobile on the Design of Park Roads," *Landscape Architecture* 13 (October 1922): 28.

11. For general works on the roadside beauty movement, see John A. Jakle, *The Tourist: Travel in Twentieth-Century North America* (Lincoln: University of Nebraska Press, 1985), 126–33; Warren James Belasco, *Americans on the Road: From Autocamp to Motel, 1910–1945* (Cambridge, MA: MIT Press, 1979), 89–90; and Hans Huth, *Nature and the American: Three Centuries of Changing Attitudes* (Berkeley: University of California Press, 1957), 202. See also "Roadside Improvement—A National Movement Well Under Way," *American City* 41 (May 1929): 100–102.

12. Department of the Interior, *Report of the Director of the National Park Service, 1924* (Washington, D.C.: Government Printing Office, 1924), 14.

13. Paul S. Sutter, *Driven Wild: How the Fight Against Automobiles Launched the Modern Wilderness Movement* (Seattle: University of Washington Press, 2002), provides valuable insights into the reactions against autos in national parks, national forests, and other public lands. Ethan Carr, *Wilderness by Design: Landscape Architecture and the National Park Service* (Lincoln: University of Nebraska Press, 1998), describes how the Park Service and landscape architects attempted to integrate autos and roads with the wilderness settings of national parks.

14. Shankland, *Steve Mather*, 284.

15. Ibid., 9.

16. Stephen T. Mather, *Progress in the Development of the National Parks* (Washington, D.C.: Government Printing Office, 1916), 5; Department of the Interior, *Report of the Director of the National Park Service, 1918* (Washington, D.C.: Government Printing Office, 1918), 60.

17. Shaffer, *See America First*, 127–29.

18. Mather, *Progress in the Development of the National Parks*, 5.

19. Shankland, *Steve Mather*, 78; Department of the Interior, *Report of the Director of the National Park Service, 1920* (Washington, D.C.: Government Printing Office, 1920), 37–40; "The National Park-to-Park Highway Tour," *National Parks Association Bulletin* 12 (October 2, 1920): 1–2. See also Shaffer, *See America First*, 118–19.

20. Department of the Interior, *Report of the Director of the National Park Service, 1920*, 37–38; "Report of the Director of the National Park Service, 1917," in Department of the Interior, *Annual Reports of the Department of the Interior, 1917*, vol. 1 (Washington, D.C.: Government Printing Office, 1918), 802. See also Ronne C. Shelse, "The Pageant Highway," *Mentor* 12 (July 1924): 29–35.

21. "Main Traveled Roads in the Sunset Country," *Sunset* 39 (July 1917): 43, 82.

22. William Charles Bettis, *A Trip to the Pacific Coast by Automobile: Camping All the Way* (Toledo, OH: Booth Typesetting Company, c. 1922), 36.

23. "Report of the Director of the National Park Service, 1917," 800–801, 835; Department of the Interior, *Report of the Director of the National Park Service, 1920*, 42–46; Department of the Interior, *Report of the Director of the National Park Service, 1921* (Washington, D.C.: Government Printing Office, 1921), 48–50; Thomas R. Cox, *The Park Builders: A History of State Parks in the Pacific Northwest* (Seattle: University of Washington Press, 1988), 57–58.

24. Department of the Interior, *Report of the Director of the National Park Service, 1924*, 11–15. In 1927, Congress committed $51 million to continue the program over a ten-year period. See Department of the Interior, *Report of the Director of the National Park Service, 1929*, 31–32.

25. Department of the Interior, *Report of the Director of the National Park Service, 1919* (Washington, D.C.: Government Printing Office, 1919), 81–82. Visitation statistics can be found in the director's annual reports for the years 1917–1930. See also Theodore Catton, *Wonderland: An Administrative History of Mount Rainier National Park* (Seattle: National Park Service, 1996), 220–46.

26. This summary of the agency's views on the circle highway is drawn from Department of the Interior, *Report of the Director of the National Park Service, 1919*, 80–82; and Erwin N. Thompson, *Mount Rainier National Park: Historic Resource Study* (Denver: National Park Service, 1981), 202–204.

27. Department of the Interior, *Report of the Director of the National Park Service, 1919*, 81–82, 215; Stephen T. Mather to Asahel Curtis, February 19, 1921, Asahel Curtis Papers, box 1, file 35, University of Washington Libraries, Seattle (hereafter UW).

28. William H. Peters to Stephen T. Mather, June 9, 1922, box 15, file 61, Mount Rainier National Park Archives, Tahoma Woods, Washington (hereafter MORA Archives). For Tomlinson's views on the road program, see Owen A. Tomlinson to Stephen T. Mather, May 8, 1924, and Owen A. Tomlinson to Stephen T. Mather, August 28, 1924, RG 79, entry 6, box 137, file 12–7, National Archives, Washington, D.C. (hereafter NA); and Owen A. Tomlinson, "Development of Our National Park," *The Mountaineer* 17 (December 1924): 40–43.

29. Tomlinson, "Development of Our National Park," 40–43. See also Tomlinson to Mather, August 28, 1924.

30. Tomlinson to Mather, August 28, 1924.

31. Carr, *Wilderness by Design*, 218–19.

32. For a comprehensive history of road construction at Mount Rainier, see Richard H. Quin, "Mount Rainier National Park Roads and Bridges," Historic American Engineering Record, HAER No. WA-35, Library of Congress, Washington, D.C., 1992.

33. Department of the Interior, *Report of the Director of the National Park Service, 1919*, 81–82; Department of the Interior, *Report of the Director of the National Park Service, 1921*, 24, 77; Department of the Interior, *Report of the Director of the National Park Service, 1924*, 47, 116. See also Richard H. Quin, "Carbon River Road," Historic American Engineering Record, HAER No. WA-120, Library of Congress, Washington, D.C., 1992, 2–5. For a summary of the Carbon River Road's troubled development, see Owen A. Tomlinson to Bert H. Burrell, July 31, 1925, and Bert H. Burrell to Horace M. Albright, August 15, 1925, RG 79, entry 22, box 16, general correspondence file, NA.

34. T. H. Martin to Senator S. H. Piles, February 16, 1921, Curtis Papers, box 1, file 35, UW; Mather to Curtis, February 19, 1921; Department of the Interior, *Report of the Director of the National Park Service, 1921*, 78.

35. See, for example, Department of the Interior, *Report of the Director of the National Park Service, 1924*, 14.

36. Carr, *Wilderness by Design*, 175, 218. See also Tomlinson to Burrell, July 31, 1925; and Burrell to Albright, August 15, 1925.

37. C. R. Short, "Location Survey Report on West Side Highway," c. 1929, RG 79, entry 26, box 3, file: location survey reports, NA. See also Quin, "Mount Rainier National Park Roads and Bridges," 42–43.

38. Sutter, *Driven Wild*, 9–18.

39. Catton, *Wonderland*, 230, 247–60; Shankland, *Steve Mather*, 120–27; Asahel Curtis to Stephen T. Mather, January 4, 1926, Curtis Papers, box 3, file 10, UW; Asahel Curtis to Horace M. Albright, December 20, 1926, Curtis Papers, box 3, file 40, UW.

40. Mather, "National Parks on a Business Basis," 430–31. The Sierra Club is quoted in Alfred Runte, *Yosemite: The Embattled Wilderness* (Lincoln: University of Nebraska Press, 1990), 144.

41. The Mountaineers, "Administration of the National Parks," November 1922, RG 79, entry 22, box 16, file: Administration, NA; J. F. Beede to Rainier National Park Advisory Board, June 21, 1927, Curtis Papers, box 4, file 19, UW.

42. Quotation is from the Mountaineers, "Administration of the National Parks," 4. For descriptions of the various visitor activities at Mount Rainier, see Catton, *Wonderland*, 14, 274–78, 292–98, 304–12.

43. See, for example, the Mountaineers, "Administration of the National Parks."

44. Curtis to Albright, December 20, 1926; Owen A. Tomlinson to Stephen T. Mather, June 11, 1928, RG 79, Central Classified Files, box 382, file 601, pt. 7, NA. The Mountaineers' proposal is quoted in Tomlinson to Mather.

45. "1926 Outline of Park Development," Mount Rainier National Park, attached to Owen A. Tomlinson to Thomas C. Vint, August 19, 1927, RG 79, Central Classified Files, entry 29, file 600, NA; Tomlinson to Mather, June 11, 1928; Arno B. Cammerer to Owen A. Tomlinson, August 18, 1928, RG 79, Central Classified Files, box 382, file 601, pt. 7, NA.

46. Department of the Interior, *Report of the Director of the National Park Service, 1924*, 14. See also Stephen T. Mather, "A Glance Backward at National Park Development," *Nature Magazine* 10 (August 1927): 112–15.

47. Sutter, *Driven Wild*, 20.

48. Roderick Nash, *Wilderness and the American Mind*, 3rd ed. (New Haven: Yale University Press, 1982), 182–87.

49. Paul S. Sutter, "'A Blank Spot on the Map': Aldo Leopold, Wilderness, and U.S. Forest Service Recreational Policy, 1909–1924," *Western Historical Quarterly* 29 (Summer 1998): 187–215. See also Aldo Leopold, "Conserving the Covered Wagon," *Sunset* 54 (March 1925): 21, 56.

50. Arthur E. Demaray to Owen A. Tomlinson, July 19, 1928, and Arno B. Cammerer to Owen A. Tomlinson, August 18, 1928, RG 79, Central Classified Files, box 382, file 601, pt. 7, NA.

51. Information on the tramway can be found in RG 79, Central Classified Files, box 394, file 900.05, NA; information on the Paradise scenic road can be found in RG 79, entry 26, box 3, file: location survey reports, NA. The subjects are also covered in Catton, *Wonderland*, 235–37, 278–80; and Carr, *Wilderness by Design*, 222, 224–25.

52. T. H. Martin to Asahel Curtis, January 17, 1928, Curtis Papers, box 5, file 3, UW; Beede to Rainier National Park Advisory Board, June 21, 1927.

53. Robert Sterling Yard, "Economic Aspects of Our National Park Policy," *The Scientific Monthly* 16 (April 1923): 380–88; [Robert Sterling Yard], "National Parks System to Assume Its Higher Status," *National Parks Bulletin* 45 (October 24, 1925): 1–2; Robert Sterling Yard, "Standards of Our National Parks System," *National Parks Bulletin* 51 (December 1926): 1–4. See also Sutter, *Driven Wild*, 100–141; and John C.

Miles, *Guardians of the Parks: The History of the National Parks and Conservation Association* (Washington, D.C.: Taylor and Francis, 1995).

54. John C. Merriam, "Suggestions Relating to Purpose and Educational Program of Crater Lake National Park, 1929," in *Reports of John C. Merriam on Studies of Educational Problems in National Parks*, Save-the-Redwoods League Collection, box 2, file: John C. Merriam Writings, 1930, Bancroft Library, University of California, Berkeley. see also Department of the Interior, *Report of the Director of the National Park Service, 1930* (Washington, D.C.: Government Printing Office, 1930), 17–22; and Stephen R. Mark, *Preserving the Living Past: John C. Merriam's Legacy in the State and National Parks* (Berkeley: University of California Press, 2005).

55. George Vanderbilt Caesar, "National Parks or City Parks?" *Saturday Evening Post* 200 (October 22, 1927): 54.

56. Asahel Curtis to T. H. Martin, January 3, 1928, Curtis Papers, box 5, file 1, U W. Last quotation is from Caesar, "National Parks or City Parks?" 54.

57. Martin to Curtis, January 17, 1928.

58. Horace M. Albright, "The Everlasting Wilderness," *Saturday Evening Post* 201 (September 29, 1928): 28, 68; Horace M. Albright and Robert Cahn, *The Birth of the National Park Service: The Founding Years, 1913–1933* (Salt Lake City: Howe Brothers, 1985), 202–3.

59. Albright, "Everlasting Wilderness," 68.

60. For Mather's overall views on roads as shaped by professionals such as landscape architects, see Carr, *Wilderness by Design*, and Linda Flint McClelland, *Building the National Parks: Historic Landscape Design and Construction* (Baltimore: Johns Hopkins University Press, 1998). For the Park Service's basic philosophy on park roads and other developments, see Franklin K. Lane to Stephen T. Mather, May 13, 1918, reprinted in Dilsaver, *America's National Park System*, 48–52; Herbert Work, "Statement of National Park Policy," March 11, 1925, reprinted in Dilsaver, *America's National Park System*, 62–65; and National Park Service, Press Release, March 12, 1925, box 15, file D22, MORA Archives.

61. For evolving ideas of nature and science, see Donald Worster, *Nature's Economy: A History of Ecological Ideas*, 2nd ed. (New York: Cambridge University Press, 1994). Landscape architects were actually aware of their influence on natural systems. Landscape architect Frank A. Waugh thought that the "ecology of the roadside" was a fruitful field of study only beginning to take shape in the early 1930s. See his "Ecology of the Roadside," *Landscape Architecture* 21 (January 1931): 81–92. For details on naturalistic design, see McClelland, *Building the National Parks*, 174–87.

One of the most insightful recent studies on the relationship between nature and artifice, which informs my interpretation, is Jennifer Price, *Flight Maps: Adventures with Nature in Modern America* (New York: Basic Books, 1999), 114–24.

62. Henry V. Hubbard and Theadora Kimball, *An Introduction to the Study of Landscape Design* (1917; New York: Macmillan Co., 1924), 219–20, quoted in McClelland, *Building the National Parks*, 183–85. For other treatments of landscape design on public lands, see Frank A. Waugh, *Recreation Uses on the National Forests* (Washington, D.C.: Government Printing Office, 1918).

63. See McClelland, *Building the National Parks*, esp. 195–233, for the details of road design, construction, and treatment. Quotations from 201, 1, 4, respectively.

64. Albert H. Good, ed., *Park and Recreation Structures*, 3 vols. (Washington, D.C.: National Park Service, 1938; repr., Boulder, CO: Graybooks, 1990), 5. The first volume, which was later expanded to three, was titled *Park Structures and Facilities*.

65. Carr, *Wilderness by Design*, 1–9.

66. Albright, "Everlasting Wilderness," 63.

67. Department of the Interior, *Report of the Director of the National Park Service, 1925* (Washington, D.C.: Government Printing Office, 1925), 33, 102. For a detailed history of the Nisqually Road renovation, see Richard H. Quin, "Nisqually Road," Historic American Engineering Record, HAER No. WA-119, Library of Congress, Washington, D.C., 1992, 17–27. Tomlinson is quoted in Quin, "Nisqually Road," 24; Albright quote is from Horace M. Albright to Arno B. Cammerer and Arthur E. Demaray, July 24, 1930, RG 79, Central Classified Files, box 380, file 204–020, pt. 1, NA.

68. General design details for this and other roads are covered in McClelland, *Building the National Parks*, 195–233. Insights into the actual design can be found in the resident landscape architect reports for Mount Rainier. See, for example, RG 79, Resident Landscape Architect Reports, 1927–1940, box 10, file: Mount Rainier 1927, and file: Mount Rainier 1929, National Archives–Pacific Sierra Region, San Bruno, California (hereafter NA-PSR).

69. E. A. Davidson, "Landscape Work in Connection with the Development of the Yakima Park Area, Including the Approach Highway within Mt. Rainier National Park," A Report to Thomas C. Vint, Chief Landscape Architect, c. 1932, no pagination, administrative files, National Park Service, Pacific West Regional Office, Seattle, Washington. Davidson summarizes the project's history, incorporating direct quotations from correspondence and completion reports related to the road's construction and design. All quotations in this paragraph are drawn from Davidson's report. Evidence for Tomlinson's support of the project can be found in Tomlinson, "Development of Our National Park," 40–43; Mount Rainier's "1926 Outline

of Park Development"; and Department of the Interior, *Report of the Director of the National Park Service, 1929*, 114–15.

70. Quotations from Davidson, "Landscape Work in Connection with the Development of the Yakima Park Area," no pagination. For further insight into the road's construction, see E. A. Davidson, Report to Chief Landscape Architect, October 10 to November 15, 1929, RG 79, Resident Landscape Architect Reports, box 10, file: Mount Rainier 1929, NA-PSR. McClelland, *Building the National Parks*, 314–18, discusses the significance of the road and its design innovations. The new landscape protection specifications are mentioned in Department of the Interior, *Report of the Director of the National Park Service, 1929*, 164–65.

71. Horace Albright, "General Planning," draft memorandum, February 1929, RG 79, entry 17, NA, cited in Carr, *Wilderness by Design*, 226.

72. Ibid.; Department of the Interior, *Report of the Director of the National Park Service, 1929*, 163.

73. Ernest A. Davidson to Thomas C. Vint, October 8, 1929, and Horace M. Albright to Owen A. Tomlinson, May 21, 1931, Preston Macy Papers, box 1, file 1, UW; Albright to Cammerer and Demaray, July 24, 1930.

74. Carr, *Wilderness by Design*, 240, 227–47. I am indebted to Ethan Carr's treatment of the evolution of master planning as well as landscape architecture in the national parks. See also Henry V. Hubbard, "Landscape Development Based on Conservation, as Practiced in the National Park Service," *Landscape Architecture* 29 (April 1939): 108–9; and Thomas C. Vint, *National Park Service Master Plans* (Washington, D.C.: American Planning and Civic Association, 1946; reprinted in *American Planning and Civic Comment*, April–June 1946).

75. Horace M. Albright to Owen A. Tomlinson, July 16, 1929, RG 79, Central Classified Files, box 380, file 204–020, pt. 1, NA; National Park Service, "Master Plan for Mount Rainier National Park, 1931," Master Plans, 1931–1965, MORA Archives. The term "master plan" was not adopted officially until 1932. Until then, plans were referred to as development outlines.

76. Albright to Tomlinson, July 16, 1929.

77. Department of the Interior, *Report of the Director of the National Park Service, 1926* (Washington, D.C.: Government Printing Office, 1926), 109; Department of the Interior, *Report of the Director of the National Park Service, 1930*, 7–8, 129, 136.

78. Robert N. McIntyre, "Chronological History of the Mather Memorial Parkway," September 12, 1952, file D30, MORA Archives; Lilian Gustin McEwan, "The Mather Memorial Parkway," typescript, c. 1939, Washington State Conservation Society, box 6, file 4, UW.

79. National Park Service, "Master Plan for Mount Rainier National Park, 1931."

80. See, for example, Catton, *Wonderland,* 499–502.

81. For accounts of the West Side Road's history see Catton, *Wonderland,* 504–5, 597–98; and Quin, "Mount Rainier National Park Roads and Bridges," 42–43. Davidson is quoted in Quin, 43.

82. See, for example, Thomas C. Vint, "Wilderness Areas: Development of National Parks for Conservation," in *American Planning and Civic Annual,* Harlean James, ed. (Washington, D.C.: American Planning and Civic Association, 1938), 69–71. Planners employed a number of terms to convey restricted use of parklands, such as "sacred area" and "research area," along with "wilderness area." See Carr, *Wilderness by Design,* 241–42.

3 / WILDERNESS WITH A VIEW:
OLYMPIC AND THE NEW ROADLESS PARK

1. Thomas Wolfe to Elizabeth Nowell, June 15, 1938, in *Selected Letters of Thomas Wolfe,* Elizabeth Nowell, ed. (London: Heinemann, 1958), 304–5.

2. Thomas Wolfe, *A Western Journal: A Daily Log of the Great Parks Trip, June 20–July 2, 1938* (Pittsburgh: University of Pittsburgh Press, 1951), 61–62, 5.

3. Robert Marshall to Irving M. Clark, March 19, 1935, Irving M. Clark Papers, box 1, file 40, University of Washington Libraries, Seattle (hereafter UW); "Mr. Ickes—Your National Parks," *National Parks Bulletin* 13 (December 1937): 3–4.

4. James J. Flink, *The Automobile Age* (Cambridge, MA: The MIT Press, 1988), 131; John Ise, *Our National Park Policy: A Critical History* (Baltimore: Johns Hopkins Press, 1961), 429. See also Marguerite S. Shaffer, *See America First: Tourism and National Identity, 1880–1940* (Washington, D.C.: Smithsonian Institution Press, 2001), 311–20, for the transformation of tourism in the years leading up to and after the postwar era with the rise of mass tourism and the emphasis shift from cultural to recreational experience.

5. Alfred Runte, *National Parks: The American Experience,* 2nd ed., rev. (Lincoln: University of Nebraska Press, 1987), 116–17, 130–40.

6. Elmo R. Richardson, "Olympic National Park: Twenty Years of Controversy," *Forest History* 12 (April 1968): 7, 12.

7. Donald C. Swain, "The National Park Service and the New Deal, 1933–1940," *Pacific Historical Review* 41 (August 1972): 312–32; Donald C. Swain, *Wilderness Defender: Horace M. Albright and Conservation* (Chicago: University of Chicago Press, 1970), 205. See also Conrad L. Wirth's autobiography, *Parks, Politics, and the People* (Norman: University of Oklahoma Press, 1980) for his involvement in the Park Ser-

Notes to Chapter 3

vice's New Deal programs and his role later as director of the agency. For a study with more national scope, see Phoebe Cutler, *The Public Landscape of the New Deal* (New Haven: Yale University Press, 1985).

8. Neil Maher, "Auto Tourism, Wilderness, and the Development of Great Smoky Mountains National Park," in *Making Protection Work: Proceedings of the 9th Conference on Research and Resource Management in Parks and on Public Lands*, David Harmon, ed. (Hancock, MI: The George Wright Society, 1997), 48–50; Linda Flint McClelland, *Building the National Parks: Historic Landscape Design and Construction* (Baltimore: Johns Hopkins University Press, 1998), 229–30, 378–79.

9. Paul S. Sutter, *Driven Wild: How the Fight Against Automobiles Launched the Modern Wilderness Movement* (Seattle: University of Washington Press, 2002); James M. Glover, "Romance, Recreation, and Wilderness: Influences on the Life and Work of Bob Marshall," *Environmental History Review* 14 (Winter 1990): 34; Robert Marshall to Irving M. Clark, December 27, 1935, Clark Papers, box 1, file 40, UW.

10. Timothy Mark Davis, "Mount Vernon Memorial Highway: Changing Conceptions of an American Commemorative Landscape," in *Places of Commemoration: Search for Identity and Landscape Design*, Joachim Wolschke-Bulmahn, ed. (Washington, D.C.: Dumbarton Oaks, 2001), 161; Timothy Mark Davis, "Mount Vernon Memorial Parkway and the Evolution of the American Parkway" (PhD diss., University of Texas at Austin, 1997), 665–72; Robert Marshall to Laurie D. Cox, January 20, 1938, RG 95, entry 86, box 66, file: U-Recreation Areas, Primitive 1936–1939, National Archives, Washington, D.C. (hereafter NA).

11. William P. Wharton, "The National Primeval Parks," *National Parks Bulletin* 13 (February 1937): 3–5; Swain, "National Park Service and the New Deal," 327–28.

12. Richard W. Sellars, *Preserving Nature in the National Parks* (New Haven: Yale University Press, 1997), 91–93. For a specific example, featuring the modernization of Tioga Pass Road in Yosemite, see R. L. McKown to George M. Wright, October 8, 1935, RG 79, entry 35, NA.

13. Davidson opposed the completion of the West Side Road in Mount Rainier. See, for example, Richard H. Quin, "Mount Rainier National Park Roads and Bridges," Historic American Engineering Record, HAER No. WA-35, Library of Congress, Washington, D.C., 1992, 43.

14. *New York Times*, May 14, 1933, quoted in Swain, "National Park Service and the New Deal," 330.

15. T. H. Watkin, *Righteous Pilgrim: The Life and Times of Harold L. Ickes, 1874–1952* (New York: Henry Holt and Company, Inc., 1990), 469–72, quotation from 469; Glover, "Romance, Recreation, and Wilderness," 35; Harold L. Ickes, "Please Save

Great Smoky," *The Living Wilderness* 2 (November 1936): 6; Maher, "Auto Tourism, Wilderness, and the Development of Great Smoky," 51; Sutter, *Driven Wild*, 231–34.

16. Ickes often participated in settling ongoing disputes within the agency about the location of, and proposals for, roads. See Theodore Catton, *Wonderland: An Administrative History of Mount Rainier National Park* (Seattle: National Park Service, 1996); Frank A. Kittredge to Director, October 18, 1929, and Horace M. Albright to Solinsky, August 9, 1933, history files, Crater Lake National Park Archives, Crater Lake, Oregon.

17. Swain, "The National Park Service and the New Deal," 319–20, 330; Ben W. Twight, *Organizational Values and Political Power: The Forest Service versus the Olympic National Park* (University Park: Pennsylvania State University Press, 1983).

18. See, for example, Irving Brant, *Adventures in Conservation with Franklin D. Roosevelt* (Flagstaff, AZ: Northland Publishing, 1988); Richardson, "Twenty Years of Controversy"; and Carsten Lien, *Olympic Battleground: The Power Politics of Timber Preservation* (San Francisco: Sierra Club Books, 1991).

19. National Park Service, "The Master Plan: Olympic National Park—Washington," c. October 1938, 1, 3–4, RG 79, Central Site Files—Olympic National Park, 1927–1953, box 129, file 600 (Master Plan, 1939), National Archives–Pacific Sierra Region , San Bruno, California (hereafter NA-PSR).

20. National Park Service, "The Master Plan: Olympic National Park," 5.

21. Harold Ickes's Seattle address of August 26, 1938, is reprinted in "'Keep It a Wilderness'—Ickes," *National Parks Bulletin* 14 (December 1938): 9–13, 29.

22. Arno B. Cammerer, "Standards and Policies in National Parks," in *American Planning and Civic Annual*, Harlean James, ed. (Washington, D.C.: American Planning and Civic Association, 1936), 17–19.

23. Ibid., 19.

24. Ibid., 19–20.

25. Thomas C. Vint, "Wilderness Areas: Development of National Parks for Conservation," in *American Planning and Civic Annual, 1938*, Harlean James, ed. (Washington, D.C.: American Planning and Civic Association, 1938), 69. See also Ethan Carr, *Wilderness by Design: Landscape Architecture and the National Park Service* (Lincoln: University of Nebraska Press, 1998), 242. The Copeland Report, authored by Robert Marshall, was a report to Congress officially titled *A National Plan for American Forestry*.

26. Vint, "Wilderness Areas," 70–71.

27. McClelland, *Building the National Parks*, 230; Carr, *Wilderness by Design*, 184–86; Henry V. Hubbard, "Landscape Development Based on Conservation as Practiced in the National Park Service," *Landscape Architecture* 29 (April 1939): 108.

28. Horace M. Albright, "Memorandum for the Secretary," July 17, 1933, quoted in Carr, *Wilderness by Design*, 186.

29. Irving Brant, *The Proposed Olympic National Park* (Emergency Conservation Committee Publication No. 35, April 1934), 2–3, RG 95, National Archives–Pacific Alaska Region, Seattle (hereafter NA-PAR). The Emergency Conservation Committee generated numerous publications in defense of the Olympics, among other conservation issues. A copy of this pamphlet is in RG 95, Olympic National Forest, box 99759, file: LP, Boundaries Olympic National Park, Pamphlets and Magazines, NA-PAR.

30. Rosalie Edge, *Roads and More Roads in the National Parks and National Forests* (Emergency Conservation Committee Publication No. 54, March 1936), 6–7, Rosalie Edge Papers, box 21, file 36, Denver Public Library, Colorado. For an early statement about the Forest Service's view of recreation, see Henry S. Graves, "Memorandum on Mount Olympus National Monument," January 20, 1915, RG 95, box 99759, file: L, Boundaries, Olympic, Mount Olympus National Monument, 1905–1916, NA-PAR.

31. P. S. Lovejoy to Forest Supervisor, December 22, 1911, Henry S. Graves to District Forester, January 7, 1916, and D. F. Houston to A. F. Lever, December 20, 1916, RG 95, box 99759, file: L, Boundaries, Olympic, Mount Olympus National Monument, 1905–1916, NA-PAR.

32. B. F. Beezley, "Report of Investigation to Determine Eligibility of Dosewallips–East Fork Route and North Fork Elwha Routes for Classification as Forest Highways" (Bureau of Public Roads, September 1926), 4–5.

33. Fred W. Cleator, "Report on Olympic National Forest Recreation Plan," June 10, 1929, in *Recreation Atlas: Olympic National Forest*, Olympic National Forest Headquarters, Olympia, Washington.

34. Robert Sterling Yard, "The Third Greatest American Tree," *The Living Wilderness* 2 (November 1936): 4–5; W. H. Horning, "Proposed Mount Olympus National Park," *The National Parks Bulletin* 13 (February 1937): 9; Fred W. Cleator, "Report on Olympic Primitive Area," April 10, 1936, p. 10, RG 95, box G-1, file: U Classification, Olympic Primitive Area, NA-PAR. Figures for the primitive area's size can be found in Acting Chief, Forest Service, "Proposed Mount Olympus National Park, State of Washington" [comments on H.R. 4724, 75th Cong.], May 17, 1937, RG 95, Olympic National Forest, box 99758, file: National Monument Correspondence, 1937, NA-PAR.

35. Cleator, "Report on Olympic Primitive Area," 10.

36. Yard, "Third Greatest American Tree," 5; Horning, "Proposed Mount Olympus National Park," 9–10; H. L. Plumb to Regional Forester, July 17, 1934, RG 95, Olympic National Forest, box 99758, file: L, Boundaries, Olympic, Mt. Olym-

pus National Monument, 1932–1934, NA-PAR; Olympic Peninsula Development League, "Resolution," May 25, 1935, RG 95, Olympic National Forest, box 99758, file 5, NA-PAR.

37. Cleator, "Report on Olympic Primitive Area," 10; Acting Chief, Forest Service, "Proposed Mount Olympus National Park, State of Washington"; Henry A. Wallace to Rene L. DeRouen, August 13, 1937, RG 95, Olympic National Forest, box 99758, file: National Monument Correspondence, 1937, NA-PAR.

38. Rosalie Edge, "Roads and More Roads," 3; Willard Van Name to Irving M. Clark, June 5, 1934, Clark Papers, box 1, file 22, UW.

39. Van Name to Clark, June 5, 1934.

40. Van Name to Clark, June 5, 1934. Van Name was responding to Clark's desire to urge protection of the Olympics using the definition of wilderness as roadless and untouched by motorized transportation as written by Marshall in the 1933 Copeland Report.

41. For these and other themes in the history of the Olympic Peninsula and what is now Olympic National Park, see Gail Evans, *Historic Resource Study: Olympic National Park* (Seattle: National Park Service, 1983), 247–315.

42. Harry F. Guiles, *Beauties in the State of Washington: A Book for Tourists* (Olympia: F. M. Lamborn, Public Printer, 1921), 81–89; "The Last Wilderness . . . A *Post-Intelligencer* Motorlogue," *Seattle Post-Intelligencer*, December 7, 1924; "Peninsula Road to Unfold New Scenic Wonders," *Seattle Times*, July 26, 1931; "Olympic Wilds Beckoning Many Northwest Tourists," *Seattle Times*, May 17, 1938; Walter A. Averill, "Building a Highway Across the West Slope of the Olympic Peninsula," *Pacific Builder and Engineer* 37 (August 1, 1931): 24–31.

43. Phil S. Locke to Henry S. Graves, October 9, 1914, RG 95, Olympic National Forest, box 99759, file: L, Boundaries, Olympic, Mount Olympus National Monument, 1905–1916, NA-PAR. See also William B. Greeley, "Recreation in the National Forests," in *Picturesque America: An Illustrated Volume with Descriptive Text*, John F. Kane, ed. (New York: Union Library Association, 1925), 33–41.

44. Irving M. Clark, "Roadside Improvement," c. 1940, Washington State Planning Council Records, box 88, file 9, Washington State Archives, Olympia; Arno B. Cammerer to Ferdinand A. Silcox, July 15, 1935, and Ferdinand A. Silcox to Arno B. Cammerer, October 18, 1935, RG 95, entry 86, file: U-Recreation, NA; Acting Chief Forester to Regional Forester, March 18, 1936, RG 95, Olympic National Park, box G-1, file: U Classification, Olympic Primitive Area, NA-PAR.

45. Emergency Conservation Committee, "Proposed Olympic National Park," 4–5. See also the Mountaineers, Inc., and the Washington Alpine Club, "Mount Olympus National Park: A Consideration of the Objections to Its Establishment,"

c. 1936, RG 95, Olympic National Forest, box 99759, file: LP, Boundaries, Olympic National Park, Pamphlets, Magazines, NA-PAR; and Margaret Thompson, "A Real or a Sham Park in the Olympic Peninsula?" *Skylines: Bulletin of the Northwest Conservation League* 2 (January 1937): 13.

46. Brant, *Adventures in Conservation with Franklin D. Roosevelt*, 91.

47. C. J. Buck to Chief, Forest Service, November 13, 1937, and Ferdinand A. Silcox to Regional Forester, November 22, 1937 (see attached anonymous letter), RG 95, Olympic National Forest, box 99758, file: National Monument Correspondence, 1937, NA-PAR. See also Lien, *Olympic Battleground*, 177–78.

48. Fred J. Overly to Acting Superintendent, Olympic National Park, November 8, 1938, RG 79, Central Sites Files, Olympic National Park, 1927–1953, box 129, file 600 (1939), NA-PSR.

49. Preston Macy to Regional Director, March 15, 1939, RG 79, Central Sites Files, Olympic National Park, 1927–1953, box 129, file 600 (1939), NA-PSR.

50. E. Lowell Sumner Jr. to Regional Director, April 26, 1939, RG 79, Central Sites Files, Olympic National Park, 1927–1953, box 129, file 600, pt. 2, NA-PSR.

51. Frank Kittredge to Arthur Blake, January 5, 1939, RG 79, Central Sites Files, Olympic National Park, 1927–1953, box 129, file 600, pt. 2, NA-PSR; Regional Director to Director, October 23, 1939, RG 79, Central Sites Files, Olympic National Park, 1927–1953, box 140, file 630, pt. 1, NA-PSR.

52. Kittredge to Blake, January 5, 1939.

53. Arthur E. Demaray to Regional Director, June 26, 1940, RG 79, Olympic National Park—Land Acquisition Files, 1938–1953, box 8, file 630, NA-PSR.

54. Davis, "Mount Vernon Memorial Parkway and the Evolution of the American Parkway," 702–7; Thomas C. Vint to Director, December 14, 1944, RG 79, Olympic National Park—Land Acquisition Files, 1938–1953, box 2, file 600, NA-PSR.

55. Preston P. Macy to Regional Director, December 10, 1943, and Hillory A. Tolson to Chief Counsel Moskey and Chief of Lands Wirth, January 17, 1944, RG 79, Olympic National Park—Land Acquisition Files, 1938–1953, box 8, file 630, NA-PSR; Ise, *Our National Park Policy*, 391–92.

56. Fred J. Overly to Regional Director, January 11, 1946, RG 79, Central Sites Files, Olympic National Park, 1927–1953, box 140, file 630, pt. 4, NA-PSR; "Skiers Discuss Park Development with Rep. Jackson," *Port Angeles Evening News*, November 23, 1948.

57. Preston P. Macy to Regional Director, December 8, 1948, RG 79, Central Sites Files, Olympic National Park, 1927–1953, box 130, file 600, pt. 6, NA-PSR; Arthur E. Demaray to F. W. Mathias, May 21, 1935, RG 95, Olympic National Forest, box 99758, file: Boundaries, Olympic National Park, NA-PAR.

58. Arthur Garrett to Henry M. Jackson, February 16, 1949, and Preston Macy

to Regional Director, February 28, 1949, RG 79, Central Sites Files, Olympic National Park, 1927–1953, box 130, file 600, pt. 7, NA-PSR. See also W. C. Struble, "Preliminary Investigation Report, Olympic National Park: Staircase–Graves Creek Road," September 1949, RG 79, Central Sites Files, Olympic National Park, 1927–1953, box 130, file 600-01, NA-PSR.

59. Struble, "Preliminary Investigation Report."

60. Preston P. Macy to Regional Director, March 22, 1949, George Welch to Owen A. Tomlinson, March 24, 1949, Owen A. Tomlinson to Arthur Garrett, March 25, 1949, and Owen A. Tomlinson to Director, March 25, 1949, RG 79, Central Sites Files, Olympic National Park, 1927–1953, box 130, file 600, pt. 7, NA-PSR.

61. Newton B. Drury to Regional Director, April 12, 1949, and Ben H. Thompson to Director, September 8, 1949, RG 79, Central Sites Files, Olympic National Park, 1927–1953, box 130, file 600, pt. 7, NA-PSR; Gunnar O. Fagerlund to Superintendent Preston Macy, May 8, 1950, and Arthur E. Demaray to Regional Director, July 25, 1950, RG 79, Central Sites Files, Olympic National Park, 1927–1953, box 141, file 630, pt. 6, NA-PSR.

62. Demaray to Regional Director, July 25, 1950; Fagerlund to Macy, May 8, 1950.

63. Owen A. Tomlinson to Director, June 26, 1950, and Preston Macy to Regional Director, May 24, 1950, RG 79, Central Sites Files, Olympic National Park, 1927–1953, box 141, file 630, pt. 6, NA-PSR.

64. Macy to Regional Director, May 24, 1950.

65. Conrad L. Wirth to Jack Westland, February 17, 1953, RG 79, Central Sites Files, Olympic National Park, 1927–1953, box 141, file 630, NA-PSR. For the Mission 66 program and a personal account of his role, see Conrad L. Wirth, *Parks, Politics, and the People*, 237–84. For a more probing analysis, see Ronald A. Foresta, *America's National Parks and Their Keepers* (Washington, D.C.: Resources for the Future, Inc., 1984), 52–57.

66. Richard M. Leonard to Conrad Wirth, April 5, 1955, and Thomas J. Allen to Richard M. Leonard, c. May 1958, RG 79, Olympic National Park, 1954–1962, box 5, file D-30, NA-PAR.

67. Leonard to Wirth, April 5, 1955.

68. National Park Service, "Olympic National Park, Mission 66 Prospectus," May 11, 1956, pp. 2–4, 80–81, and National Park Service, "Mission 66 for Olympic National Park," February 20, 1957, pp. 1, 3, 7–8, 10, RG 79, Olympic National Park, 1954–1963, box 4, file A98, pt. 1, NA-PAR.

69. Ibid.

70. Eivind T. Scoyen to James E. Murray, August 7, 1956, RG 79, Olympic National Park, 1954–1963, box 5, file D30, pt. 1, NA-PAR.

71. Fred M. Packard to Russell B. Long, April 20, 1956, R G 79, Olympic National Park, 1954–1963, box 4, file A98, pt. 3, N A - P A R.

72. In the early 1950s, the battle to protect Echo Park in Dinosaur National Monument from a dam project rejuvenated the wilderness campaign of the previous generation. It contributed to the decade-long legislative odyssey that produced the 1964 Wilderness Act, which would classify "wilderness" for all public lands as roadless.

73. National Park Service, *The National Park Wilderness* (Washington, D.C.: National Park Service, 1957). These quotations are drawn from an earlier edition of the brochure written by Howard R. Stagner, entitled "Preservation of Natural and Wilderness Values in the National Parks," 2, March 1957, R G 79, Olympic National Park, 1954–1963, box 4, file A98, pt. 1, N A - P A R. This version varies little from the final, published version.

74. Howard Stagner, "Preservation of Natural and Wilderness Values," 3.

75. Ibid.

76. Ibid., 10.

77. Ibid., 20–21.

78. Olympic National Park, "Special Report on Summer Use of Hurricane Ridge," November 1959, 2–7, R G 79, Olympic National Park, 1954–1963, box 13, file D18, N A - P A R.

79. Ibid., 2, 4.

80. Ibid., 10–12, 14; National Park Service, "Mission 66 Edition Master Plan for Olympic National Park," May 19, 1961, 11, R G 79, Olympic National Park, 1954–1963, box 15, file D18, N A - P A R.

4 / A ROAD RUNS THROUGH IT:
A WILDERNESS PARK FOR THE NORTH CASCADES

1. Jack Kerouac, *The Dharma Bums* (1958; New York: Penguin Books, 1980), 222.

2. Samuel P. Hays, *Beauty, Health, and Permanence: Environmental Politics in the United States, 1955–1985* (New York: Cambridge University Press, 1987), 2–5, 13, 22–24, 34–35; Mark W. T. Harvey, *A Symbol of Wilderness: Echo Park and the American Conservation Movement* (Albuquerque: University of New Mexico Press, 1994).

3. Hal K. Rothman, *Saving the Planet: The American Response to the Environment in the Twentieth Century* (Chicago: Ivan R. Dee, 2000), 131–57; Adam Rome, "'Give Earth a Chance': The Environmental Movement and the Sixties," *Journal of American History* 92 (September 2003): 525–54.

4. The quotation is from the caption of a photo of Glacier Peak accompanying

the article "Will We Discover the Northern Cascades in Time?" *Sierra Club Bulletin* 42 (June 1957): 13–16.

5. Grant McConnell, "The Cascades Wilderness," *Sierra Club Bulletin* 41 (November 1956): 24.

6. Stephen Fox, *John Muir and His Legacy: The American Conservation Movement* (Boston: Little, Brown and Company, 1981), 206–12.

7. [Robert Marshall], "Three Great Western Wildernesses," *The Living Wilderness* 1 (September 1935): 10. Marshall contributed this piece anonymously.

8. Keith A. Murray, "Building a Wagon Road Through the Northern Cascade Mountains," *Pacific Northwest Quarterly* 56 (April 1965): 49–56; [Marshall], "Three Great Western Wildernesses," 10–11.

9. Robert Marshall, "The Problem of the Wilderness," *The Scientific Monthly* 30 (February 1930): 141–43, quotation from 141. See also Paul S. Sutter, *Driven Wild: How the Fight Against Automobiles Launched the Modern Wilderness Movement* (Seattle: University of Washington Press, 2002), 206–7.

10. This is not to say that Marshall did not value as wilderness those lands modified or inhabited by native peoples. See, for example, Marshall's conception of Alaska wilderness in Theodore Catton, *Inhabited Wilderness: Indians, Eskimos, and National Parks in Alaska* (Albuquerque: University of New Mexico Press, 1997), 133–56.

11. William Cronon, "The Trouble with Wilderness; or, Getting Back to the Wrong Nature," in *Uncommon Ground: Toward Reinventing Nature*, William Cronon, ed. (New York: W. W. Norton and Company, 1995), 78–80, quotation from 78.

12. Robert Marshall to Irving M. Clark, November 12, 1938, RG 95, Acc. 70B825, FRC 75835, file: Wilderness and Primitive Areas: North Cascades Primitive Area, Federal Records Center–Pacific Alaska Region, Seattle (hereafter FRC-PAR). For a general summary of the Ice Peaks issue, see Conrad Wirth to Assistant Secretary of the Interior, July 19, 1956, box 14, file: Legislation—National Parks and Forests, Thomas M. Pelly Papers, University of Washington Libraries, Seattle (hereafter UW).

13. David A. Clary, *Timber and the Forest Service* (Lawrence: University of Kansas Press, 1986): 100–104; Robert Marshall to Irving M. Clark, May 18, 1938, box 1, file 40, Irving M. Clark Papers, UW; Robert Marshall to Irving M. Clark, November 12, 1938, and Robert Marshall to C. J. Buck, November 12, 1938, RG 95, Acc. 70B825, FRC 75835, file: Wilderness and Primitive Areas: North Cascades Primitive Area, FRC-PAR. See also "Management Plan for the Glacier Peak Wilderness Area, Mount Baker and Wenatchee National Forests," U.S. Forest Service, Department of Agriculture, 1965, RG 95, Acc.# 73A898, FRC# 25219, FRC-PAR.

14. Harold K. Steen, *The U.S. Forest Service: A History* (Seattle: University of Washington Press, 1976), 259–71.

15. Paul Hirt, *A Conspiracy of Optimism: Management of the National Forests since World War Two* (Lincoln: University of Nebraska Press, 1994), 44–215, first quotation from xlviii. Michael P. Cohen, *The History of the Sierra Club, 1892–1970* (San Francisco: Sierra Club Books, 1988), 192–211, second quotation from 199.

16. U.S. Forest Service, "Preliminary Proposal for a Glacier Peak Wilderness Area," February 7, 1957, RG 95, Acc.# 73A89A, FRC# 25219, file: Glacier Peak Wilderness Area, 1956–1958, FRC-PAR; Philip Hyde, "The Wilderness World of the Cascades," *The Living Wilderness* 22 (Spring 1957): 9–16.

17. See, for example, a report by the Mountaineers, "Recommendations for the Proposed Glacier Peak Wilderness Area," April 1, 1956, and Philip H. Zalesky, "Glacier Peak Wilderness Area," c. 1956, Mountaineers Papers, box 2, Glacier Peak file, UW. See also Grant McConnell to Patrick Goldsworthy et al., July 10, 1956, John Seiker (Chief, Forest Service Division of Recreation and Lands) to Edgar Wayburn (Sierra Club), October 18, 1956, and Polly Dyer, "North Cascades-Glacier Peak," June 11, 1958, typescript, Philip Zalesky Papers, box 2, unlabeled file, UW.

18. See, for example, the film *Wilderness Alps of Stehekin*, released in 1958 and produced by David Brower. A narrative version of the film can be found in David R. Brower, "Wilderness Alps of Stehekin," *The Living Wilderness* 23 (Autumn 1958): 18–24.

19. J. Herbert Stone, "Glacier Peak Wilderness Proposal (1959)," *The Living Wilderness* 24 (Autumn 1959): 10–12; David R. Brower, "Crisis in the Northern Cascades: The Missing Million," *Sierra Club Bulletin* (February 1959), quoted in *The Living Wilderness* 24 (Spring 1959): 35; "Glacier Peak Designated," *The Living Wilderness* 26 (Autumn–Winter 1961): 36–40.

20. Susan E. Georgette and Ann H. Harvey, *Local Influence and the National Interest: Ten Years of National Park Service Administration in the Stehekin Valley, Washington*, Publication No. 4, Environmental Field Program (Santa Cruz: University of California, 1980); Gretchen A. Luxenberg, *Historic Resource Study: North Cascades National Park Service Complex* (Seattle: National Park Service, 1986). See also, David Louter, *Contested Terrain: North Cascades National Park Service Complex, An Administrative History* (Seattle: National Park Service, 1998), 10–11.

21. Grant McConnell, *Stehekin: A Valley in Time* (Seattle: The Mountaineers, 1988), 9.

22. Ibid., 12–13.

23. Leo Marx, *The Machine in the Garden: Technology and the Pastoral Ideal in America* (New York: Oxford University Press, 1964), 3–11, 23–33, 221–26.

24. Brower, "Wilderness Alps of Stehekin," 18, 20.

25. Hal K. Rothman, *Devil's Bargains: Tourism in the Twentieth-Century American West* (Lawrence: University Press of Kansas, 1998), 202–4.

26. The system was eventually expanded to 42,500 miles. James J. Flink, *The Car Culture* (Cambridge, MA: MIT Press, 1975), 190.

27. John Diggins, *The Proud Decades: America in War and Peace, 1941–1960* (New York: W. W. Norton and Company, 1988), 181–85; Hays, *Beauty, Health, and Permanence,* 90–92; Kenneth T. Jackson, *Crabgrass Frontier: The Suburbanization of the United States* (New York: Oxford University Press, 1985), 246–49.

28. Lewis Mumford, *The Highway and the City* (1953; New York: Harcourt Brace Jovanovich, Inc., 1963), 234–35. See also Adam Rome, *The Bulldozer in the Countryside: Suburban Sprawl and the Rise of American Environmentalism* (Cambridge: Cambridge University Press, 2001).

29. John M. Findlay, *Magic Lands: Western Cityscapes and American Culture after 1940* (Berkeley: University of California Press, 1992) 36–39; William O. Douglas, *My Wilderness: The Pacific West* (Sausalito, CA: Comstock Editions, 1960), 121–22.

30. Harvey, *A Symbol of Wilderness,* 258, 288, for quotations; Runte, *National Parks,* 171, for figures.

31. David Brower, quoted in Richard W. Sellars, *Preserving Nature in the National Parks: A History* (New Haven: Yale University Press, 1997).

32. For a brief summary of landscape architecture and this aspect of Park Service design, see Ethan Carr, "Setting Sail on the Ship of State: Landscape Architecture in the National Park Service," *CRM* 19, no. 9 (1996): 5–9. See also Carr's longer work, *Wilderness by Design: The Landscape Architecture and the National Park Service* (Lincoln: University of Nebraska Press, 1998); and Linda Flint McClelland, *Building the National Parks: Historic Landscape Design and Construction* (Baltimore: Johns Hopkins University Press, 1998). For a treatment of modern architecture in national parks, see Sarah Allaback, *Mission 66 Visitor Centers: The History of a Building Type* (Washington, D.C.: National Park Service, 2000).

33. Alfred Runte, *Yosemite: The Embattled Wilderness* (Lincoln: University of Nebraska Press, 1990), 192–97. Runte maintains that the Tioga Road exemplifies the pressures placed on Park Service management from commercial interests, which all too often came at the expense of the park's natural environment.

34. Ansel Adams, "Tenaya Tragedy," *Sierra Club Bulletin* 43 (November 1958): 1–4, quotation from 3. Much of Adams's impressions about the road and its changes can be found in the twenty-one photographs and captions accompanying this article. For the Sierra Club's position on the road, see Richard M. Leonard to Conrad Wirth, April 5, 1955, RG 79, Olympic National Park, box 5, file D30, National Archives–Pacific Alaska Region, Seattle (hereafter NA-PAR). Wirth, of course, believed such criticism unfair, especially since the Sierra Club had supported the

agency's road program in Yosemite in the past. Conrad L. Wirth to Harold Bradley, December 9, 1958, ibid.

35. Sellars, *Preserving Nature in the National Parks*, 191–94.

36. Grant McConnell to David R. Brower, May 15, 1958, RG 79, Acc.# 71A1071, FRC# 8639, file L58, North Cascades–Glacier Peak Wilderness, FRC-PAR.

37. David R. Brower to Grant McConnell, July 11, 1958, ibid.

38. Brower, "Crisis in the Northern Cascades," 10; Patrick D. Goldsworthy to Henry M. Jackson, December 3, 1958, North Cascades Conservation Council Papers, box 13, file 7, UW; Richard E. McArdle to Thomas M. Pelly, August 24, 1959, Pelly Papers, box 14, unmarked file, UW. The Sierra Club's proposal, endorsed by the North Cascades Conservation Council, can be found in the council's press release "Cascades National Park Proposed by Conservationists," February 16, 1959, Warren G. Magnuson Papers, box 103, file 21, UW.

39. J. Michael McCloskey, ed., *Prospectus for a North Cascades National Park* (Seattle: North Cascades Conservation Council, 1963). See also Cohen, *History of the Sierra Club*, 310–12.

40. McCloskey, *Prospectus for a North Cascades National Park*, part 3, 5.

41. Ibid., 3–5.

42. Ibid., 5.

43. Ibid., 13–15.

44. Ibid.

45. Cohen, *History of the Sierra Club*, 312–13.

46. *Wall Street Journal*, June 24, 1966, cited in James J. Flink, *The Automobile Age* (Cambridge, MA: MIT Press, 1988), 176–77. Flink believes that preservationists' concerns bordered on hysteria over what he called the "Yosemite fallacy." Yosemite was unique given its proximity to two major population centers, San Francisco and Los Angeles, and its relatively short and narrow valley, which accommodated more automobile tourists than any other park. See also Alston Chase, *Playing God in Yellowstone: The Destruction of America's First National Park* (Boston: Atlantic Monthly Press, 1986), 203–8, for a critique of Mission 66 and Park Service development practices.

47. Edward Abbey, *Desert Solitaire: A Season in the Wilderness* (New York: Ballantine Books, 1968), 60.

48. Department of the Interior and Department of Agriculture, *The North Cascades: A Report to the Secretary of Interior and the Secretary of Agriculture* (Washington, D.C.: U.S. Departments of Interior and Agriculture, October 1965), 79 (hereafter *Study Report*). "Eldorado Peaks country" was the new name ascribed to the disputed Cascade Pass area. For a sense of the animosity between the two

departments over the study report's recommendations, see Orville L. Freeman to Stewart L. Udall, November 9, 1965, and Edward C. Crafts to Stewart L. Udall, December 25, 1965, Stewart L. Udall Papers, box 156, file 5, University of Arizona, Tucson.

49. *Study Report*, 90.

50. Michael Fromme, *Regreening the National Parks* (Tucson: University of Arizona Press, 1992), 70–72, Hartzog quotations from 72. See also Hartzog's autobiography, George B. Hartzog Jr., *Battling for the National Parks* (Mount Kisco, NY: Moyer Bell Limited, 1988).

51. *Study Report*, 90, 108–9. See figure 46 on page 108 for Hartzog's grand scheme.

52. U.S. Senate, Committee on Interior and Insular Affairs, Subcommittee on Parks and Recreation, *Hearings on S. 1321, A Bill to Establish North Cascades National Park . . .* , 90th Cong., 1st sess., 1967, 20 (hereafter *Hearings on S. 1321*). For Udall's record, see Thomas G. Smith, "John Kennedy, Stewart Udall, and New Frontier Conservation," *Pacific Historical Review* 64 (August 1995): 335, 351.

53. Robert Shankland, *Steve Mather of the National Parks*, 2nd ed. (New York: Alfred A. Knopf, 1954), 207–8. See also Runte, *Yosemite*, 157; and Theodore Catton, *Wonderland: An Administrative History of Mount Rainier National Park* (Seattle: National Park Service, 1996), 278–80, 431–32, 593–94.

54. *Hearings on S. 1321*, 21.

55. Ibid., 22–23.

56. U.S. House, Subcommittee on National Parks and Recreation, *Hearings on H.R. 8970, A Bill to Establish North Cascades National Park . . .* , 90th Cong., 2nd sess., 1968, 951 (hereafter *Hearings on H.R. 8970*).

57. A. Starker Leopold et al., "Wildlife Management in the National Parks," March 4, 1963, reprinted in Department of the Interior, *Administrative Policies for Natural Areas of the National Park System* (Washington, D.C.: Government Printing Office, 1970), 104, 99–112. For the Park Service's change in policy, see George B. Hartzog Jr. to All Field Offices, September 22, 1967, in Department of the Interior, *Administrative Policies for Natural Areas of the National Park System* (1970), 113–16.

58. Frederick Clements's succession theory had a powerful hold on the way ecologists viewed the natural world: as a place in which all life eventually moved, even if disturbed, toward a long period of stability. The scientists who wrote the Leopold Report displayed this view, though after World War II it would begin to lose dominance. See, for example, Michael G. Barbour, "Ecological Fragmentation in the Fifties," in Cronon, *Uncommon Ground*, 233–55. Theodore Catton has argued recently that the traditional national park model—the paradigm of parks as

"vignettes of primitive America"—does not apply to the parks of Alaska. These lands were not "primordial wilderness, but a series of socially shaped landscapes." Catton, *Inhabited Wilderness*, 217. Likewise, Mark Spence has argued that the first parks of the continental United States were cleansed of their native inhabitants in order to be preserved as primordial wilderness. Mark Spence, *Dispossessing the Wilderness: Indian Removal and the Making of the National Parks* (New York: Oxford University Press, 1999), 3–8.

59. *Hearings on S. 1321*, 23, 24.

60. *Hearings on H.R. 8970*, 957.

61. Ibid., 953, 959.

62. *Hearings on S. 1321*, 22.

63. *Hearings on H.R. 8970*, 959.

64. *Hearings on S. 1321*, 23.

65. *Hearings on S. 1321*, 67–68.

66. Ibid., 92.

67. Robert A. Irwin, "Call to the Wilderness," in *1965 World Book Year Book* (repr., Chicago: World Book—Childcraft International, 1965), 194–201.

68. "North Cascades National Park: Stehekin Road," uncataloged briefing statement, c. 1967, administrative files, North Cascades National Park Service Complex Archives, Sedro-Woolley and Marblemount, Washington.

69. *New York Times*, February 13, 1966, reprinted in *Congressional Record—Appendix*, House, February 15, 1966, A737.

70. *Hearings on S. 1321*.

5 / WILDERNESS THRESHOLD:
NORTH CASCADES AND A NEW CONCEPT OF NATIONAL PARKS

1. National Park Service, "An Interpretive Prospectus for the Skagit River Corridor of the North Cascades Complex," preliminary draft, c. 1970, administrative history files—North Cascades National Park Service Complex (hereafter NOCA), National Park Service, Pacific West Regional Office, Seattle, Washington (hereafter NPS).

2. Alfred Runte, *Yosemite: The Embattled Wilderness* (Lincoln: University of Nebraska Press, 1990), 203; Alston Chase, *Playing God in Yellowstone: The Destruction of America's First National Park* (Boston: The Atlantic Monthly Press, 1986), 208, for quotation.

3. Department of the Interior, *Administrative Policies for Natural Areas of the National Park System* (Washington, D.C.: Government Printing Office, 1970), 33.

4. Richard W. Sellars, *Preserving Nature in the National Parks: A History* (New Haven: Yale University Press, 1997), 205–6; Barry Mackintosh, *The National Parks: Shaping the System* (Washington, D.C.: National Park Service, 1985), 62–64, 68–75.

5. National Park Service, *Master Plan: North Cascades National Park Service Complex, Washington* (Denver: National Park Service, November 1970), 2, 36; National Park Service, *Wilderness Recommendations: North Cascades Complex, Washington* (Denver: National Park Service, August 1970), 1.

6. Roger J. Contor to Walt Woodward, October 19, 1968, administrative files, Yellows, North Cascades National Park Service Complex Archives (hereafter NOCA Archives).

7. Roger J. Contor, interview by author, June 25, 1996; "Statement of Roger J. Contor," Wilderness Hearings, North Cascades National Park, June 4, 6, 1970, p. 2, and Roger J. Contor, "Natural Area Management in Our Wildest National Park," March 12, 1970, Lands, Water, and Recreation Planning files, box 6, file 84, NOCA Archives.

8. John M. Findlay, "Far Western Cityscapes and American Culture Since 1940," *Western Historical Quarterly* 22 (February 1991): 26. See also John M. Findlay, *Magic Lands: Western Cityscapes and American Culture after 1940* (Berkeley: University of California Press, 1992), 14–51. For the role that suburbs played in bringing homeowners into closer contact with nature and raising environmental awareness, see Adam Rome, *The Bulldozer in the Countryside: Suburban Sprawl and the Rise of American Environmentalism* (Cambridge: Cambridge University Press, 2001).

9. National Park Service, *Master Plan*, 2–6, quotation from 6.

10. Ibid.

11. Chase, *Playing God in Yellowstone*, 206–9.

12. *Seattle Times*, September 14, 1969.

13. Walter J. Hickel to Director, National Park Service, June 18, 1969, reprinted in Department of the Interior, *Administrative Policies for Natural Areas of the National Park System* (1970), 84–89; "Park Road Standards: A Report to the Director of the National Park Service," reprinted in Department of the Interior, *Administrative Policies for Recreation Areas of the National Park System* (Washington, D.C.: Government Printing Office, 1968), 101; Roger J. Contor to District Director, July 18, 1969, administrative files, file A56, NOCA Archives.

14. Runte, *Yosemite*, 203–6.

15. "Why North Cascades Proposal Needs Revision," *The Living Wilderness*, c. 1970, excerpted copy in administrative files, NOCA Archives.

16. National Parks and Conservation Association, *Preserving Wilderness in Our National Parks* (Washington, D.C.: National Parks and Conservation Association, 1971), 119–21. See also North Cascades Conservation Council to Board Members, May 1, 1970, John Osseward Papers, North Cascades National Park Hearings, June 3–6, 1970, University of Washington Libraries, Seattle (hereafter U W); Neal A. Butterfield to Superintendent, Olympic National Park, April 17, 1968, administrative files, file L58, N O C A Archives.

17. Joseph L. Sax, *Mountains without Handrails: Reflections on the National Parks* (Ann Arbor: University of Michigan Press, 1980), 62–63.

18. Ira L. Spring to Lloyd Meeds, April 23, 1968, Lloyd Meeds Papers, box 14, file: H.R. 8970: North Cascades Correspondence, U W; Patrick D. Goldsworthy to Neal A. Butterfield, September 13, 1969, administrative history files—N O C A, N P S. Whittaker's statement can be found in U.S. House, Subcommittee on National Parks and Recreation, *Hearings on H.R. 8970, A Bill to Establish North Cascades National Park . . .* , 90th Cong., 2d sess., 1968, 400–401.

19. "Meeds Off on Park Tour; Wants It 'Pro People,'" *Skagit Valley Herald*, August 26, 1969.

20. "North Cascades Tramway Hopes Dimmed, But Alive," *Wenatchee World*, July 24, 1975.

21. "Testimony by Congressman Lloyd Meeds . . . on the Development of the North Cascades National Park," April 12, 1972, and "General Statement on Development: North Cascades National Park," February 1, 1977, Meeds Papers, box 63, file "North Cascades," U W.

22. "North Cascades Tramway 10th Priority," *Wenatchee World*, October 27, 1980.

23. Russell E. Dickenson (National Park Service) to Roy Kirk (General Accounting Office), March 24, 1980, administrative files, file L1425, N O C A Archives; Lowell White, interview by author, July 19, 1996.

24. Stewart L. Udall to Director, National Park Service, July 10, 1964, reprinted in National Park Service, *Administrative Policies for Recreation Areas*, 64–68.

25. U.S. Senate, Committee on Interior and Insular Affairs, Subcommittee on Parks and Recreation, *Hearings on S. 1321, A Bill to Establish North Cascades National Park. . .* , 90th Cong., 1st sess., 1967, 15.

26. Jacqueline Krolopp Kirn, "The Skagit River–High Ross Dam Controversy: A Case of a Canadian-U.S. Transboundary Conflict and Negotiated Resolution" (master's thesis, University of Washington, 1987); Jared Farmer, "Field Notes: Glen Canyon and the Persistence of Wilderness," *Western Historical Quarterly* 27 (Summer 1996): 211–22; Brock Evans to Henry M. Jackson, November 25, 1969, Henry

M. Jackson Papers, Acc.# 3560–4, file 91–17, UW; John A. Rutter to R. J. Brooks, December 1, 1969, North Cascades Conservation Council Papers, Acc.# 1732–2, file 1–2, UW; "North Cascades: A Wilderness Plan," *National Parks and Conservation Magazine: Environmental Journal* (October 1970): 14.

27. Sellars, *Preserving Nature in the National Parks*, 233–46. For an insightful look at the Park Service and its policies toward recreation areas, see John C. Freemuth, *Islands Under Siege: National Parks and the Politics of External Threats* (Lawrence: University of Kansas, 1991), 37–84. The Park Service produced its own document tracing the evolution of its management views as they related to North Cascades. See "A Discussion of Laws Affecting the Administration of Lake Chelan National Recreation Area," administrative files, file L76, NOCA Archives.

28. For specifics on the Roland Point development, see "Presentation for North Cascades: Lower Ross Lake and Roland Point," undated internal planning document, c. 1971, administrative files, NOCA Archives.

29. "Meeds Off on Park Tour," *Skagit Valley Herald*, August 26, 1969; "Testimony by Congressman Lloyd Meeds"; press release from Congressman Lloyd Meeds, August 21, 1972, Meeds Papers, box 63, file "North Cascades," UW; "General Statement on Development: North Cascades National Park"; White, interview.

30. "Presentation for North Cascades," North Cascades Conservation Council, Committee for the Review of National Forest and Park Service General Development and Wilderness Proposals for the North Cascades Region, to Board Members, May 1, 1970, Osseward Papers, box 7, file: North Cascades Hearings, June 3–6, 1970, UW.

31. "Presentation for North Cascades"; White, interview.

32. Lloyd Meeds to George Hartzog, March 14, 1972, Meeds Papers, box 6, file "North Cascades," UW.

33. Meeds press release.

34. National Park Service, "An Interpretive Prospectus for the Skagit River Corridor of the North Cascades Complex." The Park Service tried various phrases (e.g., "sensory deprivation of the automobile") to convince tourists to get away from cars and pavement.

35. "When Dreams Come True: A *Post-Intelligencer* Motorlogue," *Seattle Post-Intelligencer*, July 5, 1925; Keith A. Murray, "Building a Wagon Road through the Northern Cascade Mountains," *Pacific Northwest Quarterly* 56 (April 1965): 49–56. See also JoAnn Roe, *The North Cascadians* (Seattle: Madrona Publishers, 1980), for a popular account of the early highway movement.

36. John A. Rutter to Henry M. Jackson, August 12, 1970, Jackson Papers, box 107, file 20, UW.

37. North Cascades National Park, "Cascade Pass Management Plan," January 1, 1974, administrative files, file L48, NOCA Archives.

38. Ibid.

39. For insights into climbers and their relationship with nature, see Joseph E. Taylor III, "The Moral Economy of Bolts: Ethics, Egos, and Economics in Yosemite Valley," paper presented at the Pacific Coast Branch of the American Historical Association, Kanapali, Hawaii, August 7, 1999; "Cascade Road Closure Argued," *Skagit Valley Herald*, April 10, 1974; Gary J. Kuiper to D. H. Porter, April 24, 1974, Gary J. Kuiper to Regional Director, April 16, 1974 (see attached summary of public comments), and National Park Service, "Assessment of the Environmental Impact for Implementation of the Cascade Pass Management Plan," June 1974, administrative files, file L48, NOCA Archives.

40. John A. Rutter to Henry M. Jackson, November 13, 1970, administrative files, file A3815, NOCA Archives.

41. Grant McConnell, "Five Years of National Park Service Administration in the North Cascades," December 1973, administrative files, file A36, NOCA Archives.

42. Roger J. Contor to R. J. Brooks, August 12, 1970, and Roger J. Contor to Brock Evans, September 1, 1970, administrative files, file A36, NOCA Archives.

43. Contor to Brooks, August 12, 1970.

44. Roger J. Contor to Brock Evans, January 29, 1970, administrative files, file A36, NOCA Archives.

45. Contor to Evans, September 1, 1970. See also National Park Service, "North Cascades—Stehekin Transportation Plan," April 1976, administrative files, file A88, NOCA Archives.

46. Rutter to Jackson, November 13, 1970; Robert E. Ratcliffe to John A. Rutter, May 11, 1970, administrative files, file L2415, NOCA Archives; Roger J. Contor to John A. Rutter, January 28, 1970, administrative files, file L24, NOCA Archives. See also "Stehekin Visitor Transportation System, 1988," administrative files, file A88, NOCA Archives; and McConnell, "Five Years of Park Service Administration."

47. McConnell, "Five Years of Park Service Administration."

48. Sax, *Mountains without Handrails*, 76–77, 79, quotations from 79.

49. "A Scenic Road Finally Opens," *National Observer*, November 18, 1972.

50. Dickenson to Kirk, March 24, 1980.

51. For a more detailed treatment of the park's development for visitors, see David Louter, *Contested Terrain: North Cascades National Park Service Complex, An Administrative History* (Seattle: National Park Service, 1998), 78–80.

52. Keith Murray, "Building a Wagon Road through the Northern Cascade Mountains," and JoAnn Roe, *The North Cascadians*, 165–96.

53. Henry M. Jackson to A. John Carlson, May 16, 1967, and Henry M. Jackson to Hu Blonk, June 29, 1967, copies of correspondence in administrative history files—NOCA, NPS; C. P. Montgomery to Lloyd Meeds, April 10, 1967, Meeds Papers, box 14, file: North Cascades—Out of District, UW.

54. Hal K. Rothman, *Devil's Bargains: Tourism in the Twentieth-Century American West* (Lawrence: University Press of Kansas, 1998): 18–19.

55. "Park Justifies Acceleration of Highway," *Bellingham Herald*, January 10, 1968; "Cross-State Highway Key to Park Use," *Seattle Times*, October 27, 1968; "A Scenic Road Finally Opens," *National Observer*, November 18, 1972.

56. Edward C. Murphy, "Highway to Valhalla," *Washington Highways*, no. 3 (July 1969): 11.

57. Editorial, *Pacific Builder and Engineer* 78 (September 1, 1972): 14, 16.

58. William Cronon, *Nature's Metropolis: Chicago and the Great West* (New York: W. W. Norton and Company, 1991), xix.

59. Brock Evans to Peter Le Sourd, January 7, 1969, North Cascades Conservation Council Papers, box 1, file 1 (Seattle City Light 1965–1969), UW; Editorial, *Pacific Builder and Engineer* 78 (September 1, 1972): 25, 44, 45. See also Linda Nash, "The Changing Experience of Nature: Historical Encounters with a Northwest River," *Journal of American History* 86 (March 2000): 1600–1629.

60. Bob and Ira Spring, *The North Cascades National Park* (Seattle: Superior Publishing Company, c. 1975), 11; "Superintendent's Report: What's Happening in North Cascades Park," *Seattle Times*, September 14, 1969. See also Roger J. Contor to Director, Western Service Center, May 21, 1970, administrative files, file D18, NOCA Archives; Department of the Interior, *North Cascades: Joint Plan, National Park Service, Forest Service* (Denver: National Park Service, August 1974); *Wenatchee World*, June 23, 1970.

61. Contor, interview; Roger J. Contor, North Cross-State Highway Coordinating Committee Meeting, Minutes, December 3, 1969, box 1, file 25, and "North Cascades Task Force Workbook," c. 1968, box 1, file 27, NOCA Archives.

62. Lowell White to Joseph DeLeon, January 21, 1972, administrative files, file A3815, NOCA Archives.

63. Sara B. Baldwin, Gary E. Machlis, and Darryll R. Johnson, *Visitor Services Project, Report 5: North Cascades National Park Service Complex*, vol. 1 (Cooperative Park Studies Units, University of Idaho, University of Washington, 1985), 1–29, 82–84. The Park Service relied on this kind of survey, which represented a sampling of park visitors, to construct visitor profiles. The survey asked questions such as: Where do people go? What do they do? How long do they stay? The agency used surveys

returned from some 350 visitors, contacted over a period of several days, from which it determined—through statistical analysis—how the nearly 800,000 annual visitors were spending their time in the park complex.

64. Contor, interview.

65. John J. Reynolds to Regional Director, November 12, 1987, administrative files, file D30, NOCA Archives.

66. John Brinckerhoff Jackson, *A Sense of Place, A Sense of Time* (New Haven: Yale University Press, 1994), 190.

67. National Park Service, *Development Concept Plan: North Cascades Highway and Cascades Pass* (Denver: National Park Service, April 17, 1986), 1, 7.

68. Quotations are from National Park Service, "An Interpretive Prospectus for the Skagit River Corridor of the North Cascades Complex," which describes original plans for a park film. For a sample of recent reactions to the park's film, see William F. Paleck to John Toof, August 31, 1995, administrative files, file A34, NOCA Archives; William F. Paleck to Steve and Barb Rincer, August 6, 1996, and William C. Walters to Slade Gorton, January 9, 1998, administrative files, file A3615, NOCA Archives. A more thorough treatment of this subject can be found in Louter, *Contested Terrain,* 272–95.

69. For a penetrating analysis of modern relationships with nature and the role of visual media, see Jennifer Price, *Flight Maps: Adventures with Nature in Modern America* (New York: Basic Books, 1999), 207–56.

EPILOGUE

1. See, for example, Richard W. Sellars, *Preserving Nature in the National Parks: A History* (New Haven: Yale University Press, 1997), 267–90; James Sterngold, "U.S. Takes a Step to Make Its Parks Freer of Vehicles," *New York Times,* January 1, 1997; "The Great (Federal) Outdoors Is About to Get More Expensive," *New York Times,* November 27, 1996; Larry Warren, "Zion Takes Tourists out of Their Cars," *High Country News* 32 (April 10, 2000): 3. Recent management and planning documents for Yosemite and Grand Canyon can be found at the park Web sites: http://www.nps .gov/yose/planning/yvp and http://www.nps.gov/grca/transit/southrim.html.

2. National Park Service, *Visitor Experience and Resource Protection Implementation Plan: Arches National Park* (Denver: National Park Service, 1995), 1–5; personal interview with Keith Dunbar (Planning Program Leader, National Park Service, Pacific West Regional Office), interview by author, April 26, 2000; National Park Service, *Draft General Management Plan and Environmental Impact State-*

ment: Mount Rainier National Park (Denver: National Park Service, 2000), 161, 269–79.

3. Statement of Allan J. Abshez before the House Subcommittee on National Parks, Recreation, and Public Lands, *Oversight Field Hearing on the Implementation of the Yosemite Valley Plan*, 108th Cong., 1st sess., April 22, 2003, 64–67. Yosemite has recently initiated its own carrying-capacity project to address these issues further.

SELECTED BIBLIOGRAPHY

ARCHIVES

Crater Lake National Park Archives, Crater Lake, Oregon
  History files
Federal Records Center–Pacific Alaska Region, Seattle, Washington
  Record Group 95. Records of the U.S. Forest Service
Mount Rainier National Park Archives, Tahoma Woods, Washington
National Archives, Washington, D.C.
  Record Group 79. Records of the National Park Service
  Record Group 95. Records of the U.S. Forest Service
National Archives–Pacific Alaska Region, Seattle, Washington
  Record Group 77. Records of the Office of the Chief of Engineers
  Record Group 79. Records of the National Park Service
  Record Group 95. Records of the U.S. Forest Service
National Archives–Pacific Sierra Region, San Bruno, California
  Record Group 79. Records of the National Park Service
National Park Service, Pacific West Regional Office, Seattle, Washington
  Administrative files
  Administrative history files—North Cascades National Park Service Complex
North Cascades National Park Service Complex Archives, Sedro-Woolley and
  Marblemount, Washington
  Administrative files
Olympic National Forest Headquarters, Olympia, Washington
Washington State Archives, Olympia, Washington
  Washington State Planning Council records

Clark, Irving M. Papers. University of Washington Libraries, Seattle.

Curtis, Asahel. Papers. University of Washington Libraries, Seattle.

Edge, Rosalie. Papers. Denver Public Library, Colorado.

Jackson, Henry M. Papers. University of Washington Libraries, Seattle.

Macy, Preston. Papers. University of Washington Libraries, Seattle.

Magnuson, Warren G. Papers. University of Washington Libraries, Seattle.

Meeds, Lloyd. Papers. University of Washington Libraries, Seattle.

Mountaineers, The. Papers. University of Washington Libraries, Seattle.

North Cascades Conservation Council. Papers. University of Washington
    Libraries, Seattle.

Osseward, John. Papers. University of Washington Libraries, Seattle.

Pelly, Thomas M. Papers. University of Washington Libraries, Seattle.

Save-the-Redwoods League. Collection. Bancroft Library, University
    of California–Berkeley.

Udall, Stewart L. Papers. University of Arizona, Tucson.

Zalesky, Phillip, H. Papers. University of Washington Libraries, Seattle.

BOOKS, ARTICLES, GOVERNMENT DOCUMENTS

Abbey, Edward. *Desert Solitaire: A Season in the Wilderness.* New York: Ballantine
    Books, 1968.

Adams, Ansel. "Tenaya Tragedy." *Sierra Club Bulletin* 43 (November 1958): 1–4.

Albright, Horace M., and Robert Cahn. *The Birth of the National Park Service:
    The Founding Years, 1913–1933.* Salt Lake City: Howe Brothers, 1985.

———. "The Everlasting Wilderness." *The Saturday Evening Post* 201 (September
    29, 1928): 28, 68.

Allaback, Sarah. *Mission 66 Visitor Centers: The History of a Building Type.*
    Washington, D.C.: National Park Service, 2000.

Athearn, Robert. *The Mythic West in Twentieth–Century America.* Lawrence:
    University Press of Kansas, 1986.

Averill, Walter A. "Building a Highway across the West Slope of the Olympic
    Peninsula." *Pacific Builder and Engineer* 37 (August 1, 1931): 24–31.

Baldwin, Sara B., Gary E. Machlis, and Darryll R. Johnson. *Visitor Services Project,
    Report 5: North Cascades National Park Service Complex,* vol. 1. Cooperative
    Park Studies Units, University of Idaho, University of Washington, 1985.

Balogh, Brian. "Reorganizing the Organizational Synthesis: Federal Professional

Relations in Modern America." *Studies in American Political Development* 5 (Spring 1991): 119–47.

Barbour, Michael G. "Ecological Fragmentation in the Fifties." In Cronon, *Uncommon Ground*, 233–55.

Barringer, Mark Daniel. *Selling Yellowstone: Capitalism and the Construction of Nature.* Lawrence: University Press of Kansas, 2002.

Beezley, B. F. "Report of Investigation to Determine Eligibility of Dosewallips–East Fork Route and North Fork Elwha Routes for Classification as Forest Highway." Bureau of Public Roads, September 1926.

Belasco, Warren James. *Americans on the Road: From Autocamp to Motel, 1910–1945.* Boston: MIT Press, 1979.

———. "Commercialized Nostalgia: The Origins of the Roadside Strip." In *The Automobile and American Culture*, David L. Lewis and Laurence Goldstein, eds., 105–122. Ann Arbor: The University of Michigan Press, 1980.

Bettis, William Charles. *A Trip to the Pacific Coast by Automobile: Camping All the Way.* Toledo, OH: Booth Typesetting Company, c. 1922.

Brant, Irving. *Adventures in Conservation with Franklin D. Roosevelt.* Flagstaff, AZ: Northland Publishing, 1988.

Brower, David R. "Crisis in the Northern Cascades: The Missing Million." *Sierra Club Bulletin* (February 1959). Quoted in *The Living Wilderness* 24 (Spring 1959): 35.

———. "Wilderness Alps of Stehekin." *The Living Wilderness* 23 (Autumn 1958): 18–24.

Bryce, James. "National Parks—The Need and the Future." In *University and Historical Addresses*, 393–94, 397–401. New York: Macmillan, 1913. Reprinted in *Mirror of America: Literary Encounters with the National Parks*, David Harmon, ed., 123–27. Boulder, CO: Roberts Rinehart, Inc., 1989.

Caesar, George Vanderbilt. "National Parks or City Parks?" *The Saturday Evening Post* 200 (October 22, 1927): 54.

Callicott, J. Baird, and Michael P. Nelson, eds. *The Great New Wilderness Debate.* Athens: University of Georgia Press, 1998.

Cammerer, Arno B. "Standards and Policies in National Parks." In *American Planning and Civic Annual*, Harlean James, ed., 17–19. Washington, D.C.: American Planning and Civic Association, 1936.

Carr, Ethan. "Setting Sail on the Ship of State: Landscape Architecture in the National Park Service." *CRM* 19, no. 9 (1996): 5–9.

———. *Wilderness by Design: Landscape Architecture and the National Park Service.* Lincoln: University of Nebraska Press, 1998.

Catton, Theodore. "The Campaign to Establish Mount Rainier National Park, 1893–1899." *Pacific Northwest Quarterly* 88 (Spring 1997): 70–81.

———. *Inhabited Wilderness: Indians, Eskimos, and National Parks in Alaska.* Albuquerque: University of New Mexico Press, 1997.

———. *Wonderland: An Administrative History of Mount Rainier National Park.* Seattle: National Park Service, 1996.

Chase, Alston. *Playing God in Yellowstone: The Destruction of American's First National Park.* Boston: Atlantic Monthly Press, 1986.

Chittenden, Hiram M. *Yellowstone National Park.* 1895. Stanford: Stanford University Press, 1933.

Clary, David A. *Timber and the Forest Service.* Lawrence: University of Kansas Press, 1986.

Cohen, Michael P. *The History of the Sierra Club, 1892–1970.* San Francisco: Sierra Club Books, 1988.

Conzen, Michael P., ed. *The Making of an American Landscape.* Boston: Unwin Hyman, 1990.

Cosgrove, Denis E. *Social Formation and Symbolic Landscape.* 1984. Madison: University of Wisconsin Press, 1998.

Cox, Thomas R. *The Park Builders: A History of State Parks in the Pacific Northwest.* Seattle: University of Washington Press, 1988.

Cronon, William. *Nature's Metropolis: Chicago and the Great West.* New York: W. W. Norton and Company, 1991.

———. "The Riddle of the Apostles." *Orion* (May-June 2003), http://www.oriononline.org/pages/om/03–30m/Cronon.html.

———. "The Trouble with Wilderness; or, Getting Back to the Wrong Nature." In Cronon, *Uncommon Ground,* 69–90.

———, ed. *Uncommon Ground: Toward Reinventing Nature.* New York: W. W. Norton and Company, 1995.

Culpin, Mary Shivers. *The History of the Construction of the Road System in Yellowstone National Park, 1872–1966: Historic Resource Study Volume I.* Denver: National Park Service, 1994.

Cutler, Phoebe. *The Public Landscape of the New Deal.* New Haven: Yale University Press, 1985.

Davis, Timothy Mark. "Mount Vernon Memorial Highway: Changing Conceptions of an American Commemorative Landscape." In *Places of Commemoration: Search for Identity and Landscape Design,* Joachim Wolschke-Bulmahn, ed., 131–84. Washington, D.C.: Dumbarton Oaks, 2001.

————. "Mount Vernon Memorial Parkway and the Evolution of the American Parkway." PhD diss., University of Texas at Austin, 1997.

Department of the Interior. *Administrative Policies for Natural Areas of the National Park System*. Washington, D.C.: Government Printing Office, 1970.

Department of the Interior. *Administrative Policies for Recreation Areas of the National Park System*. Washington, D.C.: Government Printing Office, 1968.

Department of the Interior. *Annual Reports of the Secretary of the Interior [1903–1911]* and *Annual Reports of the Department of the Interior [1912–1917]*. Washington, D.C.: Government Printing Office, 1903–1918.

Department of the Interior. *Proceedings of the National Park Conference Held at Berkeley, California, March 11, 12, and 13, 1915*. Washington, D.C.: Government Printing Office, 1915.

Department of the Interior. *Proceedings of the National Park Conference Held at Yellowstone, 1911*. Washington, D.C.: Government Printing Office, 1911.

Department of the Interior. *Proceedings of the National Park Conference, 1912*. Washington, D.C.: Government Printing Office, 1912.

Department of the Interior. *Reports of the Director of the National Park Service*. Washington, D.C.: Government Printing Office, 1917–1930.

Department of the Interior and Department of Agriculture. *The North Cascades: A Report to the Secretary of the Interior and the Secretary of Agriculture*. Washington, D.C.: U.S. Department of the Interior and Department of Agriculture, October 1967.

Diggins, John. *The Proud Decades: America in War and Peace, 1941–1960*. New York: W. W. Norton and Company, 1988.

Dilsaver, Lary M., ed. *America's National Park System: The Critical Documents*. Lanham, MD: Rowman and Littlefield Publishers, Inc., 1994.

Douglas, William O. *My Wilderness: The Pacific West*. Sausalito, CA: Comstock Editions, 1960.

Editorial, *Pacific Builder and Engineer* 78 (September 1, 1972): 14, 16.

Edge, Rosalie. *Roads and More Roads in the National Parks and National Forests*. Emergency Conservation Committee Publication No. 54, March 1936.

Eliot, Charles W., II. "The Influence of the Automobile on the Design of Park Roads." *Landscape Architecture* 13 (October 1922): 28.

Environmental History 1 (January 1996).

Evans, Gail. *Historic Resource Study: Olympic National Park*. Seattle: National Park Service, 1983.

Farmer, Jared. "Field Notes: Glen Canyon and the Persistence of Wilderness." *Western Historical Quarterly* 27 (Summer 1996): 211–22.

Findlay, John M. "Far Western Cityscapes and American Culture Since 1940." *Western Historical Quarterly* 22 (February 1991): 19–43.

———. *Magic Lands: Western Cityscapes and American Culture after 1940.* Berkeley: University of California Press, 1992.

Flink, James, J. *The Automobile Age.* Cambridge, MA: MIT Press, 1988.

Foresta, Ronald A. *America's National Parks and Their Keepers.* Washington, D.C.: Resources for the Future, Inc., 1984.

Fox, Stephen. *John Muir and His Legacy: The American Conservation Movement.* Boston: Little, Brown, and Company, 1981.

Freemuth, John C. *Islands under Siege: National Parks and the Politics of External Threats.* Lawrence: University of Kansas, 1991.

Fromme, Michael. *Regreening the National Parks.* Tucson: University of Arizona Press, 1992.

Georgette, Susan E., and Ann H. Harvey. *Local Influence and the National Interest: Ten Years of National Park Service Administration in the Stehekin Valley, Washington.* Publication No. 4, Environmental Field Program. Santa Cruz: University of California, 1980.

"Glacier Peak Designated." *The Living Wilderness* 26 (Autumn-Winter 1961): 36–40.

"Glaciers and Gasoline: Motoring in Mt. Rainier National Park." *Sunset* 28 (January 1912): 41–47.

Glover, James M. "Romance, Recreation, and Wilderness: Influences on the Life and Work of Bob Marshall." *Environmental History Review* 14 (Winter 1990): 23–39.

———. *A Wilderness Original: The Life of Bob Marshall.* Seattle: The Mountaineers, 1986.

Goetzmann, William H., and Kay Sloan. *Looking Far North: The Harriman Expedition to Alaska, 1899.* New York: Viking, 1982.

Good, Albert H., ed. *Park and Recreation Structures.* 3 vols. Washington, D.C.: National Park Service, 1938. Repr., Boulder, CO: Graybooks, 1990.

Greeley, William B. "Recreation in the National Forests." In *Picturesque America: An Illustrated Volume with Descriptive Text*, John F. Kane, ed., 33–41. New York: Union Library Association, 1925.

Guiles, Harry F. *Beauties in the State of Washington: A Book for Tourists.* Olympia, WA: F. M. Lamborn, Public Printer, 1921.

Hartzog, George B., Jr. *Battling for the National Parks.* Mt. Kisco, NY: Moyer Bell Limited, 1988.

Harvey, Mark W. T. *A Symbol of Wilderness: Echo Park and the American Conservation Movement.* Albuquerque: University of New Mexico Press, 1994.

Hays, Samuel P. *Beauty, Health, and Permanence: Environmental Politics in the United States, 1955–1985.* New York: Cambridge University Press, 1987.

———. *Conservation and the Gospel of Efficiency: The Progressive Conservation Movement, 1890–1920.* Cambridge, MA: Harvard University Press, 1959.

Hirt, Paul. *A Conspiracy of Optimism: Management of the National Forests since World War Two.* Lincoln: University of Nebraska Press, 1994.

Horning, W. H. "Proposed Mount Olympus National Park." *The National Parks Bulletin* 13 (February 1937): 6–10.

Hubbard, Henry V. "Landscape Development Based on Conservation, as Practiced in the National Park Service." *Landscape Architecture* 29 (April 1939): 105–21.

Hubbard, Henry V., and Theodora Kimball. *An Introduction to the Study of Landscape Design.* 1917. New York: Macmillan Co., 1924. Quoted in Linda Flint McClelland, *Building the National Parks: Historic Landscape Design and Construction*, 183–85. Baltimore: Johns Hopkins University Press, 1998.

Huth, Hans. *Nature and the American: Three Centuries of Changing Attitudes.* Berkeley: University of California Press, 1957.

Hyde, Anne F. "From Stagecoach to Packard Twin Six: Yosemite and the Changing Face of Tourism, 1880–1930." *California History* 65 (Summer 1990): 154–69.

Hyde, Philip. "The Wilderness World of the Cascades." *The Living Wilderness* 22 (Spring 1957): 9–16.

Ickes, Harold L. "Please Save Great Smoky." *The Living Wilderness* 2 (November 1936): 6.

Interrante, Joseph. "A Moveable Feast: The Automobile and the Spatial Transformation of American Culture, 1890–1940." PhD diss., Harvard University, 1983.

———. "You Can't Go to Town in a Bathtub: Automobile Movement and the Reorganization of Rural American Space, 1900–1930." *Radical History Review* 21 (Fall 1979): 151–68.

Irwin, Robert A. "Call to the Wilderness." In *1965 World Book Year Book*, 189–204. Repr., Chicago: World Book—Childcraft International, 1965.

Ise, John. *Our National Park Policy: A Critical History.* Baltimore: Johns Hopkins University Press, 1961.

Jackson, J. B. *Discovering the Vernacular Landscape.* New Haven: Yale University Press, 1984.

———. *A Sense of Place, A Sense of Time.* New Haven: Yale University Press, 1994.

Jackson, J. B. and D. W. Meinig, eds. *Interpreting Ordinary Landscapes* (New York: Oxford University Press, 1979.

Jackson, Kenneth T. *Crabgrass Frontier: The Suburbanization of the United States.* New York: Oxford University Press, 1985.

Jacoby, Karl. *Crimes Against Nature: Squatters, Poachers, Thieves, and the Hidden History of American Conservation.* Berkeley: University of California Press, 2001.

Jakle, John A. "Landscapes Redesigned for the Automobile." In *The Making of an American Landscape*, Michael P. Conzen, ed., 293–310. Boston: Unwin Hyman, Inc., 1990.

———. *The Tourist: Travel in Twentieth-Century North America.* Lincoln: University of Nebraska Press, 1985.

"'Keep It a Wilderness'—Ickes." *National Parks Bulletin* 14 (December 1938): 9–13, 29.

Kendall, Carpenter. "Motoring on Mount Rainier." *Sunset* 31 (August 1913): 304–7.

Kerouac, Jack. *The Dharma Bums.* 1958. New York: Penguin Books, 1980.

Kirn, Jacqueline Krolopp. "The Skagit River–High Ross Dam Controversy: A Case of a Canadian-U.S. Transboundary Conflict and Negotiated Resolution." Master's thesis, University of Washington, 1987.

Klingle, Matthew William. "Urban by Nature: An Environmental History of Seattle, 1880–1970." PhD diss., University of Washington, 2001.

Lears, T. J. Jackson. *No Place of Grace: Antimodernism and the Transformation of American Culture, 1880–1920.* New York: Pantheon Books, 1981.

Lears, T. J. Jackson, and Richard W. Fox, eds. *The Culture of Consumption: Critical Essays in American History, 1880–1980.* New York Pantheon Books, 1983.

Lefebvre, Henri. *The Production of Space.* Trans. Donald Nicholson-Smith. Oxford: Blackwell, 1991.

Leopold, Aldo. "Conserving the Covered Wagon." *Sunset* 54 (March 1925): 21, 56.

Leopold, A. Starker, Stanley A. Cain, Clarence M. Cottam, Ira N. Gabrielson, and Thomas L. Kimball. "Wildlife Management in the National Parks," March 4, 1963. Reprinted in Department of the Interior, *Administrative Policies for Natural Areas of the National Park System*, 104, 99–112. Washington, D.C.: Government Printing Office, 1970.

Lewis, Peirce F. "America Between the Wars: The Engineering of a New Geography." In *North America: The Historical Geography of a Changing Continent*, Robert D. Mitchell and Paul A. Groves, eds., 410–37. Totowa: Rowman and Littlefield, 1987.

Lien, Carsten. *Olympic Battleground: The Power Politics of Timber Preservation.* San Francisco: Sierra Club Books, 1991.

Lillard, Richard G. "The Siege and Conquest of a National Park." *American West* 5 (January 1968): 28–32, 67–72.

Louter, David. *Contested Terrain: North Cascades National Park Service Complex, An Administrative History.* Seattle: National Park Service, 1998.

Luxenberg, Gretchen A. *Historic Resource Study: North Cascades National Park Service Complex.* Seattle: National Park Service, 1986.

Mackintosh, Barry. *The National Parks: Shaping the System.* Washington, D.C.: National Park Service, 1985.

Maher, Neil. "Auto Tourism, Wilderness, and the Development of Great Smoky Mountains National Park." In *Making Protection Work: Proceedings of the Ninth Conference on Research and Resource Management in Parks and on Public Lands,* David Harmon, ed., 47–54. Hancock, MI: The George Wright Society, 1997.

"Main Traveled Roads in the Sunset Country." *Sunset* 39 (July 1917): 43, 82.

Mark, Stephen R. *Preserving the Living Past: John C. Merriam's Legacy in the State and National Parks.* Berkeley: University of California Press, 2005.

Marshall, Robert. "The Problem of the Wilderness." *The Scientific Monthly* 30 (February 1930): 141–48.

———. "Three Great Western Wildernesses." *The Living Wilderness* 1 (September 1935): 10–11.

Martinson, Arthur D. "Mount Rainier or Mount Tacoma? The Controversy that Refused to Die." *Columbia* 3 (Summer 1989): 10–16.

Marx, Leo. *The Machine in the Garden: Technology and the Pastoral Ideal in America.* New York: Oxford University Press, 1964.

Mather, Stephen T. "A Glance Backward at National Park Development." *Nature Magazine* 10 (August 1927): 112–15.

———. "The National Parks on a Business Basis." *The American Review of Reviews* 51 (April 1915): 429–31.

———. *Progress in the Development of the National Parks.* Washington, D.C.: Government Printing Office, 1916.

McCarthy, Tom. "The Coming Wonder?: Foresight and Early Concerns about the Automobile." *Environmental History* 6 (January 2001): 46–74.

McClelland, Linda Flint. *Building the National Parks: Historic Landscape Design and Construction.* Baltimore: Johns Hopkins University Press, 1998.

McCloskey, J. Michael, ed. *Prospectus for a North Cascades National Park.* Seattle: North Cascades Conservation Council, 1963.

McConnell, Grant. "The Cascades Wilderness." *Sierra Club Bulletin* 41 (November 1956): 24–31.

———. *Stehekin: A Valley in Time*. Seattle: The Mountaineers, 1988.

McCoy, Genevieve E. "'Call It Mount Tacoma': A History of the Controversy over the Name of Mount Rainier." Master's thesis, University of Washington, 1984.

McCully, A. Woodruff. "The Rainier Forest Reserve." *The Overland Monthly* 55 (June 1910): 553–54.

Miles, John C. *Guardians of the Parks: The History of the National Parks and Conservation Association*. Washington, D.C.: Taylor and Francis, 1995.

Millis, John A. "Road into Mount Rainier National Park." In U.S. Army, *Annual Report of the Chief of Engineers, U.S. Army*, Appendix KKK. Washington, D.C.: Government Printing Office, 1904.

Mills, Enos A. "Touring in Our National Parks." *Country Life* 23 (January 1913): 33–36.

"Mr. Ickes—Your National Parks." *National Parks Bulletin* 13 (December 1937): 3–4.

Muir, John. "The Wild Parks and Forest Reservations of the West." *Atlantic Monthly* 81 (January 1898).

Mumford, Lewis. *The Highway and the City*. 1953. New York: Harcourt Brace Jovanovich, Inc., 1963.

Murphy, Edward C. "Highway to Valhalla." *Washington Highways*, no. 3 (July 1969): 11.

Murray, Keith A. "Building a Wagon Road through the Northern Cascade Mountains." *Pacific Northwest Quarterly* 56 (April 1965): 49–56.

Nash, Linda. "The Changing Experience of Nature: Historical Encounters with a Northwest River." *Journal of American History* 86 (March 2000): 1600–1629.

Nash, Roderick. *Wilderness and the American Mind*. 3rd ed. New Haven: Yale University Press, 1982.

National Parks and Conservation Association. *Preserving Wilderness in Our National Parks*. Washington, D.C.: National Parks and Conservation Association, 1971.

National Park Service. *Draft General Management Plan and Environmental Impact Statement: Mount Rainier National Park*. Denver: National Park Service, 2000.

National Park Service. *The National Park Wilderness*. Washington, D.C.: National Park Service, 1957.

National Park Service. *Visitor Experience and Resource Protection Implementation Plan: Arches National Park*. Denver: National Park Service, 1995.

"The National Park-to-Park Highway Tour." *National Parks Association Bulletin* 12 (October 2, 1920): 1–2.

"North Cascades: A Wilderness Plan." *National Parks and Conservation Magazine: Environmental Journal* (October 1970): 14.

Novak, Barbara. *Nature and Culture: American Landscape Painting.* New York: Oxford University Press, 1980.

Nowell, Elizabeth, ed. *Selected Letters of Thomas Wolfe.* London: Heinemann, 1958.

Nye, David E. *American Technological Sublime.* Cambridge, MA: MIT Press, 1994.

Olmsted, Frederick Law. "The Yosemite Valley and the Mariposa Big Trees." 1865. Reprinted in *America's National Park System: The Critical Documents,* Lary M. Dilsaver, ed., 12–27. Lanham, MD: Rowman and Littlefield Publishers, Inc., 1994.

Paxson, Frederick L. "The Highway Movement, 1916–1935." *American Historical Review* 51 (January 1946): 236–53.

Price, Jennifer. *Flight Maps: Adventures with Nature in Modern America.* New York: Basic Books, 1999.

Quin, Richard H. "Carbon River Road." Historic American Engineering Record, HAER No. WA-120, Library of Congress, Washington, D.C., 1992.

———. "Mount Rainier National Park Roads and Bridges." Historic American Engineering Record, HAER No. WA-35, Library of Congress, Washington, D.C., 1992.

———. "Nisqually Road." Historic American Engineering Record, HAER No. WA-119, Library of Congress, Washington, D.C., 1992.

Rae, John B. *The Road and Car in American Life.* Cambridge, MA: MIT Press, 1981.

Reich, Justin. "Re-Creating the Wilderness: Shaping Narratives and Landscapes in Shenandoah National Park." *Environmental History* 6 (January 2001): 95–112.

"Report of the Acting Superintendent of the Mount Rainier National Park [1906]." In *House Doc. No. 5, Annual Report of the Secretary of the Interior,* 59th Cong., 2nd sess., 1906–1907.

"Report of the Superintendent to the Mount Rainier National Park, 1910." In *House Doc. No. 1006, Annual Report of the Secretary of the Interior, 1910,* 61st Cong., 3rd sess., 1910.

Richardson, Elmo R. "Olympic National Park: Twenty Years of Controversy." *Forest History* 12 (April 1968): 6–15.

"Road into Mount Rainier National Park." In *House Doc. No. 283,* 58th Cong., 3rd sess., 1905.

"Roadside Improvement—A National Movement Well Under Way." *American City* 41 (May 1929): 100–102.

Roberts, Milnor. "A Wonderland of Glaciers and Snow." *National Geographic* 20 (June 1909): 530, 534.

Roe, JoAnn. *The North Cascadians.* Seattle: Madrona Publishers, 1980.

Rome, Adam. *The Bulldozer in the Countryside: Suburban Sprawl and the Rise of American Environmentalism.* Cambridge: Cambridge University Press, 2001.

———. "'Give Earth a Chance': The Environmental Movement and the Sixties." *Journal of American History* 92 (September 2003): 525–54.

Roper, Laura Wood. *FLO: A Biography of Frederick Law Olmsted.* Baltimore: Johns Hopkins University Press, 1973.

Rothman, Hal K. *Devil's Bargains: Tourism in the Twentieth-Century American West.* Lawrence: University Press of Kansas, 1998.

———. *Preserving Different Pasts: The American National Monuments.* Urbana: University of Illinois Press, 1989.

———. *On Rims and Ridges: The Los Alamos Area Since 1880.* Lincoln: University of Nebraska Press, 1992.

———. "'A Regular Ding-Dong Fight': Agency Culture and Evolution in the NPS-USFS Dispute, 1916–1937." *Western Historical Quarterly* 20 (May 1989): 141–61.

———. *Saving the Planet: The American Response to the Environment in the Twentieth Century.* Chicago: Ivan R. Dee, 2000.

Runte, Alfred. *National Parks: The American Experience.* 2nd ed., rev. Lincoln: University of Nebraska Press, 1987.

———. "Pragmatic Alliance: Western Railroads and the National Parks." *National Parks and Conservation Magazine* 48 (April 1974): 15–21.

———. *Yosemite: The Embattled Wilderness.* Lincoln: University of Nebraska Press, 1990.

Sadin, Paul. "Demon, Distraction, or Deliverer?: The Impact of Automobile Tourism on the Development, Management, and Use of Mount Rainier National Park, 1907–1966." Master's thesis, University of Idaho, 2000.

Sax, Joseph L. *Mountains without Handrails: Reflections on the National Parks.* Ann Arbor: University of Michigan Press, 1980.

Scharff, Virginia. *Taking the Wheel: Women and the Coming of the Motor Age.* New York: Free Press, 1991.

Sellars, Richard W. *Preserving Nature in the National Parks: A History.* New Haven: Yale University Press, 1997.

Selected Bibliography

Shaffer, Marguerite S. *See America First: Tourism and National Identity, 1880–1940*. Washington, D.C.: Smithsonian Institution Press, 2001.

Shankland, Robert. *Steve Mather of the National Parks*. 2nd ed. New York: Alfred A. Knopf, 1954.

Shelse, Ronne C. "The Pageant Highway." *Mentor* 12 (July 1924): 29–35.

Smith, Michael. *Pacific Visions: California Scientists and the Environment*. New Haven: Yale University Press, 1987.

Smith, Thomas G. "John Kennedy, Stewart Udall, and New Frontier Conservation." *Pacific Historical Review* 64 (August 1995): 329–62.

Soulé, Michael E., and Gary Lease, eds. *Reinventing Nature? Responses to Postmodern Deconstruction*. Washington, D.C.: Island Press, 1995.

Spence, Mark. *Dispossessing the Wilderness: Indian Removal and the Making of the National Parks*. New York: Oxford University Press, 1999.

Spring, Bob and Ira. *The North Cascades National Park*. Seattle: Superior Publishing Company, c. 1975.

Steen, Harold K. *The U.S. Forest Service: A History*. Seattle: University of Washington Press, 1976.

Stone, J. Herbert. "Glacier Peak Wilderness Proposal (1959)." *The Living Wilderness* 24 (Autumn 1959): 10–12.

Sullivan, Michael. "The Tacoma Eastern Railroad—Linking Puget Sound and Mount Rainier National Park." *Columbia* 13 (Winter 1999–2000): 34–39.

Sutter, Paul S. "'A Blank Spot on the Map': Aldo Leopold, Wilderness, and U.S. Forest Service Recreational Policy, 1909–1924." *Western Historical Quarterly* 29 (Summer 1998): 187–214.

————. *Driven Wild: How the Fight against the Automobile Launched the Modern Wilderness Movement*. Seattle: University of Washington Press, 2002.

Swain, Donald C. "The National Park Service and the New Deal, 1933–1940." *Pacific Historical Review* 41 (August 1972): 312–32.

————. *Wilderness Defender: Horace M. Albright and Conservation*. Chicago: University of Chicago Press, 1970.

Thompson, Erwin N. *Mount Rainier National Park: Historic Resource Study*. Denver: National Park Service, 1981.

Thompson, Margaret. "A Real or a Sham Park in the Olympic Peninsula?" *Skylines: Bulletin of the Northwest Conservation League* 2 (January 1937): 3–15.

Thomson, C. G. *The Rim Road—A Wonder Drive*. Portland, OR: Scenic America Company, c. 1924.

Tomlinson, Owen A. "Development of Our National Park." *The Mountaineer* 17 (December 1924): 40–43.

Twight, Ben W. *Organizational Values and Political Power: The Forest Service versus the Olympic National Park*. University Park: Pennsylvania State University Press, 1983.

U.S. House. Subcommittee on National Parks and Recreation. *Hearings on H.R. 8970, A Bill to Establish North Cascades National Park . . .* , 90th Cong., 2d sess., 1968.

U.S. House. Subcommittee on National Parks, Recreation, and Public Lands. *Oversight Field Hearing on the Implementation of the Yosemite Valley Plan*, 108th Cong., 1st sess., April 22, 2003.

U.S. Senate. Committee on Interior and Insular Affairs. *North Cascades-Olympic National Park, Hearings on Study Team Report of the Recreational Opportunities in the State of Washington, February 11 and 12, 1966*. 89th Cong., 2d sess., 1966.

U.S. Senate. Committee on Interior and Insular Affairs. Subcommittee on Parks and Recreation. *Hearings on S. 1321, A Bill to Establish North Cascades National Park. . . .* 90th Cong., 1st sess., 1967.

Vint, Thomas C. *National Park Service Master Plans*. Washington, D.C.: American Planning and Civic Association, 1946; reprinted in *American Planning and Civic Comment* (April–June 1946).

———. "Wilderness Areas: Development of National Parks for Conservation." In *American Planning and Civic Annual*, Harlean James, ed., 69–71. Washington, D.C.: American Planning and Civic Association, 1938.

Watkin, T. H. *Righteous Pilgrim: The Life and Times of Harold L. Ickes, 1874–1952*. New York: Henry Holt and Company, Inc., 1990.

Waugh, Frank A. "Ecology of the Roadside." *Landscape Architecture* 21 (January 1931): 81–92.

———. *Recreation Uses on the National Forests*. Washington, D.C.: Government Printing Office, 1918.

Wharton, William P. "The National Primeval Parks." *National Parks Bulletin* 13 (February 1937): 3–5.

White, Richard. "'Are You an Environmentalist or Do You Work for a Living?': Work and Nature." In Cronon, *Uncommon Ground*, 171–85. New York: W. W. Norton and Company, 1995.

"Will We Discover the Northern Cascades in Time?" *Sierra Club Bulletin* 42 (June 1957): 13–16.

Williams, John H. *The Mountain That Was "God."* New York: G. P. Putnam's Sons, 1911.

Wilson, William H. *The City Beautiful Movement*. Baltimore: Johns Hopkins University Press, 1989.

Wirth, Conrad L. *Parks, Politics, and the People*. Norman: University of Oklahoma Press, 1980.

Wolfe, Thomas. *A Western Journal: A Daily Log of the Great Parks Trip, June 20–July 2, 1938*. Pittsburgh: University of Pittsburgh Press, 1951.

Worster, Donald. *Nature's Economy: A History of Ecological Ideas*. 2nd ed. New York: Cambridge University Press, 1994.

Yard, Robert S. "Economic Aspects of Our National Park Policy." *The Scientific Monthly* 16 (April 1923): 380–88.

———. "National Parks System to Assume Its Higher Status." *National Parks Bulletin* 45 (October 24, 1925): 1–2.

———. "Standards of Our National Parks System." *National Parks Bulletin* 51 (December 1926): 1–4.

———. "The Third Greatest American Tree" *The Living Wilderness* 2 (November 1936): 3–6.

INDEX

On the Road Again: Montana's Changing Landscape
by William Wyckoff

*Public Power, Private Dams: The Hells Canyon
High Dam Controversy,* by Karl Boyd Brooks

*Windshield Wilderness: Cars, Roads, and Nature
in Washington's National Parks,* by David Louter

WEYERHAEUSER ENVIRONMENTAL CLASSICS

*The Great Columbia Plain:
A Historical Geography, 1805–1910*
by D. W. Meinig

*Mountain Gloom and Mountain Glory: The Development
of the Aesthetics of the Infinite,* by Marjorie Hope Nicolson

Tutira: The Story of a New Zealand Sheep Station
by Herbert Guthrie-Smith

*A Symbol of Wilderness: Echo Park and the American
Conservation Movement,* by Mark W. T. Harvey

*Man and Nature: Or, Physical Geography as Modified
by Human Action,* by George Perkins Marsh;
edited and annotated by David Lowenthal

Conservation in the Progressive Era: Classic Texts
edited by David Stradling

CYCLE OF FIRE BY STEPHEN J. PYNE

Fire: A Brief History

World Fire: The Culture of Fire on Earth

*Vestal Fire: An Environmental History, Told through Fire,
of Europe and Europe's Encounter with the World*

Fire in America: A Cultural History of Wildland and Rural Fire

Burning Bush: A Fire History of Australia

The Ice: A Journey to Antarctica

9 780295 990217